M000188595

Colored Cold

To Catherine)
Let it Out...
Let it Go...
Let God

Wanda Wade

Colored Cold

Wanda Wolfe with Robert Titus

TATE PUBLISHING
AND ENTERPRISES, LLC

Colored Cold
Copyright © 2013 by Wanda Wolfe with Robert Titus. All rights reserved.

No part of this publication may be reproduced, stored in a retrieval system or transmitted in any way by any means, electronic, mechanical, photocopy, recording or otherwise without the prior permission of the author except as provided by USA copyright law.

The opinions expressed by the author are not necessarily those of Tate Publishing, LLC.

Published by Tate Publishing & Enterprises, LLC
127 E. Trade Center Terrace | Mustang, Oklahoma 73064 USA
1.888.361.9473 | www.tatepublishing.com

Tate Publishing is committed to excellence in the publishing industry. The company reflects the philosophy established by the founders, based on Psalm 68:11,
"The Lord gave the word and great was the company of those who published it."

Book design copyright © 2013 by Tate Publishing, LLC. All rights reserved.
Cover design by Allen Jomoc
Interior design by Caypeeline Casas

Published in the United States of America
ISBN: 978-1-62295-013-3
1. Biography & Autobiography / Women
2. Family & Relationships / Abuse / Domestic Partner Abuse
13.01.10

Acknowledgments

Dedicated to my mother and sons.

Table of Contents

Introduction

My mother, right before her passing, handed me thirteen handwritten pages that represented her life. She titled these pages *How to Survive the Storms of Life*. Thirteen handwritten pages had come from the depths of her pain-ridden heart. She passed away before completing the task and goal she set for herself. A couple of years after her death, my brother, Buddy, circulated her writing among her children. Sadly, Mama's written words were disjointed, as if her pain had overcome her. I wrote this book for my mother—my friend. She would have wanted me to speak and not be silent. She would have expected me to write and possibly help the next generation. This present generation has little or no concept of either the hardships we endured or sacrifices we made to pave rugged roads so they could have a better life. It is a generation colored cold with an unspoken vow to love thy self only. I wrote this book for my three sons, who frequently refer to me as a man, for they have only seen the man in me. I penned these words for all of the fatherless children of the world. Finally, I wrote this memoir to reaffirm the virtuous woman inside of me.

The purpose of this book is to shed light on the impact of the Messiah syndrome. It examines the very delicate and fragile life of an innocent child, abused and neglected by her father, thus thrusting her into a forty-eight-year journey in search of this important, intended male role model. It sets the writer out on a misguided journey to find her father through a series of abusive relationships and traumatic events. This book will walk the reader through the life of a fatherless child and the damage that is done to the child's self-concept and self-esteem.

It will also examine the hypocrisy that many times exists in the church by uncovering and exposing the dark secrets that lie hidden systematically beyond the veil of religion. It will portray the importance of having a personal and intimate relationship with the Creator and offers suggestions on what to do when the church fails you. It is one artist's and female entrepreneur's story of self-determination and failing forward. My intention in writing this book is to invoke provocative conversation about the potential danger of secret closets and its silent but violent impact on the secret keeper's life.

Finally, this memoir examines and clarifies the characteristics of healthy and appropriate boundary lines—a woman's God-given right to say "No"— with a focus on being true to oneself by examining your own baggage and releasing the load that does not belong to you. It is a book of encouragement, offering suggestions on how to take lemons and make raspberry lemonade and how to find the missing ingredients.

God has chosen the weak things of the World to put to shame the things which are mighty; and the base things of the world and the things which are despised, God has chosen, and the things which are not, to bring to nothing the things that are, that no flesh should glory in his presence.

1 Corinthians 1:27-29

Sticks and Stones
May break my bones
But Words will Never Hurt me.

When I Die,
You will cry
For All the Things
You called me…

Daddy

E very plant needs watering, or it wilts and dies…
Somewhere along my journey, I read that the power of life and death is in the tongue. The famed author Iyanla Vanzant spoke of the impact and power of words… Words stick to furniture, telephones, walls, curtains, and even to our clothing. They seep into our being…accumulating, producing unwritten chapters, and engineering soul wars that measure the magnitude of World War II within.

"Worthless and a failure—not like the other kids. Look at Bill, Buddy, and Sis. You're headed for disaster. Your future will be nothing. You're going nowhere. You're going to be a nobody." I'd heard so many negative things about myself. The rejection was engraved in my fragile heart. This harmful commentary associated with me was tightly woven into a web of deception that held so strong, even I eagerly accepted a guilty verdict.

I grew up feeling odd as if there was something wrong. I didn't know what it was, but *something* was—and I was sure of that— something was amiss. One quart shy, as if God left out a key ingredient in the recipe of *Me*.

When I was an infant, my father and mother slept with me between them. While smoking in bed, Daddy fell asleep with his Lucky Strike cigarette in his hand and, with his palm upward and the fired side of the cigarette on my chest, branded me for the rest of my life. My mother always contended this severe burn on my chest was an accident, but deep in the dark corners of my heart, I did not believe her. From the very beginning, I was sure that my father did not love me. The words still bring tears to my eyes, stretching the fabric of my being…

Broken...

Every little girl needs a daddy, but mine wanted no part of me. I cannot even begin to impart how painful it was for me to experience life without him. The words "my father did not love me" would ultimately define my very existence. I unknowingly hid these words where no one could find them; *not even me.* With lies in my hands, I started out on life's journey with a burned and broken spirit.

The cold look in Daddy's eyes said, "Stay away from me. There is something wrong with you." I became invisible. When I accidently came close to him, he reminded me that I was an unacceptable child. The *defining moment* of my father's cruelty and intolerance toward me happened in the middle of a repair project of our dilapidated house. Daddy, kneeling on his knees, hammered away at a nail in the wooden floor. I innocently got on my knees with him. He angrily raised the hammer and shouted with his stutter, "G-git out of the way or I'll h-hit you in the head with this G-god damn hammer." Those words of my father rang like a Sunday school church bell for years in my heart.

Tall, handsome, but disconnected, Daddy, around the house, was a quiet man. I rarely saw him smile or heard him laugh out loud. Around town, he was just the opposite. He was popular, well respected, and widely known for his candid sense of humor and occupation. Both whites and blacks alike respected my father—a rare occurrence in the sixties for an African American man. Daddy was the town's mortician. Every dead black body in and around that part of Arkansas was touched by my father before it hit the cold ground.

Daddy spent all his life working for Sanders Funeral Home. Mr. and Mrs. Sanders were from New Orleans and had settled in Marianna years ago. The Sanders boasted light skin and could almost pass for white. They had three children and lived in a big brick building at the top of a hill in the heart of Marianna. Even though they lived in our town, they set themselves apart from the rest of the city. Sporting the finest of cars and material things, they were the wealthiest black family in that part of eastern Arkansas. To them, my father was not just their mortician, he was a close friend and considered kin. Though they treated Daddy like family, this kinship did not extend any further than him. His poor wife and nine children were viewed as *puppies under the table*; we were always given the scraps. Mrs. Sanders gave us raggedy clothes, leftover food from wakes, worn-out red carpet, and embalming sheets, stained with dead folks' blood and excrement. The bloodstained sheets that had been used during the embalming process were washed and sent home with my father. We looked at the stains, jumped in bed, and went to sleep. Any object considered damaged was passed on to our family. From tattered, broken beds to dogs so old the Sanders no longer wanted to care for them, they gave, and we gratefully acknowledged the crumbs. Outside of Tootie, who I found in the graveyard at church, all of my childhood pets came from the funeral home. The Sanders went out of their way to make us feel even smaller than we already were.

Mr. and Mrs. Sanders purchased all of their hearses and company cars to match in sky blue. They purchased my father's car in sky blue as well, thus giving the notion to other African Americans in our town that the Wolfe family was wealthy. There was no way to dispel this rumor, because we lived so deep in the woods. In reality, we lived in extreme poverty. And while Mama struggled to feed us, I saw my father as a man with two very separate lives. One was his life with the Sanders, where he was afforded the best of clothes, women, cars, and money. The other life was not so clear to me. I, along with the rest of my siblings, knew the town's mortician, yet we all struggled to tie ourselves to this enigma of a figure we called *Daddy*.

Daddy was unbearably cold and detached from the opposite spectrum of his duplicitous life. He said only what needed to be said. I never saw him engaged in small talk nor offer a compliment. He had no tolerance for annoyances. Once, one of our dogs was barking on our porch in the middle of the night, awakening my father. With no warning, Daddy got out of bed, grabbed his shotgun, and shot a hole through the door, killing the poor animal and silencing its worrisome bark. We cried over the loss of our dog. The next morning, Daddy was silent as if the night before never happened. A hole the size of a cantaloupe rested in the door for many years. In the winter, we covered its void with plastic to keep the brutal weather out. This gaping hole stood as an ominous reminder that my father was not to be disturbed. It would be decades before he repaired the damaged door. Like the hole left in the door, the hole in my heart would go unattended for years to come as well.

There were many occasions where I feared for the life of my pet. If my dogs barked, I covered their mouths and shielded their faces by draping my body over theirs and squeezing my small frame through the tiny black hole that led me under the house. Every living thing looking to hide from my father's cruelty hid under our house, from cats who escaped the death row ride down to the lake in a securely knotted Kroger sack, to spiders, snakes, and other strays. By hook or crook, I made my way underneath as well. Even though I sat—enveloped by the damp, musty darkness— somehow the vast emptiness of space felt safer than above ground.

Like the poor dog, my father disciplined me with ruthless punishments for slight infractions. My older brother, Buddy, referred to another brother, Bobby, and I as the black sheep in the Wolfe family. In those days, I didn't know what that meant, but I understood not to get in my father's way. I knew not to make him angry. Once, he grabbed me for some minor offense and stepped on me, holding me down with his foot, beating me with an extension cord until I peed on myself. I lay there, breathless on the floor, in my own sweat and urine. I felt so helpless and alone. Yes, I was surely a fatherless child. At a very young age, I started to think of creative ways to die. With my heart erratically pounding and tears flowing as if the Hoover Dam had burst, early on I would consistently remind myself that I did not want to do this thing called life.

Every Sunday, Mama woke us up in the wee hours of the morning to make sure we were ready and on time for church. My sister, Kay, and I would roll over and kick each other in discontent, eventually getting up. And amidst our other siblings, we washed our faces and brushed carelessly through our nappy hair. We tried to make pretty ponytails out of tangled wool. Beleaguered by little water and no toiletries, we always gave up, twisting our hair in ugly plaits and throwing on already dirty hand-me-down dresses.

After dressing, we all packed our bodies into Daddy's shiny blue car, heading off to morning worship. Singing at three or four churches a Sunday, we would not return home until late at night. We traveled down rural dusty roads to each event. Each Sunday, poor people from every direction came and waited on the church ground for service to start. Stout women with skirts pulled far above their waists stood watching as their bellies tried to push pass their dresses. These same women, when it was time for church to begin, rushed and pressed hard against each other to make it to the front of the sanctuary. The best seats in the house resided there. Mama always made her way to the beat-up piano. She was the musician and the choir director all in one.

After the congregation sat, a portly, black man hurried to the pulpit. With sweat resting upon his oversized nose, we all felt the weight of Reverend Hogan's worth as he brushed pass us. By the time he made it to his seat, the sweat on his forehead poured from his face and down his neck, saturating his shirt. With a handkerchief in his pocket, Reverend Hogan always ignored the heat and opted to use the cloth as a prop for his sermons.

No preacher was authentic in those days unless he carried with him a dingy handkerchief to wipe his forehead. Once his words hit the *amen corner*, he would stop right smack dab in the middle of his sermon and wipe the sweat from his face. In the beginning of his sermon, when Reverend Hogan got up out of his seat to preach damnation to our unworthy souls, his words were clear and audible. However, on each Sunday, at the same time—when the same group of women in the same corner shouted, "Amen," our Pastor started to almost sing his words with a funny, coughing sound at the end of each decree. As the noise in the crowd built to an unbelievable crescendo, he would pull off his tattered coat, exposing his already wet shirt. Once his coat came off, he would pick up one of the wooden chairs, throw it across his left shoulder, and run from one end of the pulpit to the other, screaming, "I'm carrying my cross in the heat of the day!" Every Sunday, the same women lost themselves in the aura of the moment, crying, screaming, and shouting that their salvation was real. Like rice, beans, and potatoes, church was a staple in the black community. Unlike today, we knew that our well-being and unity could only be found within the walls of the sanctuary and school.

Mothers during those years carried their children to church, and every child sat with his parents during service. Occasionally we sang "I know I Got Good Religion! Certainly Lord." In those days, black children *knew* and were afraid of God. Even though the preacher screamed words of fire and brimstone, there was a measure of moderation and logic to his messages. He always admonished us as young people to live and do right by our fellowman. I, as a young girl, never felt comfortable doing wrong. As the song had said, "It was a good religion!"

From the time I was three, I helped my mother lead songs for a choir she named The Eagle Nest Spirituals. Mama took all nine children, even our detached father, and told us to sing. It was my first exposure to music.

Mama loved singing, for music was her only escape. Through the words of her songs, she showed us that the sound of music could heal the deepest wound. Every evening, we gathered around the potbelly, wood stove and practiced as a family on songs for

Sunday. This would be the only intimate time we spent together. We all sang our hearts out, knowing that it was Mama's desire for excellence. One day, during rehearsal, Mama told us the story of how she started singing.

At the age of three, she sang church hymns with Grandpa Tom after he came home in the evenings from the cotton field. He could not believe that her voice was so strong at such an early age. Grandpa was so amazed that he took her to church and sat her on his lap while they sang duets together. The strength of Mama's voice blew their audience away. She memorized complex lyrics, never stuttering a single word, belting out notes of a veteran opera singer. With Grandpa showing her off, Mama sang wherever they went.

My mother told us how she wanted to learn to play the piano all her life but was too poor to take lessons. When she was thirty-eight, my brother, Buddy, bought her an old raggedy piano. For hours, Mama sat, pulling the sounds from her mind out of the piano. She taught herself as well as me to play. Many times, while she felt her way through the music, I sat myself beside her, listening intently as she hit the black and white keys.

On one special occasion, she carefully lifted the door of her piano and showed me the magic inside. Once she hit the key, a little wooden hammer hit a string and produced a flat, but beautiful sound. I sat in awe of her as she made up chords and wrote her own songs. Though the music she played was simplistic, it was amazing to listen to her.

On Sunday evenings, our family traveled miles through rural Arkansas to singing programs. These services proved to be the same, regardless of the church. We sang all the songs we spent hours practicing the week before. The church screamed and shouted as Mama ran up and down the aisle. She always did that when she got *happy*. Mama was not the only one; other women felt the burning of their spirit and shouted so hard they fainted, falling on the floor, causing their dresses to come up over their heads.

Ushers raced and placed smelling salt in their noses, bringing them back to the reality of their impoverished world.

After belting out five or six songs, the service would break for offering. Daddy, looking forward to his cigarette and women break, always waited impatiently for this part of the service. The church would instantly become as bare as a deserted island. Even the holiest of the holy, waiting to escape the tithe, left their pews and abandoned the sweltering heat inside. While the offering basket was being passed, they got up, tilted their heads down, put up their Baptist finger and tiptoed outside, excusing themselves. Daddy, along with other men, stood outside the building, smoking and flirting. Women, especially the broken Mary Magdalenes, looked on in great expectation of wasting their precious oils from their alabaster boxes. Kay and I raced out of church also, taking the pennies we had stolen to buy a cold drink from the sweaty, fat lady guarding the aluminum tub filled with soda pop and ice. Almost everyone left the sanctuary during offering…everyone except Mama. With all posts abandoned, my mother stayed behind and watched to make sure that all the deacons and moneychangers were on the up and up.

We were so poor. I don't think this reality was ever erased from my mother's mind. Although she cared about the worship service, Mama never forgot why we traveled those dusty roads on Sunday nights. There were days, months, and years at a time where Daddy left home and lived with other women, leaving her to fend for herself. Mama had to cook outside because we had no gas. She would build a fire under a huge cast iron skillet and cook fatback, frying hoecakes in the oil left behind. Forced to learn to survive, Mama found singing an avenue to generate capital. She created and led our family singing group to make money so she could buy groceries and propane gas to cook our food. Behind a good singing program, Mama had a few dollars to cook inside for her children.

After offering, our family would go up once more and sing a few more songs to end the program. When service ended, the deacons and my mother (with my father looking on), would recount the money and divide it 50/50. I always prayed for a good outcome. If Mama got lots of change, I felt confident that, when we got home and she fell asleep, I could lift my share, which usually was no more than a quarter. Every Sunday night I waited for Mama to fall into a deep slumber. I quietly crawled in the dark beside her bed where she kept her purse. I clumsily retrieved what felt like quarters to my touch—just enough to buy vanilla sandwich cookies on Monday morning before school. But you could never get anything past my mother in regards to money. The next morning, she recounted her money down to the penny. If anything was missing, she would question my sister and me. Kay was a bit more skillful in getting away with the loot, whereas I looked guilty from the start. It was as if my mother could see straight through me. With her tiny, piercing eyes glaring into mine, she pronounced me guilty. I learned to tread my way through my childhood...guilty.

Surrounded by rice, soybean, and cotton fields, Lee County was, and continues to be, one of the poorest counties in the United States. The small community we lived in consisted of just a few families. Our house sat miles and miles away from civilization on the end of a hidden dirt road. It felt like we were cut off from the rest of the world. The closest city was the county seat, Marianna, Arkansas, a town mostly made up of lower middle class whites, poor blacks, and government housing projects. They all looked wealthy to me.

We went to school with tattered clothing all the time. Our coats were hand-me-downs that were either too small or too big. We wore our shoes until our toes popped through the front. With no socks on, our feet were always showing through the soles and hitting the ground. During the winter months, our rooms were colder than outside. There was one bed for the five boys and one for the four girls. My oldest sister, Sophie Mae, always took the heavy clothes iron and heated it over the wood stove to warm her feet! To complicate our already dire living conditions, we all peed in the bed! Every morning we woke up to the smell of urine and a wet bed. If, by chance, I made it through the night without peeing, my sister, Kay, would pee and roll me over in hers to make it look like it was me. Daddy would come in, find the bed wet with urine, and beat the life out of me. He would beat, beat, and beat some more until he ran out of breath. "Do it again!" he'd say, "Do it again!" I could not help my overactive bladder; I would go back the next night and do it again. Almost every day I took a whipping for mine or someone else's crime!

I had gotten on my knees one day and prayed to God that Mom and Dad would move us out of the sticks and into the projects. I had also prayed that Mom would get in line like every other sane woman to get us some government cheese. *What is the big deal*, I remember thinking. The people in the projects lived well. They had running water, a bathtub, a washing machine, and a real refrigerator. Why did we have to be so different?

Daddy and Mama always put a padlock on the kitchen door before they left for work. There were locks everywhere there was food. First, there was a big lock at the entrance to the kitchen, and then once we got past that, there were chains and locks on the freezer and icebox that held red smoke links, lunchmeat, eggs from the hen house, and other perishables. My parents wrapped a chain around the freezer to prevent the nine siblings from raiding the food. With nine hungry bellies in the house, and them working all day, food scavenging was inevitable. Mama and Daddy believed that locks were their only option.

There was a small room in the corner of the kitchen that my parents called a pantry. This room was filled with shelves that held gobs of canned blackberries, peaches, pickles, okra, and cha-cha. Daddy secured this room with two master locks. My siblings and I had spent our whole childhood picking okra with socks on our hands to avoid the itchy, razor-sharp branches. The tall stalks covered our heads as we tried to pick our way to the end of the row.

We picked even the peaches from Mr. Johnson's orchard and stuck our hands in dangerous rattlesnakes' homes to pick blackberries. We worked in the hot sun to gather food only for our parents to lock away. It didn't seem fair.

There was no food around to be mustered, but Kay and I always found a way to get in and out when in desperation. Whether it was going through the window from the outside or squeezing our tiny bodies through the gaping holes left on the barely hinged doors, we would exhaust every measure to eat. One day, I crawled through the window into the kitchen, then into the pantry. There were beautiful jars of yellow peaches and purple blackberries everywhere. My mother had rows and rows of canned goods waiting to be robbed. There was food everywhere. I shuddered at the thought of eating her delicious blackberries. That previous night, she had opened *one* jar and rationed out a tiny amount to each child. My tongue was still purple from the berries that I had eaten the night before. They were so delicious.

Mama canned with precision, cooking and preserving her fruits and vegetables to perfection. Each one of the jars was carefully boiled and sterilized before putting the mixture inside. There were beautiful, shiny jars all around me. I nervously reached up to grab a jar of blackberries, knocking the glass beside it off the shelf and onto my foot, breaking my big toe! Purple mixed with blood, spread everywhere as I hobbled back out the window in pain. When I made it to the backdoor of our house, I sat on the steps, crying and holding my foot. My sister Sophie Mae reprimanded me and put spider web on my toe to clot the bleeding! That would be all the medical attention I received for this injury. For the next month, I limped around with a crooked big toe. I guess my parents felt that was punishment enough for the crime I committed.

Our family lived in a house that sat on cinder blocks. There were huge, open spaces, separating the house and the ground, and holes in parts of the floor of our house. The dark space in between gave safe boarding to stray dogs, rats, cats, and a myriad of weird-looking insects . There was dampness all around. This dampness made the dark corners under the house a paradise for dangerous things. We were constantly killing black widows, and sometimes snakes would make their way through the empty spaces in the floor into our home! On one occasion in the middle of our choir rehearsal, a huge black chicken snake crawled from under the house into our living room. When he got a whiff of us, and we got whiff of him, he slowly crawled back to the open space and made his way back under the house before Daddy could get his gun. The snake moved slowly as if he felt he had just as much right to the house as we did!

Inside our house, large buckets sat in corners, waiting their turn to catch the rain from our leaky roof. When the storms came, Daddy would calmly tell us to get all of the buckets and strategically place them under the holes, adorning the ceiling of our house to catch the water.

The journey from *dirty* to *clean* was a tedious one. When it was time to wash our clothes, we pulled grimy water from Mr. Turner's pond to fill an aluminum tub. Before drawing it, we beat the water with a stick, shocking it, to scatter the amoebas, insects, and tadpoles. It was already filthy, but we scrubbed what little clothes we had on a washing board, squeezing them out with our hands and hanging them to dry in the wind. In the wintertime, we hung them outside in the freezing rain and wind. Instead of drying, they became stiff as a corpse. We had no choice. Even though they were wet and cold around the waistband, we put them on and wore them anyway. I did not understand why my father, being the town's mortician, could not afford to move us to the projects. Why did we have to go outside to an outhouse laced with black widows, maggots, and centipedes? We had to walk at least an eighth of a mile to get to this dreadful place. If it was daylight outside, we reluctantly found our way, but when night fell, we went outside in the dark, standing as close to the house as possible and did whatever was necessary to alleviate ourselves.

One night, I walked outside into the pitch-black darkness to relieve myself. Dogs seemed to come from everywhere. Filled with an unimaginable fear, I fell over into my own excrement, severely cutting my hand on a broken Coke bottle. I could feel the blood as it gushed from my hand and ran down in between my fingers. I stumbled to get away from the dogs. As I struggled to get back inside the house, I looked back and saw that all the dogs were left behind, fighting over my feces. By the time I made it in the house, my dress was saturated with blood. The cut on my hand and wrist was so deep that, in today's world, I probably would have been hospitalized. Instead, Sophie Mae once again grabbed spider web from a corner in the house and spread it over my wound to clot the bleeding. We were not as lucky as Mama and Daddy, who owned a chamber pot. Through the night, they used the bathroom in it and emptied it when morning arrived.

Spider webs and black soot from the potbelly stove were the remedy for all injuries that were associated with blood. Sophie Mae, who was going to be a nurse, doctored on all of us when an accident happened. On many occasions, I clumsily stepped on rusty nails. I would hobble back to where Sophie Mae was, and she would roughly yank the nail out of my foot and dress the wound with spider web. In those days, Tetanus shots were unavailable to us. The folk in our town called Tetanus *Lock Jar*. Their cure for this disease was to stay away from rusty nails.

One day I was playing outside and accidently stumbled into a red wasp nest. The angry wasp lit into my body, stinging me in my face. I ran frantically, looking for my sister. My face was so swollen, I couldn't explain my injury. No spider webs this time! She looked at me, shook her head, and walked away. Sophie Mae got pleasure out of seeing her patients scream as she performed surgery and patched them up. Today she is the head nurse in a trauma unit in one of Austin's largest hospitals.

The well we pulled our drinking water from stood just one hundred yards north of our house. Though close, the process of drawing water was grueling. The smell of dead rats and snakes that had taken their final plunge in the cistern exploded in the air the moment we removed the makeshift tin overlay. We covered our noses and let the chained bucket down until we filled it to its brim. After pulling it up and out of the well, we sifted our drinking water through the embalming sheets from the funeral home. Each corner of the sheet was held up by one person, leaving slack in the center, while another person poured the dead rat water on top and waited for it to drain through into a huge drum.

Outside of going to school, we were cut off from the rest of the world until Sunday when we went to church. Our school bus traveled a good ten miles down a beautiful, scenic, winding, paved highway, adorned with dogwood and magnolia trees, only to dump us off on a dusty, dirt road. The moment we stepped off the bus, the smell of Mr. Jim Rhone's hogs hit our noses. We walked at least a mile to make it home.

One day on the way home, Kay and I saw a tiny snake. We ran, found a jar, and captured it. We made our way home holding our schoolbooks on top of the jar to make sure the snake did not escape. When we arrived home, we were so excited to show our older brother Larry. He took one look at the snake in the jar and was furious because we were so careless. It was a baby rattlesnake. He carefully shook it from the jar, took a garden hoe, and cut it in half.

We had our own little social enclave of poor blacks that lived nearby. A few hundred yards from where the dirt road began was a fence that marked Mr. Jim's property. The sound and smell of hogs told us we were nearing his land, which consisted of a dilapidated trailer where he brought women from town. We would see them come and go. Women in church hats as broad as the hood of his car squeezed through the front door of his streamline trailer.

Further down the road was the forbidden house where Lula Grunge lived. My mother warned us that Mrs. Lula was evil. She was a big woman and extremely backwoods. She always wore an apron that we were sure she slept in. She chewed tobacco, dipped snuff, and cussed like a sailor. Mrs. Lula poisoned our dogs, taunted Mama, and even threatened to kill us if we got in her way.

She had a grown daughter, Mrs. Kathleen, who lived with her. Mrs. Kathleen's three children also lived in the forbidden house.

When I was eight, Sodom, the oldest of the children told me he had a secret. He asked me if I wanted to know why he and his siblings called my Daddy '*Good O' Wolf*'. I never even thought about the nickname they had for Daddy. When they wanted something from him, they would start their sentence with, "Good O Wolf, Can we... Sometimes they shortened it and just called him, Good O. They said it with such pride, almost boastful. That day, Sodom leaned over and with a big grin, told me that my father and his mother, Mrs. Kathleen, were lovers. He whispered that my Daddy loved his mother more than he loved Mama. Sodom called him *Good O*, because Daddy was so good to him, and he believed he could get anything he wanted from my father. Sodom and his family made sure that each one of my nine siblings knew we were second-class citizens.

Since our house sat down the road past Mrs. Lula's house, we had to walk by her place every day to get to the highway. Mama, in a dignified stance, walked with her head high and, regardless of the circumstance, maintained her composure. The moment she reached the forbidden house, Mrs. Lula seethed hatred and shouted insults. "You no betta dan me, woman. Look at cha, wit your head hell up like you special. Well now, guess what, your husband been comin' to my house in da nite visitin' with my girl. How dat make you feel?" Mrs. Lula always ended her seething with her arms akimbo, her massive breasts puffed out, and a nasty splat of snuff and tobacco juice from her puffy black cheeks.

When insults fell short, Mrs. Lula took hatred to another level. She coaxed my sister, Kay, onto her porch and offered to comb her hair. She worked some foul smelling chemical into Kay's scalp, causing her hair to fall out. She poisoned Buddy with an egg sandwich specifically made for him. He almost died for his unwillingness to let Sodom *ride piggy* on his back.

When Mama came close to Mrs. Lula's house, she never took the bait. She always walked past at the same pace. Daddy's affairs were no secret, yet Mama wanted to keep our family together. Every time one of the children from the forbidden house called my Daddy *Good O'*, you could see the pain in her face. They were angry that Mom and her children existed. Mrs. Lula spent many hours standing on her porch, glaring at Mama.

Short, heavyset, with skin colored carbon-cold black, Mrs. Lula proudly wore a nose cut by something jagged and sharp. The rumor was that while she was picking blackberries in the woods, a rattlesnake slammed its fangs into her face, leaving the bridge of her nose sunken with an unsightly gash. Rarely seen standing up, Mrs. Lula spent most of her time leaning over the banister of her front porch or sitting in her rocking chair, plotting. She never left her post. In the morning when we passed by her house, heading for the school bus, she was there. In the evening, she was still there, making nasty remarks to us as we headed back home. Each day, Mama reminded us to look the other way and never be disrespectful. She also warned us not to go in Mrs. Lula's house. "Bad things will happen," she said.

There were times when the command not to go up the road to Mrs. Lula's house was just too hard to obey. Even though we knew that our disobedience would bring trouble, her evil aura beckoned us. Mrs. Lula's house was filthy and smelled of cat urine; still it was a loose environment, and there were fun things to do. There were four grandchildren living in her house—Sodom, Anna, Cassie, and a tobacco-chewing toddler named Tillie. They had the latest in clothing, music, and toys; most of them bought by our own daddy. When the beckoning was too loud to ignore, we secretively made our way up the sometimes-muddy road into their house.

One day while Mama and Daddy were away at work, Cassie came down to our house and asked Kay and I to come and play a game of *Simon Says*. We raced up to their house. Mrs. Lula was in her usual spot sitting in her chair, spitting tobacco juice into giant slobber puddles on her porch and waiting for us to arrive. I was just a child, yet I was wise enough to be apprehensive about playing this game, because Mrs. Lula was involved.

All the children ran to get in position for the game. Mrs. Lula instructed me to stand in a certain spot. I moved as she sat smugly in her rocking chair. She played the role of Simon, saying, "Raise your arms." We all raised our arms. Simon says, "Scream to the top of your voice," she shouted. We all screamed as loud as we could. "Simon says, 'Clap your hands,'" she proceeded. We all clapped our hands enthusiastically. The laughter was loud and intense. "Simon says, 'Take two steps forward.'" We all took two steps forward. "Simon says, 'Take four steps backward.'" All the kids started to step backward. I took four steps backward. There was cold and wet all around me. The stench was suffocating. My feet and ankles were covered in cow manure. Mrs. Lula had instructed her grandchildren to cover up a giant pile of feces behind me for me to step in. I stumbled into the pile and got the moist patty on my hands. As I started to cry, I inadvertently got some on my face. Mrs. Lula's grandchildren were doing only what they were told. This woman had actually taken the time and wasted her precious energy to attempt to break my spirit by employing her grandchildren to aid her in working mischief through a game of *Simon Says*! There was laughter all around, so much that I couldn't think. I lost myself.

While Mrs. Lula laughed with the rest of the children, I sunk into my invisible corner. I faded into nowhere, into nothing, disconnecting with my surroundings. Life was unbearable. I was in my own world, distrusting of everyone. I tried to avoid the forbidden house after that. They always seemed to find a way to pull me back.

The worst torment to come from Mrs. Lula's house happened when my baby brother, Chuck, died...

When Mama gave birth to Chuck, word came back to us that he was very ill and probably would not make it through the night. All of Mrs. Lula's grandkids came to our house and sat with us in a wide circle. We had a prayer ritual that we would do when someone was sick. It was an odd congregation of the black families around us. A powerful feeling—almost voodoo-like—descended upon us all. Each one of us would send up well wishes for that person. As we began to send up prayers for Chuck, everyone in the circle seemed to join in with well wishes. Sodom, Anna, Cassie, and all my siblings petitioned the darkness around us for a good ending. When the prayer chain reached me, I sat up straight and said, "Oh God, I hope my brother Chuck lives." Tillie, Mrs. Lula's four-year-old granddaughter, sat next to me with a wad of chewing tobacco in her mouth. In the middle of her spitting, she uttered the words "I don't. I hope he dies!" We were all terribly shocked at what we heard. Everyone sat quiet and still; you could hear a pin drop. I think we all were attempting to digest the weight of her words.

Chuck was only a baby, but the hatred that Tillie and her family had for Mama and her children knew no age. As she sat, slumped in her chair, spitting her worn out tobacco in a tin cup, Tillie had a look of disgust on her face. I was beyond angry, but I knew that Mama would not tolerate any contempt or disobedience. If word got back to her that I was being rude, a switch from the willow tree would be waiting. In anguish, I sat, silently hoping for a better outcome. But before the night was out, Chuck passed away into my invisible world. I walked away from the circle filled with hatred and condescension for the tobacco-spitting toddler Tillie.

After Chuck died, Mama—without the help of Daddy—buried him in a small shoebox at Eagle's Nest Cemetery, not far from our house. Everyone said he died of a condition called *Cat Guts*. I had no idea what that meant. *What is Cat Guts?* I only know that I spent years grieving for a brother I never knew. I convinced myself that, had Chuck been here, he would have protected and looked out for me. However crazy it sounds, at a very early age, my subconscious kicked into survival mode and never shifted gears again.

Daddy had been living with Ms. Emma Tee for almost a year when Chuck died. When Mama gave birth to Chuck, she was all by herself. When she brought the baby home, he lived a little over a week before he passed away. All of the grieving that Mama did was done alone! Her eyes were swollen from crying, and her breasts were engorged with milk. With no baby to suck the milk out and relieve her of the pain, she quietly picked me up, sat me on her lap, and placed her breast in my mouth! With tears in her eyes, she said to me, "Baby, you gon' have to help me. Chuck is gone, so I want you to suck the milk out ya Mama's breast. You mustn't swallow it, 'cause it'll make you sick. Once the milk hits your mouth, I want you to spit it in this jar!" Looking up and into my mother's pain-ridden eyes, I pressed down on her nipple and drew the milk from her breast. My mouth filled up with an awful-tasting liquid. I gagged as I fought to spit the milk into the dingy jar! For an entire year, I sucked my mother's breast until she stopped producing milk!

* * * *

Not long after Chuck's death, Tillie accidentally drank Kerosene oil. Many thought she would die. The adults rushed her to the hospital while all the kids gathered at Ms. Lula's house, once again, in a wide circle to send up prayers and well wishes. Everyone expressed his or her desire for a good outcome. All the people before me said somberly, "I hope she lives, I hope she pulls through, Lord, give her strength, I hope she makes it..." I never forgot what Tillie said in Chuck's prayer circle, and I never forgave her.

When my turn came, I sat up straight and with unexpected anger said, "I hope she dies, because she prayed for my brother Chuck to die, and he did. So, I hope she dies." Everyone in the circle sat stunned and disappointed in me. I was disappointed, later on that night, when Tillie came home from the hospital alive. She heard the story of my *not-so-well* wishes. Tillie's family was crazy, and I should not have fed the flames of the feud. During a petty argument between Kay and me a few weeks later, Mrs. Lula asked Kay if she would like to give me the same sandwich that made Buddy sick. "That will shut her up," she promised with a pleasant voice that made Kay's skin crawl. Kay told them that she didn't think that was a good idea. Sometime later in the day, Kay came back to me and told me that I was lucky that she didn't take them up on their offer. It was weird, but I didn't feel so lucky!

* * * *

My mother had only an eleventh grade education. Who knows what she would have become had she graduated from high school. She had an unbelievable strength and an incredible perception of the world around her. People fed off her as she shaped our family into who we became. Mama had vision and could see past the physical birth of her children. With guts and determination, in the midst of extreme poverty, she had expectations for her kids. While many African American parents were succumbing to what was becoming known as *the system*, my mother refused welfare. Even when Daddy was living with other women, even when we did not have enough food to eat, Mama would not stoop to welfare. She stood in line for government cheese and lunchmeat *only one time*. Afterward, she refused to go back. We could have eaten well every day, but with dignity, Mama refused to rely on free help.

I would sometimes pray, "Oh God, please let my mother get in the government cheese and spam line," always to no avail. She was adamant about being independent and teaching her children to stand on their own strength. Her thought process went totally against the grain. We were a black family living in the sixties, and there was poverty everywhere, yet our mother said with sincerity,

"No government, no cheese." I did not understand it at that time, but she understood what her responsibilities were to her children. She prided herself in the fact that she was not on welfare, that she was self-reliant and raising responsible children. My mother, in spite of our extreme poverty, provided us with many lessons.

Mama was a strong Christian woman who dedicated a major amount of her time to serving others from a Christian perspective; nevertheless, there was another side to her. She would listen to a daily broadcast as she worked and took care of her house chores. While I was playing outside I could hear an eloquent voice announce from her radio, "And now, the honorable Elijah Mohammed." During these times, Mama closed her door. Though I knew that the shutting of her door meant *For Grown Up Ears Only*, I stopped what I was doing, raced inside, and stood silently at the entranceway, trying to hear the fragile voice as it transformed itself into a mighty thunder. The walls were so perfectly paper-thin, and I could hear every word he said. After the introduction, Elijah Mohammed's tiny voice became a giant presence in Mama's bedroom. I could hear him talking of black people making their own way. He talked of a crippled society and the unforeseen dangers of relying on the government to put food on the table. He admonished African Americans to start their own businesses and shop within their own community. He demanded that black people stand on their own two feet, free from the shackles of government handouts. Mama read her Bible all the time, but she listened to that advice. My mother had the answer to lift us out of poverty. She even knew how to deal with racism. The answer was always: education, education, education. Her obsession with our future made me wonder about her past.

*   *   *   *

Mama's father, Grandpa Tom, owned a little Beatnik store across the street from Anna Strong Elementary, where Kay and

I attended school. The neighborhood frequented his store to buy tamales, cookies, chips, and soda. I never thought twice as I ran into Grandpa's store to get tamales. He had not one ounce of Hispanic blood in him, but to this day, for me, good tamales are based on how my Grandfather's tamales tasted.

Grandpa Tom was a pillar of the black community in Marianna. One of the first black business owners, he was well known in our town. Black entrepreneurs in the late fifties and early sixties were as rare as the Haley's comet.

While I knew Grandpa Tom, I did not know anything about his parents. Like so many black families, the family history only went back a few generations. *Where was Grandpa Tom from?* The answer to that question is likely lost in the wind, but his will to survive goes much deeper than what the natural eye can see. My knowledge about my ancestors stops with my grandfather, but stretches back further than the slaves stacked on top of one another on ships destined for America and other distant lands.

One thing I did know about Grandpa Tom was that he hated Daddy. It had not always been this way. They started out as close friends. That union would only last a brief season. Long before Daddy met Mama, he was a married man with children. At sixteen, my mother was angry with Grandpa, because he, like so many other poor blacks, took her out of school to work the cotton fields to help provide for the family. Wanting to become a teacher, Mama was devastated over his decision. Even though she was close to her father, Mama was mad and threatened to leave home forever. She needed to escape the norm. She moved in with Grandpa's twenty-eight-year-old friend, James Edward Wolfe and his wife. The rest is history. Mama and Daddy became involved. His ex-wife and children moved back to Detroit, and without divorce papers, my parents married. As a wedding gift, Grandpa gave my Mama part of his land to live on, but he never forgave his new son-in-law.

Not long after their nuptials, Grandpa Tom went berserk, mortgaging the land right from up under her. With tears in her eyes, Mama proclaimed, "We have no money." Grandpa said, "I don't care where ya'll go! You got no food? Well...now you got no land and no house! Let's go! You need ta git up off the land and go wherever!" Because Daddy was in and out, Mama had to find a way to take care of her children. Grandpa's words forced Mama to plant greens, peas, tomatoes, corn, and a host of other vegetables to sell to the public to survive. Even though he was cruel to her, when Mama found him running down the road with no clothes on, chasing a rabbit, she called on friends to help get him to a nursing home. That day Grandpa Tom flew right over the Coo Coo's nest! Not long after his nudity incident, he died.

My grandfather's distaste for Daddy partially explains why we were so disconnected from our relatives. It was an awful cycle in the making. While both my parents stressed the importance of education, subjects on extended family, the value of relationships between brothers, sisters, uncles, aunts, and cousins were never discussed. Mama and Daddy had no idea that their children would grow up even more disconnected from their siblings than they were.

On Daddy's side of the family, we knew that one of his brothers was disgruntled with his relatives. His name was Clarence. As a teenager, he left home never to return. We, by no means, knew the details of his discontent, but one thing we knew was that it was as if Uncle Clarence never existed. No one ever mentioned his name. Already a cycle of brokenness and misconception was being birthed; relatives were being lost within the ranks. We learned quickly that we were *not* our brother's keeper. These negative, silent teachings shaped each one of the nine children into loners. It would be years later, at a small family reunion, when we would meet the grandson of Uncle Clarence. Searching through the archives of the wind, our cousin, Derrence felt that he had found some of the missing pieces to his life. It was a horrible thing for me to think about. What could have made Uncle Clarence so mad that he disconnected himself from his entire family? He left his parents and siblings! What could have caused him to feel so alone in his life? Why did Daddy's parents not look for their child? The components needed to build a strong family unit were *as gone* as Uncle Clarence, the day he walked out the door; nobody cared.

Like Uncle Clarence, my brother Bobby left the same way. He was the other black sheep. We both wore darker skin than the rest of the children, and Daddy could not stand the sight of us. One night in the summer, Daddy became so furious with the appearance of Bobby that he picked him up and threw him down the steps of the front porch. With Bobby struggling to get up and retrieve his balance, Daddy stood on the porch with a gun in his hand, waving it and telling my brother to get away from his house and never come back. That night, the wind blew silently against Bobby's face as he disappeared into the night. It would be thirteen years before we saw him again. While we waited and wondered, Mama always reassured us, "Naw baby, Bobby is not dead. If he was, God would have shown me." The possibility of normalcy in our family was unlikely.

*   *   *   *

Mama was eighteen years when she gave birth to my brother, Bill. I am not sure what age my parents married, but with my mother being a child, and my father being twelve years older than her, their marriage had to be engineered by Daddy. While these stories are hard for some of my siblings to digest, I find them worthy of penning for lessons in life. My parents were not perfect people nor were the circumstances around them. They did what they knew, making decisions based upon the information they had, which was not much. Daddy made many mistakes, but he was a product of his time—a time where whites dominated blacks, men dominated women, and *everyone* dominated young black women.

I knew the pains of growing up as a little African American girl in the sixties and seventies, but imagine growing up in the twenties and the thirties, where total segregation and racism existed, a white America with blacks just trying to stay alive. My parents grew up in a hate-filled society. To wake up black had to be extremely tough. I am sure that circumstances helped to color my father's life *cold*. Imagine growing up before December 1955, when Rosa Parks refused to give up her seat to a white man. My father was thirty-seven when this monumental event happened. In 1943, during the Detroit riots, he was twenty-five. In 1938 when the headquarters of the NAACP hung a flag that read "A Man Was Lynched Yesterday," my father was twenty; my mother was only eight. In 1930, when a huge crowd in Indiana gathered to witness the lynching of Tom Ship and Abe Smith, my mother was being born. My father was just a twelve-year-old kid. I can't even begin to conceive what it was like for the both of them. To hear the voice of God amidst so much pain is miraculous in itself. My father's world was cold. He grew up in a world of hate. How else could he be? As I envision their lives, I am in awe I can even say I had a man I could call *father*.

Daddy was a proud man and well respected in our small town. He was highly esteemed by blacks and whites alike. I never once saw my father disrespected because of the color of his skin. He had a reputation of being a no-nonsense man when it came to racial intolerance.

Years ago, Kay told me the story of our father being left alone to tend to his younger brother. While crossing a country road, holding his baby brother's hand, a white driver tried to run the two children down. Daddy—scared for his life—let go of his brother's hand, and dove out of the way. He watched from the ditch as the man plowed the truck into his little brother. The driver shouted racial slurs as he sped away. When Daddy thought it was safe to come out, he crawled out of the ditch and onto the road, picking his brother up. He cried as he cradled the child's mangled body in his arms, and, right there before his very eyes, Daddy watched his little brother die. He developed a severe stutter after this incident. I believe that conditions and circumstances colored my father *cold*.

Born into Violence

While my generation was far from the tumultuous era of my parents, I was born into violence. In 1954, six years before I made my entrance into this world, the U.S. Supreme Court ruled that segregation in public schools was unlawful. Three years after this unprecedented decision, in 1957, The Arkansas State Capitol became infamous for its refusal to allow nine African American students into the still segregated Little Rock Central High School. Arkansas Governor, Orval Faubus, used the state's National Guard, armed with bayonets, to stop their entrance into the school. This incident put Arkansas on the U.S. map while a reluctant President Eisenhower placed the National Guard under a federal court order to escort the students into the building. Even though segregation was against the law, our governor was not ready to see integration happen. Rather than submit to the law, at the end of the school year, he shut down the entire education system.

By 1960, the year I was born, African Americans were staging sit-ins in segregated public places all across the United States. While I was still sleeping on embalming sheets and fishing stinking animal water out of the well, Dr. Martin Luther King was fighting for racial equality. He was on the lips and minds of blacks and whites all across my small town.

When I was a toddler, state administrators in all parts of the country were willing to go the gamut to maintain segregation. Like Governor Faubus and Alabama's George Wallace, (who stood in the doorway of the University of Alabama to defend segregation in his state), administrators withdrew services and closed public facilities to maintain the color line. Thousands of

African Americans, organized by Dr. King, marched through the streets of Birmingham, protesting inequality and boycotting its downtown retail stores. The demonstration enraged the city of Birmingham so much that Police Chief Bull O'Connor arrested almost one thousand children and young adults. The media captured Bull, himself, releasing police dogs on innocent black children. It also captured footage of Birmingham's Fire Department, plowing helpless protesters onto the ground by turning their powerful water hose on them. These images stunned the world and ultimately helped to desegregate Alabama. In the fall of that same year, Dr. King organized a march on Washington, D.C. With a crowd of over 250,000 people listening, he delivered his famous *I have a dream* speech before the Lincoln Memorial. I was only three years old. Kay was five and Buddy was thirteen.

In 1964, when I was four, President Johnson signed the Civil Rights Act, outlawing discrimination in employment and public facilities based upon the color of a person's skin. And in 1965, the Voting Rights Act was signed into law, opening the polls and giving blacks the right to vote. Crossing into uncharted territory, America was in turbulent water.

In April of 1968, while Kay and I were playing under the mimosa tree, my mother came, screaming out of the house, and onto the front porch, saying that Martin Luther King was dead. She heard it over her transistor radio in the kitchen. A white man, named James Earl Ray, had shot him at the Lorraine motel. Mama cried as she fell to her knees, "He's gone! A white man murdered Dr. King! He's gone!" I was just a kid, but somehow understood the tears and stress on my mother's face. The morgue shipped Dr. King's body back to Atlanta, laying him to rest. Just like that...our Moses was gone! I was almost eight years old. Our future looked bleak and impossible.

Out of all the places Dr. King traveled, he was shot and killed in Memphis, Tennessee. The spot was only forty miles from my hometown. He was staging a march and protesting the working conditions and discriminatory practices of the city toward black sanitation employees. The world, upon hearing the news of his death, looked on as America tore itself apart. Massive riots broke out in over one hundred U.S. cities.

We saw Dr. King as our only hope, because he was not afraid of the violence that was sure to come. Moreover, when Martin died, we knew that there would never be another man of his character. People were afraid and had every right to be, but Martin was such an enigma that he convinced protesters to go, even in the midst of their fear. Whatever accomplishment he made, black people were sure that the federal government would not hold up to their end of the bargain anyway. To blacks across America, Martin Luther King *was* the movement. The day he was killed, most felt the dream of equal rights died with him. It took years for us to realize that many people of different creeds and colors walked alongside him. Not only that, but there were people like Malcolm X and even Angela Davis who were helping to set the gauge and momentum in the plight of blacks in America.

After Dr. King passed, Arkansas never looked the same again. So much was happening in the world, yet in Arkansas, we were still picking cotton. This tradition stretched back centuries. The only thing missing from the old days were the shackles and the whip.

Each year, Mr. Buddy Meredy—the meanest and tallest black man I had ever known—came to the end of the road near our house with a huge bus to pick up cotton choppers and pickers. From young to old, black people lined up, waiting to work the fields for three dollars a day. I, at eleven years old, along with some of my siblings, got up at the break of dawn and walked down our dusty road to the end of the lane, and waited for Mr. Meredy's bus to pick us up as well. It wasn't actually his bus, but he drove it and made us believe it belonged to him. In actuality, it belonged to a wealthy white man, who owned thousands of acres of land, filled with millions of rows of cotton. Once on the bus, Mr. Meredy drove miles to get to the fields. I closed my eyes and hoped we would never arrive, but all good things must come to an end.

To let us know we were there, Mr. Meredy screamed, "Hurry up an' git on off that bus, lazy ol' good fo nothin niggas!" By the way he talked to us, it was hard to believe that he was as black as the rest of us.

We worked the fields from sunrise to sunset with minimal rest, while the scorching heat blackened my face even more. We lugged our heavy cotton sacks on our backs, and if we chopped or picked too slow, Mr. Meredy came running down the cotton row screaming demeaning words at us. The only thing missing was a whip in his hand and gun on his hip.

In the heat of the day, Mr. Meredy would bring a huge, Igloo cooler, holding ice-cold water and a copper dipper down our row. The dipper was similar to a soup ladle, except its purpose was to hold the water as it was being released from the cooler. We waited as he went, one-by-one, empting the crystal clear water into the dipper, quenching the thirst of the exhausted workers, then passing the makeshift cup on to the next person. Many of the workers chewed tobacco or dipped snuff. With our bodies drained of energy from the sweltering heat, we all drank behind each other, never giving germs or sanitation a second thought.

Chopping cotton was my first connection with work. If my parents felt that the fields were demeaning, we never knew it. They placed a high value on working and making an honest living. If we were to get new clothes and shoes, we had to work. The cotton fields were as good as any place to start.

One day while Kay and I were working the fields, a huge cottonmouth lay on the ground between us. The moment Kay caught a glimpse of the snake, she screamed and ran franticly toward the other workers.

"Snake!" she screamed. The pitch of her voice was so intense that it caused everyone else to scream and run in the opposite direction.

Mr. Meredy shouted back, "What the hell is goin' on up yonder? Y'all niggas git back up in nare and git ta' work."

Someone screamed back at him, "We aint goin' no where! That Wolfe gal done seen a cottonmouth!"

Mr. Meredy went into the field, searching for the snake. After a few minutes passed, he came running toward us with a huge, dead snake hanging from his hoe. He laughed as he told the other workers, "See, this aint nuthin but a lil bitty o' snake. It wuttin' nuttin to be sked of." With sweat pouring from his face, he dropped the snake, grabbed Kay and I and drug us back to the bus. Mr. Meredy, struggling to handle both of us, picked us up and threw us into the seat and said, "Y'all stay yawls asses up here on dis here bus and don't u come down! Don't y'all show up ever again on my cotton pickin' bus. And don't ya say one mo mumblin' word!" We never went back to the cotton field again!

* * * *

In 1971, we found ourselves in a city filled with turmoil. Racially divided, the politics of segregation turned Marianna into a ghost town. I was eleven years old and in the sixth grade. It was a terribly hard time for our city, but oddly, the best year of my school experience. There was a boycott of stores and the education system, because many whites in our town were hell bent on keeping things just as they were. White people rose to protect the segregation laws, but a mysterious moral majority lifted their heads and demanded change. I was too young to know who the moral majority was, but these brave people walked, talked, and ate in places they were not welcome. They challenged the age-old rule of *Separate but Equal* and fought for a better life for us all. People were saying that the small town of Marianna was worse than certain cities in Alabama. There was a rumor going around town that Marianna's Fire Department, like Birmingham, had actually opened their hose on its black high school students, forcing them to their knees on the ground. Mama and Daddy kept the tiny black and white television off to shield our innocent ears. Neither I, nor my siblings knew if this was true; everything was confusing. If we asked questions about adult affairs, they promptly told us to leave the room. In fact, the only thing we knew for sure was the importance of education, education, education. "If you want to win in this situation," Mama and Daddy warned, "get an education." And so, in the middle of the boycott of Marianna's downtown retail stores and the school system, we went to school—amidst angry blacks and whites. White people were angry that blatant racism was being exposed. Black people were angry, because they seared in poverty, and this day had been too long time coming. African Americans looked at my parents as if they were betraying our race, because of their decision to keep us in school. In fact, not only did Mama make us go to school, but she continued working at Strasburg's, a Jewish clothing store in the heart of our deserted town.

Clearly, Mama found herself caught between two diverse ideologies: Martin Luther King and Malcolm X. Those days when she privately listened to Elijah Mohammed speak of independence and self-determination had saturated her being. Martin affected her also with his calm and reserve. His impact upon the black race was then, and continues to remain, incalculable. Martin, all his life, was a peaceful man and practiced the same, wherever he went. When he observed Mahatma Gandhi obtain rights for his people through peaceful demonstrations, Martin followed suit. Malcolm X was different; he was a peaceful man as well, but believed that we, as African Americans, should gain our freedom "By any means necessary." Because Mama was an independent thinker, she listened and weighed the value of *all* words. She, more so than Daddy, was passionate about her beliefs. She marveled about her right to choose to support the boycott or not. Had the boycott been about retail stores and materialistic things only, Mama would have supported the efforts of the people. However, this was about the education and long-term well-being of her children. On this occasion, Mama chose the philosophy of Malcolm X for all of us, including Daddy. What my parents did during these chaotic times was unprecedented. Word spread fast of their unwillingness to support the black cause.

One hot afternoon, a white van came hurrying around the curb of our dusty road, producing a fog so dirty and dense we swore a level three tornado was on its way. A dark cloud of dust from the road raced with the van to see which would make it to our house first. Once they reached our home, three men sat for a moment in the hot truck to allow the dust to settle. The look on their faces told of their fear as sweat pushed through their nicely pressed shirts. They briefly talked amongst themselves. It was as if they were wondering how they ended up in a third world country in the heart of Arkansas. Poverty stretched as far as their eyes could visibly embrace.

The three men were news reporters and had come unannounced, finding Mama on the front porch, washing our clothes on the washboard by hand. Her wig was unkempt and positioned toward the north. With pants under her long skirt, this attire was Mama's favorite in those days. Kay and I played in the yard as a white man slowly opened the door of his van. With sweat pouring from his face, he cautiously stepped down from his vehicle, wiping his forehead with a crisp, white handkerchief. After hesitating, he advanced toward Mama. As he was walking, two other white men got out, walked around, and opened the door to the back of the van to retrieve their camera equipment. Mama, almost as fast as their door opened, shouted from the porch, "How are you? What can I do for you?"

The reporter walked into our yard and said, "We heard that you are one of the people who's keeping your kids in school during this boycott."

She responded, "I am one of those people, and I will be happy to talk to you once I go in the house, take a bath, and put my wig on right!" The reporter looked agitated at her words, but before he could speak, Mama said, "The whole world is in a complete mess. Now what you all came to see was some poor, poverty-stricken woman using broken English. I will be happy to talk to you, but you are going to have to let me go in my house to make myself pretty. I can't be looking like this on TV."

The white men looked at each other and agreed that she looked good enough for what they were doing. Immediately, Mama's countenance changed. She shot back, "I'm sure I do look good for what you all are doing. You want me to get on your camera with my wig on backward and show the good folk across America what niggas in Arkansas look like. Well I tell you what you need to do... pack up your stuff and git going as fast as you can. I don't wanna have to use that ol' shotgun in the corner of my living room." Kay and I sat quietly in the grass while Mama saw the men to their truck. I was in awe. I didn't even know she knew anything but broken English. When she was talking to these men, her grammar was flawless. I sat in the grass, wanting to hear more of her and then more of her, but the white men drove away and Mama said, "Ya'll come on and git in the house."

There were only seven black children in my sixth grade class, and everyone moved cautiously along. Most black families in Marianna chose to keep their children home. We were all fearful of reprisals and backlash, but my parents were self-determining thinkers. They pushed us through the broken education system. All of our classmates whose parents chose to hold them out of school would graduate one year behind us. Though criticized, my parents stayed the course. I was lost in translation, and the personal attention I received in this small classroom reshaped how I saw myself. I gained momentum and was beginning to excel. I was ahead of others; forget that it was by forfeit or default, I was excelling.

By 1972, our school was integrated, and I moved on to seventh grade. I could, for the first time in my life, get on the bus and sit on the same seat as a white child, drink from the same water fountain, and even use the same restroom. Nonetheless, we saw the fallout and collateral damage from a year of racial tension. The students held back had a difficult time catching up. Children much smarter than me were one year behind me. Many succeeded by going to summer school, but some did not. Those unable to catch up graduated one year behind their class. Many local whites didn't come back at all. A private school was set up for whites refusing to go to school with blacks. This school stands even until this day. Marianna became a ghost town. On windy days while sitting, waiting for my father at the funeral home, I watched the trees blow and empty their leaves onto the bare streets. Neither whites nor blacks patronized merchants in our towns. Stores closed never to reopen again. The price of equal rights was costly.

Expanding my Horizons

That year, in the seventh grade, Aunt Sophie asked Kay and me to come and spend the summer in New York. She sent plane tickets, and off Kay and I flew to the big city. Let no one say that people are of no essence or that one's actions cannot influence, for my aunt was of great influence in my life. The summer of '72 was life altering and served as a catalyst to facilitate change in how I viewed myself. My thought process would never be the same.

Aunt Sophie was Daddy's sister. She lovingly referred to him as *Jimmy* and was always attentive to his needs. I found my love for my father through her affectionate words toward him. She was articulate, with no trace of a southern drawl. When Aunt Sophie was a teen, she moved from poverty-ridden Arkansas to New York and became a nurse. She fell in love and married the man of her dreams, who treated her like the queen she was. Her husband passed away years before our visit to New York, but her heart was forever entwined in his. I had only seen pictures and heard endearing stories of their love for one another. Sometimes, when she was talking about him, I could feel the spirit of his love enveloping us. Theirs was a love so grand that it even survived death and promised to protect us through the dark night.

New York was an avalanche of firsts. I took my first plane, saw my first skyscraper, road my first train, and tasted my first banana split, right around the corner from Aunt Sophie's house. I closed my eyes and savored it, as the vanilla ice cream, strawberries, pineapple, nuts, and bananas mixed in a smorgasbord of goodness in my mouth. Never had I tasted such wonder. I tasted my first mango with Aunt Sophie. She carefully peeled it and shoved a small piece into my unsuspecting mouth. As the rarity of sweetness hit my taste buds, I swallowed slowly and asked, "Aunt Sophie, what is that?"

She smiled and simply replied, "It's mango, sweetheart." I went to my first movie theater in New York. Every day, my cousin Billy, Kay, and I caught the bus from Laurelton to Manhattan. We went from one theater to the next, watching kung fu movies and black exploitation films. We left early in the morning staying out until after sun down. Life was so good, and I never wanted to see those dusty roads of Arkansas again. The subway, tall skyscrapers, and my aunt Sophie were all I needed in life. Buildings that reached into the heavens, touching the base of the sky and resplendent lights, brought the city to life, and I was a part of it.

It was a summer filled with instructions on how to sit, how to speak eloquently, how to communicate with all walks of people, from the ultra-rich to the toothless drug-heads swimming through the ghetto. There were instructions on how to groom myself and how to take care of my skin. It was also a vacation filled with grammar lessons and table etiquette. When Kay and I made mistakes, Aunt Sophie would lovingly correct us. She consistently reminded us why our communication skills were important. With a kind and soft voice she said, "Baby, education is important, but it is nothing if you lack the ability to communicate your needs to those around you!" She reminded us that the possibilities were limitless with a world opening up, she promised, if we were willing to work hard.

Aunt Effie, another sister of my father, lived in the same house. She was kind, but reserved and stingy. If Aunt Sophie sent us to the store with a twenty-dollar bill to buy mangos, she would tell us upon return, "Sweetie, put that in your pocket." Aunt Effie, on the other hand, would send us with just enough money to purchase an item and upon our return would ask, "Didn't I have something coming back to me?" We hated going to the store for Aunt Effie. She was not only stingy, but quiet. She rarely spoke to us. With Aunt Sophie showering Kay and I with love, it did not matter. I felt like I could conquer the world.

That summer we found out that plums and Indian peaches were not the only fruit in the world. We tasted papaya, star fruit, and even guava. While Marianna slept, we walked down long, white stairs to an underground train. Underneath the bustling city, the subway zipped us to Madison Square Garden and Coney Island beach. I ate my first slice of pizza at Coney Island and tasted the frozen deliciousness of an Italian ice while looking up at the Empire State Building.

Nearing the end of my stay, Aunt Sophie presented me with a charm bracelet adorned with diamonds, rubies, and pearls—all the jewels her husband had given her over the years of their marriage. She pointed out what each jewel represented: anniversaries, birthdays, and Christmases. She placed the bracelet on my skinny wrist as a token and confirmation of her love for me and charged me to keep it safe until we returned to each other. Whether it was two years or twenty, I was to guard it with my life. The gift was not just valuable in a monetary sense, but was also full of sentiment, representing her life and her undying love for me. In a way, she passed on her life to me through that little bracelet.

Summer ended and Aunt Sophie placed Kay and me back on the plane back to Arkansas. With tears in my eyes, I put my left hand on my right arm, coveting my bracelet and remembering her words, "Protect it with your life until I see you again." I held my dearest aunt in my heart and would never forget my time with her. As the plane lifted off the runway at LaGuardia Airport, I fingered the jewels of the bracelet, remembering each story she told. I looked out the window of the plane and tried to wish away the muddy roads of Arkansas.

*   *   *   *

Two days after my return home, I woke up to a bare arm. The charm bracelet was missing. Tears soaked my pillow as I lay on sheets, scented with embalming fluid. "Nothing there...nothing I could do!" Aunt Sophie had given me a piece of her heart. Each time she pointed to a jewel, she paused and placed her hand on my heart saying, "This diamond, this pearl, this ruby is *you*, my precious darling." Before the lesson was over, she made me feel like a child of the queen. Through the darkness of her dimly lit room, I embraced her words and felt the rarity of me. For only a few days, I believed I deserved to wear such a priceless treasure. Through my tears, I could see her going to the jeweler and having him take apart all of her necklaces and broaches to make me feel special. Nobody had ever cared enough to give me anything—nobody but Aunt Sophie—and it was gone. No one had seen it. I shrunk down and hid myself even deeper inside my secret closet. I avoided all conversation with Aunt Sophie, fearing she would ask the dreaded question, "Where is it?"

It was the first of thousands of precious things I would lose in my life.

I sunk so deep into my closet of depression that I didn't speak to Aunt Sophie for nearly a decade. It would be years before I realized I cheated myself out a precious relationship, one too rare to duplicate. I was only twelve; she would have understood, but early on, I learned to distrust those around me. Aunt Sophie, even though she was one of the most loving women I had ever known, was no exception.

The following winter, she sent a huge box of warm clothing for Kay and me. We tore through the box, claiming our clothes. I grabbed a beautiful plaid winter coat. Arkansas winters were brutal, and a thick coat was exactly what I needed. I enveloped myself in Aunt Sophie's love—but like the bracelet—by morning, the coat was missing. I searched in tears, but it was as if it never existed. That day, I walked up the long, frozen road with only a sweater to protect me from the biting wind. With my heart shattered into a million pieces, I shook as I waited for the school bus to appear. When it finally arrived, I raced inside to hide from the brittle wind. Later, in the school lunch line, I saw a boy wearing my coat! Daddy had taken my coat and given it to his mistress's son, leaving me to shiver in the cold.

He stole a piece of my life—a better life, far away in New York. It killed me to think that the coat Aunt Sophie sent was on another child's back, a coat that I desperately needed for the bitter cold, one that represented my Aunt Sophie's love. As I stared at the jacket in the lunch line, my anger grew. The boy strutted around as if he was someone special, a peacock, wiggling his shoulders, showing off his new clothes. I was a girl, and a shy one at that, but I lost it!

I grabbed the kid and punched him in the face. He fell to the floor as I tried to yank my coat off him. He fought back, but there was so much anger inside of me, the poor kid never understood what hit him. I was screaming as I was fighting, "That's my coat! My aunt Sophie sent it to me! Give me back my coat!" He kept crying out, "No, my mama gave me this coat!" A teacher came, separated us, forced me to give back the coat and sent me to the end of the lunch line. Even my father's mistress's children were more important than I was. I was left to figure out what to wear for the winter, while the boy wore my coat through the cold season. After that, I watched Daddy more closely. In the coming weeks, the light would shine so brilliantly that it would expose the great shadows and shrouds of secrecy that kept my father away from his wife and children. Mama had always known why Daddy periodically disappeared from our lives. There were times when he stayed away as long as two years. But this time, the spirit of truth was permeating through darkness, and I too began to see the light.

One afternoon, not long after the coat incident, Kay and I were walking from school to Aunt Doll's house. Related to us by marriage, Aunt Doll was one of the oldest citizens in our small town. As we headed to her house, we saw Daddy's car parked in front of a small convenience store. Even though we knew the answer was no, we went inside to ask him for candy. We opened the door to the store and walked inside. The lights were very dim and toward the back, we found our father pressed up against a heavyset light-skinned woman. It was Ms. Laraleen. She caught a glimpse of us before Daddy did and cleared her throat to alert him that they had spectators. With his arms still wrapped around her body, our father turned around and nervously glared at us. For a brief moment, he looked like a deer trapped in headlights. He shifted his body and dropped his hands down to his side, and in a panic, stuttered, "Y'all, c—an ha—ve, any—th—ing y'all want! Coo—kies, ca—ndy, pop; An—yth—ing, y'all want!" My father was caught and vulnerable. It was one of the few times in my life that I saw him giving instead of taking.

Kay and I grabbed all the pop, candy, and cookies we could carry. Once we arrived home, we told Larry the story. The three of us sat, debating whether Mom needed to know, but before we reached an agreement, Larry walked out the room and spilled the beans to Mama. Once the story was out, we were amazed. Mama was calm. She went in the kitchen and started cooking and singing as she waited patiently for Daddy to return home.

Hours later, he walked in. Daddy was so tall that he had to bend his head down to get through the barely hinged doorway. Wearing psychedelic blue pants and bright blue shoes to match, Daddy was sharp as a tack, and nobody could tell him any different. Ignoring the cold sentiment in the room, he asked, "Lindy, you got my supper ready?"

Mama walked out of the kitchen, leaned up against the living room wall, yet never spoke a word.

He repeated the question. "Lindy, you got my supper ready?" Before she could respond, Daddy said, "Hey, I need my green pants washed!"

Mama quickly answered back, "Tell Laraleen to wash them." Daddy asked, "What, did you, say?"

This would be the only time in my life that I would see my parents argue. Mama's comment sizzled like a fuse before an explosion. She shot back, "I said, 'Go tell Laraleen to wash them.' I aint washin nuthin! I need you to get out and go on back down to Laraleen's house. You ain't welcome here no more." While she screamed, "Get out!" Mama ran back into the kitchen and grabbed a cast iron skillet, raising it as if she was going to hit him. Before we knew it, Daddy was gone. After he left, Mama grabbed the tattered phone book, thumbing through for the oblivious. She picked up the phone and called Ms. Laraleen. The moment the woman answered, Mama screamed into the mouthpiece, "Slut," and hung up! Mama had reached her limits. She was not the type of woman to curse or raise her voice, but that night was her breaking point. The next morning, Daddy came home, and it was as if nothing ever happened.

Even though that was the only fight I ever witnessed between my parents, the stories that my older siblings told were epic.

One time, Daddy was in a juke joint, dancing with another mistress of his, Ms. Emma Tee. Mama, after finding out that he was night clubbing in the middle of the day, went to the town pawnshop and asked the owner, Mr. Wilbur Pennegar, for a gun. Mr. Pennegar, a white friend of Mama's, would not sell her the weapon. She was too angry, and he could tell. After much prodding and pulling from my mother, he finally gave in and handed her the pistol. Mama never knew that Mr. Pennegar emptied the chamber before releasing the gun to her. He showed her how to use it and told her to bring it back to his store after she was done.

Mama marched out of Mr. Pennegar's store and straight into the dimly lit hole-in-the-wall. Billy Holiday crooned lyrics from the jukebox 'My Man's Gone Now' as my mother quietly walked up on Daddy and Ms. Emma Tee. Without any warning, Mama jumped on Daddy's mistress, slamming her to the floor. She shoved the pistol in the woman's mouth and calmly said, "I done told you bout messin' wit' my husband." As the woman struggled and screamed for her life, Mama, in a heat of passion, pulled the trigger, expecting to empty a few rounds into the mouth of her adversary. The gun made only a hollow clicking sound as my mother looked at the woman in amazement. *By now*, she thought to herself, *Emma Tee's brains should be all over the floor!* Instead, the woman lay there breathless as Mama straddled her like a saddled horse. The dance floor cleared out like a bunch of rats fleeing a sinking ship. Daddy stood to the side, in complete shock. The cops showed up and hauled Mama to jail. Her bail was so large that Grandpa Tom had to mortgage his land to get her out. When Mama learned that Mr. Pennegar saved her life by removing the bullets from the gun, she was eternally grateful. Ms. Emma Tee was too ashamed to press charges, Daddy was too scared to run away, and Mama was too determined to keep her marriage together to let it fall apart; she loved Daddy and had gone to great lengths to keep him.

I was no different. I wanted Daddy to know I existed as well. One Sunday, on a cool, October night, driving home from church, Daddy saw a rabbit on the road. Speeding his car up, he swerved and injured the animal. The wounded rabbit struggled to make it to the thickets bracketing the road. Daddy, almost as if he had a keen sense of intuition, turned to me in the backseat and said, "Wanda, you got good eyes...go get that rabbit." Without giving it a single thought, I beat the rest of my siblings out the door and raced into the thickets trying to find my father's approval. To no avail, I looked amidst the dried branches. That rabbit, if I found him, would serve as dinner tonight. With the thought of my father smiling at my accomplishments, I got on my knees and searched even harder. I dreaded the thought of coming back empty-handed, so for twenty minutes, my heart pounded as I tried to feel my way around in the dark—nothing! Eventually I gave up and attempted to make my way back to the car. I was so immersed in my failure that I tripped over something—maybe a log, I'm still not sure—but something big enough to cause me to fall forward into the dried field of branches. A stick went into my left eye! I cried out in pain, but no one heard me. Shielding my face with my left hand, I got up off the ground and began the lonely walk back.

When I got back in the vehicle, I did not want to tell my father that I failed, but there was no getting around it. Before I could shut the door to the car, he asked," Did you get him?" Still covering my injured eye with my hand, I sheepishly told him no and slumped down into my seat. I could feel in the air frustration and discontent all around me. After hearing my answer, Daddy turned around and sat for a minute, looking straight ahead into the darkness. This short period of silence seemed to last for hours, yet it was only a matter of minutes. He quietly got out of the car and walked the thickets until he returned with the rabbit. He never said a word, but I could tell he was disappointed. I think about that night more than anything else in my childhood. It wasn't his words that hurt; it was his complete silence. It was what he didn't say! His silence was even more painful than the stick that went into my eye. The trauma done to my physical eyes could not compare to the scarring done to my emotional eyes. His silence spoke volumes of negativity to my tiny, fragile heart, and I could see nothing but failure in my future. What my father didn't say caused a swirl of self-doubt to arise in me. This same self-doubt attached itself to me and hid in obscure ways, peeking its head out at the most crucial times. That night I learned that sometimes the most painful thing a person can do is to say nothing at all.

Where there is Smoke...there is Fire...

It was as if the well-known author, Alice Walker, was peeking through my secret closet when she wrote parts of *The Color Purple*. At the tender age of twelve, a suitor at least five times my age pursued me when he assumed no one was watching. When I was walking down our dusty road, he gave me cookies, candy, nickels, and sometimes even quarters. When in church, he would slyly wink approvingly at me. His name was Mr. Benny, but I only knew him as *the old black man with the mule and buggy*. I was innocent and unsuspecting that behind his smile was something sinister.

It was a typical summer day in Arkansas, and dust was rising, mixing with the clouds. I sat on the steps of the house, waiting to see who was coming down the road. It was not the sound of a car, but of clapping hooves. When I saw the buggy, I stood up, and waited. Something deep within said that the old black man was coming for me. When he reached our house, he beckoned his mules to stop! His words, "Whoa mule," stick in my head even to this very day. Though my heart raced, I stood still. As sweat poured from his black forehead, he stepped down from his buggy. His dirty overalls were tattered, yet the clothes he held in his hands made up for his grotesque form. In his hands he held a beautiful, yellow dress and yellow, patent leather shoes to match. Never had I seen anything so striking. He gave them to me and said, "I bought these jus' fo' you."

Feeling uncomfortable, but mesmerized by the gifts, I said, "Thank—" Before I could say another word, Mama raced out of the house, grabbed the shoes and dress out of my hands, and threw them at Mr. Benny. She told him she had been watching him for weeks and she would kill him if he came near her child again!

Mama screamed, "My child ain't for sale. You better leave before I get my shotgun!" He jumped in his buggy, hitting his mules with a fierce urgency to get away from our house. Somehow, though young and innocent, I fully understood that Mama had come to save me, to save the day.

At age thirteen, I attempted to erase the ugly feelings I had about myself. I used Noxzema to clean my skin, Ambi to fade the awful black spots in my face, and, seeking independence, I decided to straighten my nappy hair.

Louise Mix, who stood barely four feet tall, opened a hair salon on the corner of Main and Chestnut, and I was her first customer. With a little small talk, she convinced me to come in and sit in her chair. I was hesitant, but an invisible tug pulled me inside. By the time I sat down, my knees were shaking like dry leaves in autumn. Louise wrapped me in a white cloth similar to Daddy's embalming sheets, opened her jar of lye, and saturated my hair with it. She then rolled my hair and placed me under the hot dryer. As the dryer became hotter, a bonfire ignited on my scalp. I sat, squirming, thinking, *I don't think it's supposed to feel like this!* A single tear fell from my eye as I fought to keep my composure. After twenty minutes passed, Louise turned the hot dryer off and removed the rollers and *everything else on my head*, everything except a few sporadic sprigs of hair attached to the plastic rollers. I was bald for the remainder of the school year. Louise gave me a dreadful afro wig to wear to hide my burned, bald scalp.

That year, I was the laughing stock of my entire class. It was the year cruel children reminded me of my lack of water to take a bath. They made fun of my raggedy clothes and reminded me, daily, of the acne and dirt on my skin. I felt so ugly and unwanted. One day, a kid named Darryl Robinson snatched the hairpiece off, exposing my bald head. He ran onto the playground screaming, "Come and get it if you want it!" Defeated and alone, I sat down on the ground and cried, cradling my burned head in my hands. It was the first time I entertained the idea of suicide. My year of independence quickly turned into my first serious bout with depression.

* * * *

That same year, in our backyard, near the outhouse and trash dump, I lost my virginity on the ground to a boy named Perry Jones. He was seventeen and I was thirteen. He convinced me that he loved me and wanted to protect me from the rest of the world. Without my consent, Perry forced himself inside me and thus began the sins of Mary Magdalene. That night, I felt like a trapped animal, helpless but wanted!

My mother repeatedly warned me to stay away from Perry. She said he was nothing but trouble. I ignored her concerns, and, surrounded by trash and the stench of garbage and excrement, I allowed Perry to penetrate my body. He roughly pushed past my underwear and painfully took what little innocence I had left. The moment he forced himself inside of me, I remembered girls talking about how good sex felt. What was wrong with me? There was nothing good about this! There was nothing romantic about it. The act itself lasted only five minutes or so. When Perry was done, he got up, pulled his pants up, and zipped his fly as he stood over me. I lay there on the filthy ground scared and wounded. He hadn't even allowed me time to say if I wanted to go forward. Days later, I found out from another Mary Magdalene that Perry's mission in life was to see how many virgins he could conquer. After deflowering a young girl, he would boast about it in school, then move on to the next.

When telling stories of my life, I would often omit Perry Jones and move on to Sam Wells. Because of our brief encounter, I felt he was irrelevant. *I was wrong!* This boy was extremely significant in helping to develop the character of my Mary Magdalene. There he was in the St. Simon church choir, singing away as he blew kisses my way. I had no idea that this puppy love experience would end in the loss of my innocence. We never talked again. For Perry, it was as if it never happened.

The Mary Syndrome

Mary Magdalene was a troubled woman who was plagued with demonic spirits. Most biblical scholars believe that she was a prostitute and adulterer, a very serious crime back then, punishable by death. I often think of her life before her incredible transformation. I imagine her broken, confused, and running from man-to-man. She was a woman looking for someone to make it all right and save her from herself. I imagine that, even in the company of others, she was alone. I can see her sitting in the darkness, sobbing in emptiness and drowning in the deep waters of her own tears. It wasn't until her promiscuous life was exposed that she was forced to deal with the true gravity of her situation. Mary, caught in a compromising position, according to the law, could only be dealt with by stoning her to death.

Many times, I have asked myself, "Where was the man in this fatal scenario?" There was never a mention of her cohort, but everyone who witnessed the incident saw Mary as completely evil and worthless to humanity. With her secret closet ripped apart for the world to see, spectators called for her death. The religious community especially closed the door in her face. These *good, sanctified, self- righteous* folks saw no redeeming qualities worth saving in Mary. While they turned their righteous backs on her, Jesus sat, writing on the ground. Right before the carrying out of her death sentence, Jesus challenged the teachers of the Mosaic Law, saying, "He who is without sin, cast the first stone!" His words caught everyone off guard! Many people have questioned the contents of his doodling on the ground. Although not completely sure, I'd like to think that Jesus opened the secret closets of all Mary's accusers by writing their sins on the ground.

Whatever He wrote, the words made Mary's accusers go away! He saved her life. There is a saying that Mary, before she met Jesus, believed that her freedom lay in the arms of the men she slept with. It was not until this great transformation that *she came to her senses* and realized that she had wasted her time and priceless oil. The misuse of her oil was symbolic of the wasting away of her life. Operating from a *position of insanity*, each time she poured herself into the arms of another man, fragmented pieces of virtue stayed behind. I believe Mary came to the end of herself when she found herself on death row. She did not want to die, yet I believe she *willed* herself into the *position of no more!* She had experienced enough physical and emotional abuse to last her another lifetime. When Jesus healed her of the many vices she possessed, she anointed his feet and *his feet only.* Out of all the characters in the Bible, especially as a young woman, I understood what happened to Mary. Perhaps I understood who Mary was, because she, like me, was drowning herself in a cesspool of self-induced exploitation and violence. Like Mary, my problem was not in how I treated others; it was how I allowed others to treat me and how I treated myself. The deflowering of her innocence must have occurred when Mary was a little girl. Someone in a position of authority had not protected her. In other words, someone that Mary loved did not know how to reciprocate that emotion and threw her to the dogs. And like me, her search for acceptance almost took her life. *I know Mary, because she was I.*

He Could Smell My Hopeless Fear

My eighth grade teacher, Mr. Allet, asked me to stay after school to help *grade papers*. He spent his time rolling his obese body up against mine and placing his hand inappropriately in my pants. I silently became a willing party. All throughout eighth grade, he kept me after school, fulfilling the sick fantasies of his mind.

While other teachers worked to prepare for the following day, Mr. Allet molested me. As with Perry, I kept quiet and shoved it into my secret closet. I felt responsible for his actions.

Sex and touching, whether appropriate or inappropriate, were not subjects discussed in our family. They were taboo. Rarely did I see my parents display any form of affection. Whatever one did in secret could easily remain a secret. If my family had been more open to sharing and talking, Mr. Allet probably would not have been able to molest and abuse me. We were all silent with so many things tucked and hidden away. I didn't understand at that time that he was a predator; I only understood what it felt like to be wanted. When the year ended and I moved on to ninth grade, Mr. Allet stopped talking to me and acted as if nothing ever happened. He quickly moved on to his next eighth grade after school project. A few years later, Alisha Miller's parents filed charges against him for sexually abusing their daughter. I often wonder how many young girls Mr. Allet molested before authorities stopped him.

By the time I reached fourteen, I was a daughter of secrets and shame, wearing an invisible veil of mourning. No one knew, or maybe they did, and looked the other way. Maybe no one cared. Much of a girl's vision for her life is directly linked to her femininity. With a distorted self-Image, her past, present, and more importantly, her future is likely to be blurred, resembling a reflection in a funhouse mirror. Her entire outlook on life can shift on a few small incidents. These incidents with men altered the course of my life.

Mr. and Mrs. Norwood, an elderly white couple, lived several miles from our house in a lake home, used only during the summer months. The rest of the year, they resided in Memphis. At thirteen, I became their maid. For twelve dollars a week, every female in the Wolfe family (except Rosa), performed housekeeping at the Norwood home. We all split our earnings with Daddy to pay for a ride to work. He demanded it. With the small amount of money left, I bought skin cream and clothes for the following school year.

With her white glove treatment, Mrs. Norwood taught me the meaning of the word *clean* by inspecting each nook of every room. She also taught me *honesty* by placing money in inconspicuous places to see if I was stealing from her. Mama always said to lift the money up, dust under it and place it back down in the same spot. I was proud of my ability to satisfy Mrs. Norwood's lofty requirements. The scent of their cottage smelled of pine and lemon. Each time after cleaning, I looked at their hardwood floors and determined that, though I lived in deep poverty, someday I would have a house like theirs. As demeaning as the job seemed, I learned how to create a sanctuary, how to meet my employer's expectations, and more importantly, how to operate with integrity. It was a priceless lesson to be trusted around someone else's wealth. Amidst all of the emotional dirt, I was gaining valuable attributes.

I entered the ninth grade with my own hair, clean skin, and new clothes. Even though meeting new people terrified me, I made friends in my freshman year. With a new image, black and white girls with bright futures accepted me into their circle. Most of them were better off than I was and lived uptown. They dressed nice, smelled good, and dated athletes. Each year they were the students voted Most Popular and Most Likely to Succeed. Enamored by the possibility of being just like them, with every breath, I hid the poverty that was sure to shroud me once my school bus dropped me off. High school looked promising, but it didn't take long for a new male to enter my life. His name was Sam Wells.

Sam Wells, the Sweat Hog

Kenneth Perkins, the captain of the football team, could not believe I was the same Wanda Wolfe. Notorious for wearing ugly afro wigs and tattered clothes, he was shocked to see me with clean skin and natural hair. Striking an immediate comradeship, he introduced me to his best friend, Sam Wells.

With fists as big as a cannonball and voted the strongest man in school, Sam was a body builder, bench-pressing 450 pounds. He also played defensive tackle for Lee High School's football team. Athletes on the opposing teams feared running into him, because of his animalistic strength. Sam was quiet, withdrawn, and unable to give direct eye contact—as if he had something to hide. He seemed curiously confused about everything in life, except football and me. Every girl, I thought, saw him as handsome and desirable. I was drawn to him instantaneously. When Sam asked me to go steady, I said yes and fell hopelessly in love with him. Little did I know, dating him would help to *color my life cold*. I knew nothing about his background, nor did I care. I liked the way he looked, and that was enough for me. I willfully stammered into a world of horrific violence.

When Sam and I walked down the school hall, he squeezed my hand so tight it almost went numb. No one had ever held onto me that firmly. I misread his tight grip for love and protection. Our first kiss was barbaric, ironically telling of the brutal future to come. Rough and depraved, Sam nearly choked me with his tongue as he gripped my hair tightly in his fist. It was a horrible experience. I grasped for breath as I attempted to gain my composure.

The star players on the football team named themselves the Sweat Hogs after a group of misfits from a popular seventies TV show, called *Welcome Back Kotter*. The sweat hogs were the most popular guys in school. They were known, not just for their agility and ability on the field, but also for their talent for playing girls. They were all cheaters. Their girlfriends were known to other classmates as the *Sweethearts*, thrusting each one of us into popularity. Our relationship quickly became one of sadistic, jealous possession.

Violence came quietly while the two of us waited for our bus. A mutual, male friend walked up and paid me a compliment about my dress. While the boy was talking, Sam grabbed my arm and discreetly dug his fingernails into my wrist. He cursed in my ear and whispered, "You better watch yourself." I bit my lip as I fought back the tears. His jealousy was becoming a sickness, clouding his opinion of me and everyone else around him. Saturated with insecurities, Sam wanted to know everything. "Where have you been? Who were you talking to? Why are you lying to me?" My self-esteem began to wither even further away. It became so low that I developed an unconscious habit of holding my head down and to the side. The insecurity I felt on the inside was beginning to peek through my secret closet. One day, Coach Coleman, a favorite teacher and mentor, confronted me about my posture. He said, "Do you know who you are? You are a Wolfe! You must never allow anything to cause you to forget this! Stand up straight and don't let me see you with your head down ever again! I expect you to succeed like Bill and Buddy!"

Buddy

Bill and Buddy, my two older brothers, graduated together in 1968. When Bill was younger, he was forced to stay home to work the fields for two years during one of my father's absences. Mama needed her oldest son to help provide for our family. Instead of being two years ahead of Buddy in school, Bill graduated alongside him. Under Coach Coleman's leadership, my brothers were captain and co captain of a winning football team. During their high school years, they had a reputation of being athletic forces. Marianna's football team was never the same upon their graduation.

By the time Sam and I started dating, everyone except Buddy had graduated and moved on. The other siblings Bill, Sophie Mae, and Bobby left so fast one would have thought there was an outbreak of Ebola in our hometown! Once they escaped, they never looked back. It was as if Marianna, Arkansas, never existed. Buddy was different. He attended Lane College in Jackson Tennessee. He was a model student and All-American through his achievements in football. After graduating from college, he taught history at a local high school in Brownsville while moonlighting as a disc jockey.

Buddy's personality was a force that pushed him through life. In the eighties, he was one of the pioneering artists of the Rap/Hip-Hop genre (Google *Super Wolf Can Do It* to see Buddy in all his early eighties glory!). West Tennessee knew him as Super Wolf; to us, he was still Buddy, my second hero. He took what Aunt Sophie started and continued the process of mentoring. He came home from Tennessee on a regular basis and connected with his siblings left behind: Larry, Kay, myself, Gary and Rosa. He chose to reach back and pull us forward. We spent all of our holidays and summers in Jackson. In 1976, Buddy married Blues Hall of Fame artist, Denise LaSalle. Eventually the two purchased a radio station and became pillars of society in their community, sharing the experience with us.

During the summer months, Buddy drove to Arkansas, took all five of us to Jackson, and enrolled each of us in summer work programs. During some of my visits, his wife, Denise, exposed me to celebrities like Anne Peebles, Rufus Thomas, The Emotions, and Lionel Richie. One day in front of the Lorraine Motel, where

Martin Luther King was killed, Denise introduced me to her friend, Bobby Blue Bland. I was awestruck when he kissed the side of my face. And when Wanda, the lead singer from The Emotions, allowed me to come backstage during one of their concerts and sample her makeup from her huge cosmetic board; I thought I would die from excitement. Buddy and Denise even took Mama and me into the recording studio and allowed us to record four songs. These were all positive, impactful events in my life. I often wonder what would have happened to me and the rest of my siblings had Buddy not been there. He was the only sibling that cared. With high standards set, Buddy hammered into our heads: "There is no option to fail." These words proved to be extremely life altering, for I would eventually model my life after him.

One day, Buddy came home to visit and found me on my way to the dentist. I was about to get a gold tooth... right smack dab in the middle of my mouth. Having saved my money for months, I was excited. Once he heard my plans, he sat me down under the mimosa tree in the front yard. "It's your money," he said, "You can spend it however you want. But know this—when I went to Detroit, people saw the gold in my mouth and knew I was a black man from the South. I had it removed for this very reason. If you want to fit the stereotype, then by all means, *Go*! But if you want a better life, just possibly a gold tooth may not be the smartest thing to spend your hard-earned money on." Afterwards, Buddy pointed out how beautiful my teeth were. I chose to keep my money and forego the gold.

Strong, resilient, and profound, my brother, Buddy, was a role model for struggling, wayward African American youths throughout Tennessee. He passionately embraced the inner city children. He utilized the radio to express the problems that existed within his community and became an example of excellence among his peers. While people watched as he rode the rugged waves of life, I had learned to smile at each interval. He was amazing in his conquest. Clearly, he chose to rise above the clouds of adversity.

Buddy was born in 1950. He was five when Emmitt Till was murdered in 1955 and five when Rosa Parks refused to give up her seat to a white man. In September 1957, when the Supreme Court outlawed school segregation in Arkansas, he was seven years old. When blacks knew Birmingham as *Bombingham*, and Police Chief Bull Conner's method of *control* for blacks was fire hoses strong enough to knock out a brick wall, my brother Buddy was only thirteen. When the Montgomery March took place from Selma to Montgomery Alabama, Buddy was fifteen years old. These activists were pushing for the rights for blacks to vote. When President Lyndon Bird Johnson listened to Martin Luther King Jr. make his argument of the importance of the Voting Rights Act in the White House in 1965, I was five; Buddy was fifteen. In 1968, while Martin Luther King Jr. lay in his casket and Andrew Young, Ralph Abernathy, and others looked on after his assassination, our beloved brother Buddy was just graduating from high school. He made a choice to share his knowledge and freedom with his siblings who lived in a dying town. He reached out in the midst of the struggles that he faced and unselfishly reached back into his past to bring us forward in time. His actions made it unacceptable to live a life of violence or mediocrity; yet violence and mediocrity was the road I began to walk.

*   *   *   *

In Marianna, the violence in my life was beginning to pick up momentum. Scars began to show up everywhere. Sam's favorite form of discipline was wringing my skin as if it were a dishtowel. I gritted my teeth and bore the excruciating pain of his fingernails going in and twisting away. This painful gesture served as a constant warning to me of a greater threat of violence to come once we were alone. When we were at his house, he was not so gentle. He was in his comfort zone and brutality was the norm. It soon became evident to me that fighting and hostility was all he knew. From the pulling of my hair to the slamming of his huge fist against my head or stomach, he accelerated his quest to conquer.

There was a history of violence in Sam's family. His father, Mr. Wells, had four brothers who beat and tortured their wives. All of their women were broken vessels. Lacking in self-worth, each one walked with her head down and avoided eye contact. They did not want the world to know that their mind, body, and spirit lay in fragmented pieces.

Sam's whole family had a backwoods mind-set. His mother, Mrs. Geneva, was a sad, obese woman who tried daily to please her husband. She was always unsuccessful. Strapped in by a house filled with small children, too many to count, Mrs. Geneva sat in her corner chair, trying to rock the pain away. If she got up, it was only to cook the greasiest of foods. I laughed at the thought of Mr. Wells croaking after eating her lard-based spaghetti and sausage. I swore she was trying to kill him off legally, making him pay for all the dirt he dealt out to her.

Out of the entire brood, one child captured my attention. His name was Marty, and he was severely mentally challenged. I'm not sure why, but Marty was as fascinated with me as I with him. Standing within a foot of me throughout the day, he followed me everywhere saying, "Joon musty…iddy musty!" It took me years to figure out that he was saying, "June's (Sam's nickname), musty, really musty!" Mrs. Geneva suffered horrific violence when she was pregnant with Marty. Mr. Wells hit his wife in her abdomen so hard that it knocked her backward, flipping her over the couch and onto the floor, damaging the fetus. No one was ever prosecuted, but everyone knew that Marty was mentally and physically handicapped because of domestic abuse.

The first few times I went to Sam's house, I lied to my parents, telling them I was at my friend, Vickie's, house. Instead, I rode the school bus, getting off on his road. Young and stupid, I do not know what I was looking for. Without giving it a second thought, I allowed myself to be weaved and entangled into a long generational cycle of abuse and violence that spanned well over forty years.

At night, at least in the beginning, Sam would ask to drive his father's car to get me home. When we first started dating, it was important to Sam to take me home. After a few months, when he became comfortable with me, he stopped caring if I made it home at all. He lived too far away for me to walk the distance; many times, I ended up staying overnight.

Sam lived in a strange house. It was a long place, resembling a shotgun house. Four rooms went down a lengthy hallway. Sam's room, back at the end of the house, became my personal chamber of horror. When we were in his room, he was free to do whatever he wanted. He would yell, scream, threaten me, and then beat me to a pulp. One night, he became angry and pushed me through a mirror. The sound of breaking glass was so loud I thought his parents would come in and stop the scuffle. His family, though— in the other rooms—turned their heads and closed their eyes while rough sex and violence took place. As complacent as Sam's parents were, it did not take long for tension to build with mine.

One night after a beating from Sam, I came home late, and Daddy met me at the door. He started to scream about the rules of his house. In sheer lack of common sense, I walked away, smart mouthing my father. As I headed down the back steps of the house, Daddy came up behind me and hit me across my shoulder with a log. The impact of the blow sent me flying down the steps and onto the ground in our backyard. Filthy from Sam's house and the dirt on the ground, I found myself crying, and even laughing at the horrible conditions around me. It would have been better to be dead! Daddy did not know and did not care what happened to make me disrespect his rules. The beating I had just taken from Sam was because I wanted so badly to come home on time. With my face in the dust, I cried into the night.

Every evening after school, I, like every other student living in my area, had to ride Sam's bus to connect with my own. The buses left Lee High to interchange at Anna Strong Elementary. Every day, Sam took his fingernails and dug them deep into my skin, warning me not to stand up. With tears in my eyes and hatred in my heart, I sat still and waited for his bus to pull away, headed for his house. Some nights I came home, and some nights I did not. Mama and Daddy always looked at me in disgust saying, "We are sick and tired of you coming in when you feel like it." I would quietly find my way to another part of the house to avoid contact with my parents. I wondered if they knew what was going on. How could they not know the truth? Many times I came home with black eyes, busted lips, swollen jaws, bruised arms and legs, and swollen noses. No one ever asked me to explain my injuries. They never said one word.

I was more familiar with Sam's home life than my own. Mr. Wells had a pigpen behind his house, and the smell of it was everywhere. When it was time to feed the hogs, Sam helped his father fill the troughs with slop while I sat quietly in his room. The smell of rancid unwashed clothes and hogs gathered in my mouth, causing me to gag. During the fall months, they slaughtered hogs. After shooting the pig in the head, Sam and his father would heat water in a huge kettle outside. At the point of boil, they would take the dead animal and drop it in the kettle, dousing it with hot water to remove the hairs from its body. Afterwards, they would string the hog up by its hind legs. Hanging the animal in mid air, they would cut his belly from top to bottom to remove its guts. He and his father would sit and pull the feces from its intestines to create chitterlings. The smell of pig blood, burning flesh, and feces filled the air around Sam's house.

After this horrible process, Sam made his way back to his bedroom without washing or bathing to have sex with me. I would silently protest by backing away, but he would grab and kiss me anyway. "Show me that you love me!" Sam demanded as he groped with his filthy hands, crushing me with his iron body. I began to associate the slaughtering of hogs with sex. I would hold my breath, declare my loyalty, and pray to God that he finished quickly. As the smell of dead hogs and boiling water engulfed my throat, I would pray, "God I know that I'm wrong, please let this end. Please help me."

When Sam was done, I wanted to wash it all away, but I was too afraid and ashamed to leave the room. Even though it was not a big deal to him, I didn't want his parents and siblings to see me. The stench of dead hogs was in my skin, my hair, all over me. One night, after a slaughtering, I made the mistake of requesting something of Sam that he was unwilling to do without a fight. "I want to go home," I pleaded with him.

"I can't take you home," he said. "I don't think my Daddy will let me drive tonight."

"I can't spend the night again," I told him. "Daddy and Mama will be so upset. They have already said they will not put up with me staying out all night anymore. Please ask your Daddy. Please." Sam left out of the room, and came back with the keys and angrily said, "Get your coat." I felt his muscles tensing as we got in the car. He was so angry. He shouted, "You gon' get me in trouble with my daddy. I can take you to Vickie's house but no further." "No," I started to cry, "I've got to go home. I can't go to Vickie's house. I've got to go home. Mama and Daddy are going to kill me. Please take me home, Sam."

He screamed out, "Dammit, I said I can't. My daddy will not let me use the car again if I go all the way out to your house.

I whimpered, "Please take me home, please, Sam, please. My parents have warned me. Please Sam, take me," and before I could finish my sentence, he hammered his fist into my face.

Many times before, he had done this very thing, and I had seen stars. But this night was different. He was like a ferocious animal. Blood gushed from my nose and mouth; my left eye shut tight within a matter of minutes. I screamed out, "Oh God, oh my God. God, please, oh God, God—help me!

Sam was frantic "I told you to shut up," he screamed. You made me do that. Please shut up so I can think. Let me see." He looked at my face and told me if I had just shut up, this would not have happened. He then sighed and said, "I'll take you back to my house, we'll get you some shades, and I'll take you home tomorrow. No one will know."

The following day, he went out and bought dark shades for me to wear. Two days later I went home, telling the lie that Vickie was driving, and when she made a sudden stop, my face went into the dashboard of her truck. My parents bought the lie, but after that fateful night, I was unable to bite or chew firm fruits such as apples and pears. I developed TMJ, which caused my jaw to lock with severe headaches. Like a trapped animal, I saw no way out, except by dying. Years later, well after these violent times, I was diagnosed with petit mal seizures.

I grew up in a world of secrets. My life with Sam was the kind of thing that was not openly discussed. In small town Arkansas, there was an unspoken agreement among some of the men of our town. I could feel it when I walked by, and people stared at my bruises. I felt it in the questioning glances—"Wonder what s*he* did to deserve that smack." And deep down, if the truth be told, I felt responsible for Sam's actions. Like his uncles' wives, I had become a broken vessel as well. I began to visualize myself obese, sitting in my own rocking chair, on welfare, accustomed to the violence. As time passed, I saw myself sinking deeper and deeper into Sam's cesspool of despair.

During my senior year, each Sweat Hog came back to his Sweetheart with a startling disclosure. One heated night on the town, they all pulled a sex train on two wayward girls. Someone, and they were not sure whom, but someone dirty had gonorrhea. They all had sex repeatedly, causing each one of us to contract the disease. Each of them carried and transmitted the STD to their girlfriend. The Sweethearts were devastated, but with a loyal code of silence, we all marched down to the city's health department and received penicillin shots in both hips. And while I tried to grapple with the appalling circumstances in my life, an old snake raised its head.

A couple of months before graduation, brown-eyed, tobacco-chewing Tillie, started to make trouble again. On the bus ride home from school, she and two other kids started to bully my younger brother, Gary. I leaned forward and told them to stop. As the other kids moved away, Tillie turned and said, "Watch your back!" She had established a name for herself as a town brawler. I leaned back and rode the rest of the way home in silence. Once the bus stopped, we all exited together, with Tillie running ahead of us. I was relieved to walk the long road in peace. I exhaled as I treaded home with my siblings.

The next morning on the bus, there was a suspicious quiet. I thought about Tillie's threat and our history together. I remembered the prayer circle.

That evening after school, we got on the bus, heading for home. The silence was even more haunting. As soon as our bus driver, Shorty, came to an intersection, a raggedy, white truck blocked its path, causing the bus to come to a halt.

Shorty opened the door to speak to the driver. Before he could say anything, an angry mob poured through the door. He yelled, "Y'all caint come on the bus. You guys get out of here!" Rosa and Gary looked on as Tillie's friends and family grabbed me by the hair, pulled me off the bus, and threw me into the street, pushing me down on the pavement. I was in a blur as seventeen children and adults beat me to a pulp.

The reason behind the beating was much more than my breaking up a fight the day before. These people were lashing out at our family. All of my siblings had gone to college while Tillie and hers stayed behind in Marianna. Everyone in the forbidden house had gotten pregnant or hooked on drugs. This fact, while it made us stronger people, also made us a target for Tillie's family to exact revenge. We were taught to better ourselves, but they believed we thought we were better than they were.

Grown women well past forty, fought like men, to bring physical harm to my body. One monstrous woman weighed over three hundred pounds. I was in a stupor and almost unconscious when someone grabbed my breast and sliced into it with their teeth. There was blood everywhere. Later on, Tillie bragged that she was the one who bit me. Shorty eventually came down off the bus, broke the fight up, picked me up off the ground, and drove me all the way down the dusty road to our house.

In the evening, Daddy came home, took my face in his hand, and carefully examined the damage. A single, long scar started at the bottom of my left eye and ended right above my top lip. Daddy stammered, "They scarred my child's face!" I had never seen him so emotional. The next day, he went to the courthouse and pressed charges against the mob of people.

When our court date rolled around, the judge asked my father to explain why he had felt the need to press charges against Tillie and her family. Daddy broke down in tears as he pulled my blouse down away from the scar on my breast and attempted to tell his story. That was the first and only time I saw my father cry. The judge looked down from his bench in apathy. His look seemed to say, "It's just a bunch of niggers fighting."

My father tried to tell the story, but with his pronounced stutter, was unable to articulate his thoughts. The judge looked at the wound, then Daddy, and said, "You have no grounds for a suit." Nothing happened to Tillie, her family, and friends. Yet, even though Daddy lost the case, I felt like a winner. I had to take a beating from Tillie and her crew, but it all seemed well worth it, because that day in court I felt the love of my father.

The Freedom of Music

At the end of my senior year, my friend Theodore and I decided to travel to Helena, Arkansas, to audition for a summer acting and singing road show. We stood in an empty, yet massive high school auditorium, waiting for our turn to sing. Theodore auditioned first, and they rejected him. I belted out three lines of *The Way We Were*, and they immediately chose me to go on the road. I was excited to leave my hometown. Most of all, I was excited about leaving Sam behind.

He dominated my life. I spent all of my money as a Sonic drive-in employee to purchase Sam's graduation cap and gown. I even purchased his tuxedo for his senior prom. With no money left for myself, I went to Mom and begged her to pay for my prom and graduation attire. She narrowed her eyes with reservation and concern but eventually gave in. I wanted it all to end, and this was the perfect opportunity to disappear.

Our ensemble traveled to parks inside of eastern Arkansas. The group of singers was eclectic. I was one of two black performers. The rest of our entourage was white. One boy was from deep in the Ozarks. He had never seen a black person in his life. When I got to know him, I discovered he was a good person. We all ate at the same table and rehearsed together for a successful production. We were learning to get along and learning to accept and embrace what true integration looked like.

We sang songs from *All That Jazz* and the *Wizard of Oz*. They issued us leotards and tutus, and I wore them proudly. All the girls were in ballerina attire, learning new words, like *plié* and *curtsy*. Each day I became more interested in theater. Singing was the one thing I had always been comfortable doing. During my high school years, I had won first place many times, competing in talent shows. Here I was traveling all over rural Arkansas, singing songs like *Tomorrow* and *If You Believe*. The music transported me to another place far away from the poverty of Marianna, far away from Sam. We belted out songs in park amphitheaters while families sprawled out on blankets, and people sat on logs. It was the best three months of my life. With incredibly grey days ahead of me, I wished away the clouds and prayed for my days in this ensemble to last forever.

Weeks of performance passed, and my abdomen seemed to push through my leotard. There was a pooch there, and every morning before and after eating, I vomited my insides out. I thought of all the physical abuse from Sam and even the beating I took from Tillie. After missing my period, I decided to go back to Marianna to be examined by the doctor who delivered Mama's babies.

Mama loved and respected Dr. Fields. Some of the other doctors in my town said that under no circumstances, would they touch a nigger woman giving birth. Even our town dentist said, "I'd rather put my hand in the mouth of a rattlesnake than place it in the mouth of a nigger!" I went back home to Dr. Fields. She was a short woman, heavyset, and a long ponytail with eyes as strong as steel. In a field dominated by men, she knew what it was like to suffer discrimination. She was white, but accepting of all races and creeds. After examining me, Dr. Fields delivered the news. "Well I know why you're getting sick." She came around, put her hand on my shoulder, and gave it a squeeze. "You are almost six months pregnant." Her words pierced my heart. I was sick and devastated. I was the first of the Wolfe children to fail. She didn't just say *pregnant* but *six months*; no longer an embryo, but a baby with limbs, a baby with a face. I was taking birth control pills, but lately I had become careless. I was more consumed with the violence around me. Pregnancy never crossed my mind.

* * * *

To uplift my spirits I took what little money I had and bought a beautiful, white sundress, then went to the funeral home and waited for Daddy. The moment we got on the highway, I sat silently in the car, wishing that the beautiful, scenic, winding road would disappear quickly, so we could get on with real living. I absolutely hated the road from Marianna to our house. It was deceptive with its peaceful, swaying trees, gorgeous ponds, and picket fences. The way the highway manipulated its twists and turns, one could not help but think it would empty you off at heaven's gate. *But…* right before its last curve, it turned a little to the left and dealt a horrible blow, delivering us to an impoverished home. And like the road, I had learned to be as deceptive about the ugliness inside of me. I hated this road and hated myself even more. I felt old, abused, exhausted, and very alone—a complete failure and mess.

Upon arriving home, I walked inside the house and, staring blankly into space, delivered the news to my parents. Daddy was silent. Disappointment was written all over his face. There was no way out. Instead of lying on a bed, I chose the living room floor, because I felt I didn't deserve any better. The bare floor was a blank slate that screamed, "You are a failure, a nothing, a nobody!" At one point, I sat up in the center of the living room and rocked like a boat adrift. Pregnant at eighteen with Sam's baby, I sat there, staring at my belly, knowing that I was trapped.

Daddy came into the living room and said, "You know you have to take care of yourself. I bought you a carton of milk." Stunned, I gratefully took the container, opened it, and drank until it was gone. I was amazed at my father. He was so kind to me at that moment. Even to this day, I associate this one kind act with him. It took me foolishly engaging in sex, becoming pregnant, and giving up on life to experience compassion from my father. Daddy understood the consequences of my irresponsible choices. With nine children of his own, he knew that my life was about to change forever. I was unprepared for the events to come.

After collecting myself, I knew I had to tell Sam. I took a long breath, picked up the telephone, and dialed his number. Only a few days before, Sam enrolled at the University of Arkansas in

Conway. College bound, he had said, "Nothing is going to hold me back!" He picked up the receiver and asked why was I home. "Sam," I began with a trembling voice, "I'm pregnant."

He shot back, "So what do you want me to do about it?"

I had no reply.

"I'm going to college," Sam continued. "What the hell do you want from me?"

"Sam, what am I supposed to do?"

"That's not my problem," he said.

After those words, our conversation ended. His bitter expressions were too cold to process.

Mama sat in her bedroom in complete silence once she heard the devastating news. She was not willing to accept failure in our family with one of her children, even if it was me. A rush of emotions washed over me. A sensation of insignificance pulled at me. Feelings can be deceptive, but at that time, at such an immature age, feelings were everything. Distress and pity resided on Mama's face. I needed her to say something, anything, but she remained quiet. In fact, over the course of the next week, she never spoke about it—not one single word. It was as if our conversation never happened. For an entire week, I lay on the wooden floor and wept silently while Mama bore her burdens alone.

Murder...By Reason of Insanity

Kay was a sophomore at Arkansas State University. When she came home to visit, and I told her about the pregnancy, she burst into questions and painful comments about my future. She reminded me of Marty, Sam's mentally challenged brother. "The abuse you went through," she warned, "could have serious effects on this baby."

I held my stomach and thought about all the times Sam hit me. I was surrounded by poverty—no washing machine, no indoor plumbing, and no money, yet I was about to have a baby by a violent man who scared me to death. I knew I would never be able to escape Marianna. Kay told me that my only option was for us was to find a place that did second trimester abortions.

Neither one of us understood the gravity of the situation. However, having the child was a more frightful thought. How would the child live? How would I provide the necessities? What would I do if the baby were like Marty? What kind of life would it have with a father like Sam? Kay and I both made up our minds that an abortion was the best and only option. If everything went as planned, I would be in college in the fall. We told Mama it was a mistake, that I was not pregnant, and that I was just picking up weight. She was relieved. I now believe she knew we were lying, but my failure was too much for her heart to handle.

Kay got on the telephone and searched high and low for a place that performed second trimester abortions. Eventually, she found a hospital in Camden, Arkansas. The cost was $630.00, an absolute fortune for poor black families in 1978. We also needed money for the bus fare. Kay lied and told Mama that I planned to enroll in school, but the financial administration said I needed $730.00 to get me started at ASU. Mama looked at us with a keen sense of concern. We could see the apprehension in her eyes. After a long, motherly pause, she agreed to give us the money. She said that the amount would totally wipe out her savings. "But anything," Mama said, "to get you enrolled in college."

My life was moving at warp speed. I was so far along that I didn't even have time to think about the horror of it all. I was making plans to kill my baby, yet everything was happening so fast; I closed my spiritual eyes and ears to the repulsion of it all. Every time I got a chance, I went in my room, closed my door, clutched my swollen abdomen, and wept. I tried my very best to act as if I was old enough and even strong enough to bear the profound weight of my choice.

Since I was nearly six months pregnant, the doctors at the hospital told me to hurry, or the procedure could not be done. Kay, after making the necessary calls, drove me to the bus station, and bid me good-bye. I begged, "You can't leave me by myself, Kay!" She reassured me, "You'll be fine! Go get on the bus! While you're at the hospital, I'll go to the administration office of Arkansas State and enroll you for the fall semester. Don't forget to take the taxi to this address." She handed me a piece of paper, containing information of how to get to the death chamber. Alone, pregnant, and unsure, I cried for every choice that led to failure in my life.

* * * *

Once in Camden, I called a taxi and waited. An old African American woman, sitting next to me said, "I know everybody in this city. You don't look like you're from here."

I foolishly replied, "No!" *And then…*from a place of stupidity that even I was amazed of, I offered up the ghost and said, "I am from Marianna, but I have been here before. A few years ago, I attended a wedding here. My oldest brother, Bill, married a lady from Camden." The woman tilted her head and looked at me with a pensive stare. The anger in her eyes made me uncomfortable. She asked, "What people do you know from here?"

I replied, "My sister-in-law's name is Ira Burk."

The old woman responded, "I know the Burks. I know Bill and Ira. Now, why did you say you were here in Camden?"

My heart dropped along with my eyes. I couldn't think fast enough.

She then said, "Oh, I know why you're here. Baby, that place is such a bad place. You ought to turn around, get back on that bus, and go home." The blank stare of her judgmental eyes cut right through my heart. I got up and walked in haste to my taxi. She shouted out, "I'll tell Ira I saw you." That day, I learned that everything hidden, in some way or another, shall be exposed.

I have always believed that most women, regardless of their ethnicity or their political or religious views, have a secret that resembles this very disclosure. It is packed away neatly in the privacy of their own secret closet. Many *right-to-lifers* have lived the very essence of my experience, yet they would never allow anyone to peek inside their glass menagerie. And though I speak against abortion today, at that terrifying moment, I was face-to-face with an awful reality of my life and chose to have this very dangerous procedure done. I was stupid, ignorant, and desperate. I had no idea what was about to take place. All I knew was that I was trapped and trying to find a way out.

I arrived at the hospital and checked in. After leading me to my room, a nurse handed me a gown and told me to undress. The moment I took my clothes off, my life and poor choices flashed before me. I had made so many mistakes. Exposed, I felt as if the whole world was watching as I removed my pants and blouse. As I covered my body with the gown, I wondered what would happen. *What had I gotten myself into? How did this partial birth thing work? Would it dissolve or melt the baby away in my stomach? How did it work?*

After examining me, the doctor told me I was almost too far along to perform the partial birth abortion, but decided to go ahead and do the procedure. A few minutes later, another nurse arrived with a stainless steel tray, holding several instruments. My fear shifted to panic. On the tray, lying amidst all the other stainless steel tools, was a long syringe. Never had I seen a needle as long as this one. I trembled as I turned my head to the side while tears in my eyes flowed like a river. The nurse slid the first skinny needle into my wrist to set up an IV. While looking away from him, I listened as the doctor explained that the long needle was filled with Saline solution, and that he needed me to lie very still as he injected it into my round abdomen. I continued to look away as he slid the huge syringe into my stomach. The moment it pierced my skin, I whimpered. After the injection was complete, the doctor left the room.

After a few minutes, the nurse returned and placed a bedpan under my naked bottom. She instructed me to stay in bed—no matter what happened! If I felt I had to use the bathroom, I was use the bedpan only. After the nurse left, there was an almost haunting quiet. Then with no warning, a dull pain began to build in my lower back. That dull ache became stronger, longer, then harder, and longer and stronger until I screamed for help, "Oh God! Help me! Help me God!" I had no idea what a contraction was! I screamed and screamed some more! The nurse came back and forth telling me coldly in a southern drawl, "I don' told ya to lay down! Once that needle goes in, ain't nuthin' that can be done. You gotta let it run its course."

I went on screaming, "What is happening to me?"

The nurse kept saying, "Lay down and keep that bedpan under your backside. We don' already told ya what to do. Now lay down and quit keeping up such a racket!"

Great flashes of pain, as quick as a camera shutter and as intense as a bonfire, snapped through my reality. Pain too great to sit, too great to lie, or stand. I ignored their instructions to stay in bed. I got up and paced the floor back and forth.

Then came a knock on the door. I weakly told the visitor to come in. It was a white Catholic priest. He said, "When I saw the name *Wolfe* on the roster, I thought it was someone that was a part of my parish, but I guess I have the wrong room. Are you okay? You seem to be in severe pain."

I burst into tears, telling him how I had made a grave mistake. I told him about the constant beatings by my boyfriend, the pregnancy, and the choice to have this procedure done. I cried and asked for forgiveness. I cried so hard that he held me up, took my small face in his hands, and asked, "Can they do anything to reverse this?"

I whimpered. "No, once the procedure is started, it has to run its course." With no concern for the color of my skin, he held my teary face tighter and said, "It's still all right. God forgives you. He has already forgiven you. I came to this room, because I thought I was visiting someone I knew. You are not the person I set out to see, but God has sent me to you. He has already forgiven you. It's already done, but *now*, you must learn to forgive yourself."

I cried with an even greater intensity. Tears soaked my hospital gown as I tried to come to grips with what I had done. I emptied my tears onto his white collar as he tried to hug me to abate my physical and emotional pain. It was useless. My tears caused reality itself to distort. My entire field of vision bowed into a twisted shape. The minister released his hug and held my hand as I writhed with pain.

Before bidding me good-bye, he said, "I don't want to leave you, but I must go. I need you to remember one thing. What's done is done. You can't change this, but you can change *you*. You have a choice of how you will live the rest of your life. You can choose to beat yourself over the head for what you did or you can choose to forgive yourself and let it go. I recommend that you learn to forgive yourself. If you don't, the world will miss a truly beautiful person!" After those words, he hugged me and left the room.

Hours passed, and I felt an urge to have a bowel movement. I shifted my body to make it go away. It would not. The urge to defecate became greater and greater until I couldn't hold it inside any longer! *I had to go!*

Riddled with pain, I got out of bed, maneuvered the IV pole, and stumbled to the bathroom. *My body felt like my only option was to go!* I sat on the toilet and pushed to relieve myself. It did not come. I pushed harder and nothing but a greater urge. I used every stomach and back muscle and pushed even harder. A huge gush came, and a giant splash hit the water in the commode. I was startled, but relieved that the pain was over. I slumped over the toilet with my face as close to my lap as I could get. As I sat on the commode, thinking about my choice to come to this dreadful place, I thought about if it were this painful to have a bowel movement, what would it feel like for the actual abortion to take place? For a brief moment, I was grateful for the calm around me. The pain had stopped, but there was something hanging from my body. I pushed the button for the nurse as I peered into the commode. "What? What is this?" I weakly shifted my body and peered in to get a better view. "Oh My god, It's a baby! It's a baby boy." I screamed so loud I couldn't hear my own voice! My baby was in the water. My life shattered all around me. "He's hanging. Dying. He's twirling in the water! I killed my baby! *Pieces of broken glass*! I killed my child! I killed my baby!" I couldn't stop screaming. The nurse came in, and I screamed, "My baby's in the commode! I didn't know! I didn't know! My baby is drowning! Help me please! Oh God help me! I killed my baby!"

The nurse rudely interjected, "Didn't I tell you to stay in bed and use the bed pan if you felt like you needed to push?"

I stood up over the commode with the afterbirth hanging. I grabbed at the walls and groped at myself. I pulled at my soiled hospital gown. I was looking for something, anything, to hold onto. Nothing! Blood was everywhere, on the lid of the commode, on the floor, and on me! "My baby is dead! I killed my baby!" The sound of my voice in my mind decreased to a whimper. The nurse, filled with apathy, instructed me to sit back down and push again over the commode to release the placenta. I quietly slumped back into a sitting position and pushed my baby's lifeline out of my body. At that moment, I silently begged for somebody, anybody, to come and save me. "Someone please help me!"

The nurse brought me a disposable bathing pan, filled with soapy water, a clean gown to put on, and a large white pad to place between my legs. We both were silent as I cleaned myself up. After I finished, she took the pan and soiled gown then left the room.

Drained of energy, all I wanted to do was hide my head under the covers. I lay motionless in bed until morning. A single thought swirled through my mind in the sterile darkness of the room. Staring at the closed bathroom door, there was only one thought, and the horror of it all played over and over. *I killed my baby, my little baby boy.* In the heavy darkness of time and space, I began to feel the weight of my choices. Debilitated mentally, I tried to fit, bit by painful bit, all of it inside my secret closet. *Murderer!*

That next morning, I talked myself out of bed, put my clothes on, and headed out the door. I went straight from the hospital to Arkansas State University. Kay, as she promised, pulled some strings and got me enrolled for the fall.

*   *   *   *

It didn't take long for Sam to find out that I was enrolled in college. Before the abortion, when I told Sam about the pregnancy, he asked me rudely, "What do you want me to do about it?" While I was devastated with his response, he was happily on his way to University of Arkansas in Conway. He didn't care what I did, because he thought I would be stuck in Marianna. Once he heard about the abortion, he said, "You killed my baby to go to college." Sam didn't care about the baby, but he was obsessed with the fact that I was going to college. He couldn't stand the thought of me being on a campus around other young men. With no warning, he changed his mind about Conway and switched to Arkansas State University to be near me.

A week later, I left Marianna and headed to Arkansas State with a major in journalism. To my dismay, Sam followed. Kay and I were roommates in a small, spartan room with two tiny beds. With Sam living in a dormitory close by, the freedom of college was tempered. I could see his dorm from my window. Not long after saying hello to a fellow friend and football player in the hallway, Sam forced me into his room and pushed me against a wall. He lost it and slammed his huge fist into my already bruised and battered abdomen. Blood was everywhere! It was just like old times. I went to the university hospital and allowed them to patch me up, hoping they would not ask too many questions.

I became full of silent anger—full of plots to disappear, to run and save my life. Sam could sense my inner rage, and in a constant fury, tried to beat it out of me. He pinched me, slammed his clenched fist up against my head, and anything else he could think of to denigrate me. Everyday, between classes, some sort of violence occurred. By the time he drug me down the dormitory hall by my hair while people were screaming for him to stop—by the time he locked me in his room, forcing the campus police to come get me out, kicked me in the stomach while I was lying in bed. *In my mind*, I was already gone. He just didn't know it.

It was raining, and Sam started up, as he had done so many times before, about other men looking at me. I protested and entered my innocent plea, but with his guilty verdict, he slammed his fist against my head. From the impact of the blow, I fell to the floor. I'm not sure what got into me, but as I was falling; I saw my spiked heel shoe. I got up off the floor with the shoe in my hand, and without thinking… I slammed the sharp heel into his top lip. A trickle of blood showed through his mustache, and at that moment, it appeared we both were lost in time.

For a period of four years, I had taken so many punches from Sam. Within that span of time, I never fought back. On this one and only occasion, I defended myself. He was shocked. His eyes shifted from white to bloodshot red. A chill raced over me as I tried to plot my exit in my mind. Time stood still as I waited for him to retaliate against me. He did not; instead, he bucked his eyes and stared blankly into space and trembled like a madman.

Suspended in disbelief, Sam, in an almost whisper, cursed and said, "Are you crazy? You made my lip bleed! You better go before I kill you!" I knew it well before he said it. I was going to die if I did not leave. Sam was eventually going to kill me. I understood that death was eminent; it would arrive. I just did not quite know when, but for sure, *death would come*. Never taking my eyes off him, I backed out of his dorm room.

With no shoes on in October, I walked in the rain. It should have felt cold, but it didn't; I could feel the raindrops hit my face. I thought of the many ways I could disappear. I plotted to preempt the inevitable.

In my five years of dating him, Sam had cheated with several girls yet maintained his control over me. I knew that he was always about Sam! After pondering over the possibilities, I decided, in the middle of the night, to go to the only place he could never get to me. If I went home, he would follow. If I ran to Jackson, he would find me, beat me, and bring me back. But if I told him I was joining the army to help pay for his college education, he would happily let me go. I rehearsed my answers to the questions I knew he was going to ask.

I called the army recruiter early Monday morning. It was barely six and still dark outside. He asked me when I wanted to leave. I said, "Yesterday!" He promised he would be at my door in a few minutes and slammed down the phone. It took him less than an hour to arrive. The recruiter picked me up and drove me from Jonesboro to Memphis to take my entrance exam. After I passed with excellence, we headed back to Arkansas State. As I exited the officer's car, I reiterated that I needed to make a swift exit. He promised to rush my papers along. "Within two weeks," he guaranteed, "you will be MIA from ASU."

I went over to Sam's place and told him that I had a proposition for him. Sitting with his two roommates, he looked somber as I broke him the news. I acted sad as if I really did not want to go, "But certainly, I have to, Sam, because I want to take care of you." I answered all his questions according to *dress rehearsal*: "With the money that I am going to send, you can even purchase a car to get around campus." I saw his expression change when I promised to send my paychecks back to him. He could not wait for me to leave. In fact, Sam helped me pack my bags!

The two weeks came fast, and I boarded the bus to Memphis with Sam on the sidelines. He waved good-bye with a request that I remember him. *How could I forget you, Sam?* Cautiously, I put my middle finger on the side panel of the window and thought unthinkable things. I was so hurt by the abuse. I did not understand that my five years with Sam would be a major catalyst in the hard drive of me. As the bus pulled away, I closed a very painful chapter in my life!

Uncle Sam
and Steve

I entered into the army, expecting to follow the dream of being a journalist. The recruiter pumped up the army experience. I wanted to be like Buddy, a radio personality. He assured me the army had just the spot in O5 Bravo. I figured it fit into my plans well enough. I traveled from Memphis to the army reception station in Fort Jackson, South Carolina. I was in a daze as I watched my life shift around me.

Once we arrived at Fort Jackson, we were funneled straight into the infirmary. Thousands of us stood with green fatigues and white T-shirts, waiting for medics who held guns that blasted medicine straight through the skin of new Army trainees. With seven shots in my arms, each one stung like an Arkansas red wasp. After a long day, I piled into a barrack room as big as an airport hangar. At night, I lay on my back, looking around at the rows of people around me, holding my stomach underneath my covers, thinking of the secret murder I'd committed. I spent a lot of my time crying quietly, never wanting to show the other soldiers my weakness. Everyone in the army—even the girls—acted tough. I tried to do the same.

Within two weeks of being in South Carolina, I met a guy my age, named Steven Franklin. He was tall, thin and handsome, with light brown skin and emotive eyes; beautiful enough to be a model. The minute we decided to date, we got our orders and both shipped out to the same state. Steve went to Fort Benning, Georgia, and I took the bus to Fort Gordon, a few hours away.

I sat quietly, riding the bus from South Carolina to Georgia. During the trip, I took out my small compact mirror and checked my makeup. Everything seemed intact. I fell asleep. Hours later, I woke up to loud screams and passengers running quickly to get off the bus. Lagging in my seat, I was left behind. I looked outside and saw the entire bus assembling in formation. It looked as if we were in the middle of nowhere. Oddly enough, I thought, *Great! The middle of nowhere is just as good as any place to start.* I straightened my hair; for even in the middle of nowhere, one had to look good. A tall, muscular man came on the bus while I was trying to check my makeup and said with a thunderous shout, "Where do you think you're going—Paradise Island or somewhere?" He put his hand in my mug and smeared my newly applied mascara onto my face. I tried to save the situation by getting up, but it was much too late. He shoved me down in the seat and shouted, "Do you know where you are, trainee?"

I said, "No!"

The sergeant shouted back, "When you address me, it is 'Yes, Drill Sergeant,' or, 'No, Drill Sergeant!' Listen here, trainee… formation began fifteen minutes ago, and you are late! Don't you ever let me catch you being late again! Do you understand? You don't move unless I say move! Do you understand?"

I whispered, "Yes, Drill Sergeant."

He screamed, "I can't hear you, trainee!"

I shouted to the top of my lungs, "Yes, Drill Sergeant!"

"Now Git down off the bus!" he screamed. I grabbed my purse, jumped up, and ran for my life!

He raced up behind me and continuing his rampage, grabbed my purse, emptied the contents on the ground and shouted, "There will be no wearing makeup here!" Holding the empty purse in the air as if it was the decapitated head of Medusa, he reiterated to the rest of the squad, "Whatever contrabands you have, leave them right here! You no longer belong to yourself; you belong to Uncle Sam and me! My name is Drill Sergeant Irizarry! I am your daddy now! I tell you when to eat, sleep, and use the latrine! Your brain no longer belongs to you! It belongs to me! I will tell you what, how, and when to think!"

Oh God, I thought to myself, *what have I gotten myself into?*

The first few days were drills. We marched and called cadence. We got up at four in the morning and ran, then ate, then ran some more. All the while, Drill Sgt. Irizarry pounded into our heads that our entire miserable lives were the value of a pile of mouse feces.

* * * *

As time passed, I was chosen to be the squad leader over the females in my unit. This motivated me to work even harder in succeeding. The army was tough, yet I felt the brutal beatings and abuse I endured were harder. I determined that whatever the mission or task, I would not abort. I was determined never to let a man beat me again.

In the wee hours of the morning, I was up and ready to serve my country. The discipline I received during this brief period in my life would influence me for years to come. I developed a will to survive in the toughest conditions. We ran and crawled in the rain, sleet, and snow. There was no down time, and no time for complaints. We moved as a team working, eating, and sleeping with the same group of people.

Drill Sgt. Irizarry determined that his covert mission for the U.S. Army was to break my will. He hated me. He let me know it every second of every day. "Trainee Wolfe," he would yell, "you are nothing! There is no way in the world you're gonna make it!" If I looked to the left, Irizarry screamed, "Get down and give me ten!" If I looked to the right, he demanded twenty! He zoomed in on me as if I were an enemy in his camp. I hated him back.

Weeks went by as slow as a thick coat of paint on a damp wall. My time in basic training was grueling. Rising in the wee hours of the morning to a blank, black sky, the darkness enveloped me. Then there were mornings where the stars were so thick in the sky they took my breath away. Tracing the Big Dipper while the rest of the world slept, we jogged in the middle of nowhere, sounding off cadence until darkness turned to light. Through the mud, flat on my belly, I crawled with my M-16 rifle cradled in my arms as if I was crawling to save my life. I smoked my first cigarette during these hours. We celebrated each obstacle course with a square and a cup of coffee.

During our final weeks of basic training, we took a long bus ride into the middle of nowhere, then a five-mile march into bivouac. I pushed myself along to meet the task of not falling by the wayside while painful charley horses strained against my calves. I fought with all my might to not let the males know I was in pain. Some soldiers, amidst the sergeants' protests, begged for rest from the hilly terrain. Once we reached our destination, we found ourselves in a remote area with signs everywhere, boasting the dangerous snakes that existed in Georgia and the severe penalty for killing one. Amidst the signs were obstacle courses as far as the eye could see.

From gas chambers, where we were put inside a building and forced to take off our masks to inhale tear gas, to grenade throwing and sharpshooting, five grueling days of war games were set in place to assess whether we truly made the grade. I achieved Expert on all but one phase of bivouac, the only one that really mattered to me. I wanted so badly to be an expert at shooting my M-16 rifle, but no matter how much I practiced, I earned the Marksman medal, the lowest one could get. The target was right there in front of me with detailed instructions of how to shoot accurately, but each time I unloaded rounds from my gun, it not only barely hit, but many times, the bullet missed altogether. Not only that, but

I was one of the few in my company that received a Marksman medal. Most of the soldiers earned either a Sharpshooter or an Expert medal. Irizarry smiled in satisfaction.

After bivouac, Irizarry, endeavored to weaken my esteem even more, attempting to give me an Article 15. The offense was small, but Articles 15s are no joke. Receiving one hinders the possibility of promotion or may cause demotion, depending on the severity or nature of the write-up. My offense was insubordination with a superior officer. In the middle of one of my push-up fiascos, I sounded off my frustration toward Irizarry's unfair picking at me. Instead of counting off, "One, Drill Sergeant! Two, Drill Sergeant," I told Sgt. Irizarry how I had had enough of his abuse. "I'm not a dog," I said.

He looked at me and told me, "Trainee Wolfe that will be one Article Fifteen for insubordination." Irizarry had waited all of basic training for this defining moment. He marched me over to the commander's office, but before he could explain his reasoning for recommending an Article 15, Lt. Brent Mossburger, our company commander, said he was in a precarious situation, because on his desk lay a letter of commendation as well. This letter merited my careful handling of weapons retrieval. He stated to both of us that his rule of thumb was to uphold his drill sergeant's recommendation, but this particular time, he felt it was necessary to go against his sergeant, because of the magnitude of praise in the letter of commendation. Our commander stepped outside the box and refused to give me an Article 15. It was unprecedented. Yet he reminded me as he handed me the letter of commendation, that I was a very lucky person, and that if I should find myself in the same predicament he would not be so kind. He told me that any type of insubordination toward my superiors was unacceptable behavior. Drill Sgt. Irizarry tested the water on our walk back to the barracks by commanding me to march at least two steps behind him. With my letter of praise in hand and my head held high, I submitted wholly to his authority.

* * * *

Steve and I wrote each other throughout basic and advanced individual training. Even though we had just met, we lied to each other, professing an undying love. We decided that, during Christmas, we would spend time together. All I knew of him was in the letters that he sent me through our twelve weeks of basic. Looking back, I realize I was not in love with Steve. I was running—running as hard as I could to get away from Sam. I ran to the army and then ran into Steve. All I could think about was how my relationship with him would put me farther away from my past.

On Christmas leave, Steve and I went to Detroit together. While sitting in the garage apartment of his father's rundown house on the east side, Steve walked in, grabbed my hand, and slid a diamond on my finger the size of an eyeball and asked me to marry him. Three days later, we went to the courthouse and took our vows. These are words and chapters that are hard to write, because I can see the stupidity in the words as I pen them. Each move I made was a move in the dark. I was plagued with an invisible illness. Just three months of letters. That was all I knew. I didn't know his family, where he went to school, or anything about his life before the army. The pattern in my life was beginning to take its own shape, but I was too broken and fragmented to look at myself. I pretended that Sam never existed, but one thing that I could not shake off was the deliberation of murdering my baby! It would be years before I came to terms with this cold act of cruelty.

We celebrated our marriage by going out to a tiny nightclub. We partied until about two in the morning; the smoky bar serving as my wedding reception and honeymoon all rolled into one. We came back to the small garage apartment behind his father's home and found the door knocked off the hinges. Someone had broken in, ransacked the entire place, and had taken the television, radio, and any jewelry they could find. Frightened at the thought of someone invading our space, I sat on the bed, quietly thanking God that the huge diamond Steve had given me was not a part of the theft. Oddly, he never expressed any fear or talked about calling the police. He was upset, but I could tell by his demeanor that burglary was the norm. Perhaps it was what he didn't say that made me feel something was not right.

The following day, while standing at the small sink washing dishes, I peered into the incredible shine that the suds had aroused in my wedding ring. I took the ring off my finger and squeezed the band. It did not give into the pressure I applied. I let out a sigh of relief, but the gnawing feeling that something was not right would not go away. I placed the ring on its side, took a frying pan, and lightly pressed against the stone. The glass in the ring shattered. I quietly went into my secret closet and acted as if everything was normal. He never even noticed I wasn't wearing the ring he had given me. I waited for Christmas leave to end so I could head back to the army. I think he was ready for me to go as well. Serving in National Guard after completing his training, Steve went back to his home in Detroit as I processed out for Frankfurt Germany.

As I was leaving Fort Gordon, Drill Sgt. Irizarry gave me a piece of advice from his heart. It felt strange coming from a man who'd told me his mission in life was to break my spirit. He said, "Private Wolfe, learn to stick to the middle. You are either too far to the right or too far to the left. A good soldier knows how to stay in the center. I've watched you for six months crawl in the mud, run as if someone was chasing you, and fight to the death to prove to all these men that you are a better soldier than them. You have lived these past months acting as if you were a man. I tried to break you because of that. You have the demeanor of a mule, not budging. At the end of your training, I became proud of you, because of your will power to resist failure. In the beginning, I was so angry when you, as a woman, ran the five-mile run to the end when many of the soldiers gave out. I told myself, 'Before this is over I will break her,' but every exercise that was put before you,

you succeeded, many times ahead of your fellow male soldiers. I don't know where your drive comes from, but I know this one thing—you will be successful if you find the center. If you don't, you will fail. I'm proud to have been your drill sergeant."

Drill Sgt. Irizarry was right. I spent six months trying to shake off Sam and my dead baby. I told myself that I would never allow another man to beat me. Through the mud, slime, rain, sleet, and snow I pushed forward as I was determined to win. In my secret closet, I laughed when the males gave out during strategic exercises. I moved from Trainee Wolfe to Pvt. Wolfe. It was a huge accomplishment, but how would I find the center when I'd never been there before?

* * * *

Once in Germany, things were different. I went from the harsh training in Georgia to a laid-back platoon in Frankfurt. Everyone around me was smoking hash and snorting cocaine. My roommate Laura—a white girl from Georgia—kept a confederate flag hanging over her bed and a tiny silver spoon on her dresser, smaller than a thimble. I marveled to myself, "The flag's not too cool, but what a cute little spoon." I had no idea it was drug paraphernalia. There were drugs everywhere, and it was uncool if you were not a part of that crowd. I playfully lifted the spoon from Laura's dresser and took it to Ray, a fellow soldier down the hall. He asked me where I got it and if I knew what it was. I told him it belonged to Laura. "You better put that back, Wanda. That's a cocaine spoon. She puts little mountains of powder on and snorts it up her nose. She'll be pissed if she finds out you got it." I put the spoon back and avoided the drug crowd.

Germany was another planet. With winding roads, misty mornings, and commuters slicing through the fog on bicycles, the weather was breezy and cool. Possibly the army and Germany served as the catalyst in keeping me from self-destructing. The discipline and even downtime I experienced during this season, I consider one of the most valuable assets of my life. I needed the structure of something seemingly larger than life controlling my comings and goings.

During the week, I worked at Bohnamas Air Force Base. On the weekends, I spent time, taking 20k walks with Ray through rural areas of Frankfort. The land on these Volks Marches stretched for miles. Windmills, stone fence hedges, and irregularly shaped meadows filled with livestock adorned the countryside. There was not a car in sight. Everyone was either walking or riding a bicycle. I found small pieces of myself on these road trips.

These tiny, fragmented pieces brought back memories of when I was a child, working for Mrs. Norwood. I saved my money for two weeks and bought an old bicycle. That bike became my saving grace. I taught myself to ride, pop a wheelie, and even maneuver down the steep hills of our winding, dusty road with my hands straight up in the air. Amidst the flowers and clean air, I was outside with nature and free. I spent a great deal of my time talking with Ray. Like Steve, he was from Detroit. Sharing similar interests, Ray and I became instant friends. He was the solemn type—always serious—and on those long walks, we philosophized about the big things: the nature of friendship, the meaning of life, and why the army always made us hurry up to wait.

Though Germany was beautiful and I felt alive, something began to change. As the months passed, I found myself drained and nauseated. I went to the infirmary and found out I was pregnant. Once again, I was numb. I wished a million times over that I had not been so careless and had chosen to use protection. The army gave me the option of staying in or leaving with an honorable discharge. Though I chose to leave, it was an odd thing, because I felt as if I was betraying my government. The conditioning that one goes through during basic and AIT is almost like brainwashing. My thinking had changed, and breaking away from the army was hard, but I still knew how to run, and running is what I did. I called Steve and shared the news. While I was neither happy nor sad, he was excited. The baby inside reminded me of my past. I became consumed with the protection of my unborn child.

From the Gullet of Detroit

When I exited the army Ray and I promised to keep in touch. In the blink of an eye, the military shipped me back across the Atlantic, out of the beautiful serenity of the German countryside and into the bowels of Detroit. The moment my plane hit American soil, I noticed an unsettling in my soul. Something was wrong! Steve stood at the terminal gate, waiting for me to exit the plane. Welcoming me with opened arms, he planted a huge kiss on my forehead. I closed my eyes and tried to wish away my fear of the future as he placed his arms securely around me and helped me into the cab. My heart pounded ninety miles a minute as the driver whisked us away to the east side of Detroit.

To my surprise, Steve's father moved out of his dilapidated house and allowed the two of us to move in. Although this monstrous house was better than the garage apartment, the carpet inside was foul, producing an acrid odor that crawled down my throat. And even though I was sick to my stomach, I was grateful. Anything was better than the bitter memories of Arkansas.

After settling in, I called my mother, telling her I was pregnant and back in the United States. Though excited, her emotions were tempered. In the same breath, she congratulated me on the baby and told me to always know I had a home in Marianna, *just in case*. I wondered why she would say that, but I said, "I will always remember." We said our usual *I love you* and hung up the phone.

* * * *

Steve hugged, kissed, and made love to me. For the briefest of moments, I felt safe. After our love making, he got up out of the bed to go to the store. While he was away, I aimlessly wandered around my new home. It did not feel like home with its dirty shag carpet, cracking ceiling, and unsettled foundation.

As I was browsing through the house, I noticed an overnight duffel bag in the corner of the bedroom. Inside were Steve's underwear and a couple of T-shirts. I searched a little more and saw an envelope. I opened it and found nude pictures of my dear husband Steve and two white women having sex. Someone else had taken the pictures. The photos were sickening. My heart beat fast, faster than I could ever remember. My mind raced, but no tears came.

A few minutes after I found the pictures, the door opened. It was Steve. I threw the photos on the bed. "Why would you do this? How could you?" I demanded. "Why?"

"I'm so sorry, Wanda. I got caught up in the moment!" he said. He swore the women in the pictures meant nothing to him; that it would never happen again. I grabbed the few clothes that had found their way out of my suitcase and tried to put them back as he protested the possibility of my leaving. He begged and begged until finally I relented. It was so ugly, the whole thing. I meant nothing to him, yet I was more concerned about what everyone would say. My family certainly would expect nothing more or even less than a systematic breakdown and malfunction when it came to me. I didn't want them to see that I was incapable of getting it right.

I wanted to leave him, but he was my husband. The potential failure of my marriage loomed on the horizon like a dust storm rolling toward a deserted town in Southern California. I tried to gain my composure as I attempted to grapple with the contextual value of the situation at hand. Facing the nature and character of my husband through each lurid scene was hard, but nowhere near as complex as facing the woman in the mirror. All I could see was failure and calamity all around me. In that moment, with those pornographic pictures lying on the bed, I saw bleak days ahead. I anticipated the phone calls to my family. "Mom, Steve, and I are not going to make it. Dad, I could not stay with him." I didn't want to face my family, so I stayed.

A month passed, and I could see my stomach growing. I touched it often to reaffirm my love for my unborn child. Protecting my baby was all I could think of. One day I started to run a slight fever. I called the doctor, and he suggested bed rest until my next appointment. I crawled in bed and covered my head as I succumbed to the silence around me. A dull ache in the base of my spine began to settle in—not a highly noticeable throbbing; just a kind of gnawing *there's something wrong* type of pain. I shifted my body on the bed and tried to find a comfortable position for me and the baby. Nothing seemed to abate or make the ache go away. I got up and went to the bathroom to urinate, and what used to be dull turned into fire and excruciating pain at the base of my abdomen and vagina. I raised my dress and placed a mirror down below to see if anything looked odd. There was swelling and inflammation everywhere. I told Steve that I needed to go to the hospital. He quickly got me to the car and raced me to the emergency room. After I told the triage nurse I was pregnant, they rushed me into a cubicle where an African doctor came and examined me. He said with concern, "Woman, you have the love disease."

"What do you mean?" I asked.

He smiled and said, "You got gonorrhea, don't you know."

I sat there, wondering just what gonorrhea had to do with love while my new husband stood across the examining room against the wall. He wore a look on his face so heavy all he could do was stare at the floor.

The doctor said he could not give me the usual penicillin shot for fear that it may damage my unborn child. Instead, he prescribed pills and told me to check back with my physician after two weeks of taking the medication. I felt a filth that no shower could wash away. I went back to Steve's house and once again, he said he was "so sorry." He must have caught the disease from one of the girls in the photos. I called my mother, and she wired me money for a bus ticket. The next day, I caught a bus home.

The STD affected my vaginal area so bad that I could barely walk, but not bad enough to keep me from running, so once again, I ran. After a fifteen-hour bus ride, I arrived in Marianna. It looked much smaller since I'd seen the world. Daddy picked me up and drove me home. I walked into the tiny house of my youth, sat on the bed, and opened a drawer to unpack my things. Inside was the white dress I purchased during my first pregnancy. Mama had kept it safe by hiding it in a drawer—like she knew I was going to wear it again. It was so white and beautiful that it took the brokenness inside of me and made me feel whole.

Marianna had not changed much. Poverty was everywhere; even Sam was there. Once he realized I was not going to be his meal ticket, Sam dropped out of college. I thought that somehow he would find a way to get near me, but Mama watched over me as a mother hen watches over her baby chicks. It was during this time that I would begin to see her in a new light. I learned that Mama always had foresight. She was a dreamer and could see the future. I thought about her words "You always have a home." She knew that things would fall apart. When I was younger, she would make wild predictions about the future. She would say, "Uncle Booker will disappear." Three days later, Uncle Booker would be gone. She had a real gift. During this time, I found out that Mama was also a nurturer and caregiver. She wanted everyone around her to feel good, flourish, and be whole. She sacrificed her own happiness to make provisions for the people she loved. Many of the things one would normally care about, Mama did not. It was during this time of closeness that I learned of her true character.

I was disillusioned by the horrific events that occurred in Detroit, but Mama helped me understand that life was hard. She said it was my responsibility to face each challenge with courage. Once again, I became my family's talking point. The grapevine words regarding my failures were beginning to travel, making their home at the dinner tables of all my siblings. My parents' telephone rang constantly with people asking for the shocking details. If Daddy answered, he would cover the mouthpiece and whisper the details. If Mama answered, she would softly tell the caller it was none of their business, but if they wanted to help, to feel free to send a donation. Mama never spoke ill of anyone.

My mother helped nurse me back to health by involving me in her life. Everyday, I went with her to help at Marianna's Senior Citizens center and Meals on Wheels. I gained knowledge and wisdom spending time around the elderly. They talked about life in the South, survival, what it was like to be white, what it was like to be black, and on, and on. There I was, back in the town I spent my entire life thinking about how to escape, yet I found myself falling in love with everything around me. Marianna was a special place, filled with people of all ranks in life. I did not

realize how blessed I was until I was afforded this opportunity to chat and investigate. The elderly talked about their past successes, failures, and current regrets. I found more small, fragmented pieces of myself in the act of serving them. The stories they told took me back to my past, reminding me of a time when I was a little girl.

I remembered Mama putting me up in front of the entire church, and me belting out an almost impossible note. The octave was so high that it shocked the congregation. Afterward, a woman in church pulled my mother aside and told her that I was a youngun' with an old soul. I think she was right. When I was with the elderly, I felt at home. They had secrets and little gifts that could help me lighten the burden of life. I picked those fragments up and moved on. Spending time with seasoned souls helped to heal many of my wounds.

I found myself even reaching out to Daddy. Regardless of the numerous mistakes he made, he was still my father and deserved my respect. I wrestled with the past as I tried to imagine developing a relationship with him. I began to see what the rest of our town saw in my father. He was a funny man. Daddy told jokes and made me laugh at things he had done in the past to make money. He had unbelievable stories to tell, and some of the ones he told were the culprit for the condition of my parents' house.

One day Daddy came across $3000.00 while on a dead body run. Three robbers had been killed in a car accident. Little did the thieves know…they were going to meet their maker and their mortician! Daddy neatly packed the corpses in his hearse, took them to the morgue, and pocketed the loot. That was the end of their story.

Daddy didn't put the cash in the bank, buy clothes, or anything else that would let people know he had come into some money. Instead, he bought a giant pile of bricks, stacking them on the side of the house with a plan to lay mortar.

These bricks sat, undisturbed, for two years, becoming a giant nesting ground for black widows and other insects.

My father found something of worth on *every one*. While picking up dead bodies, he plundered the poor souls, by empting their pockets of all valuables. If he picked up a body from a house, he looked through the drawers, under mattresses, and any other places he thought valuables were hidden. When a corpse came through the morgue with gold teeth in their mouth, Daddy would knock their teeth out and glue their mouth shut. No one ever knew the difference; *dead men don't talk*. He kept the teeth in a coffee can, stashed underneath the huge oak tree near Sanders Funeral Home. Once he filled the can to capacity, Daddy removed the contents, brought it home, and stashed it under his bed in a shoebox. As a child, I remember sneaking in Daddy and Mama's room and staring into the box of gold fillings and rare coins. There was an entire graveyard under my parent's bed.

By the time I came back to Marianna, Daddy had pulled the bricks from the side of the house and had just about finished the task of bricking their home. Laying no insulation, he took the spider-infested material from the side of the home, and slapped some mortar on the house, gluing the bricks in place. Upon my arrival, he was about ninety-five percent done. Since Daddy knew nothing about masonry, the house took on a shape of its own. There were irregular spaces left where all kinds of critters and insects crawled inside. That year, during my pregnancy, I learned the definition of fear. The spiders that found their way in through the brick holes had mutated into oversized, monster arachnids. They crawled into shoes, clothes, on top of the curtains, under tables, and in bed with me. Possessing my parents' home, these spiders took panic to a new level.

Desperate to see my surroundings, I slept with the light on. Surveying every corner of the room, I went to bed with my heart pounding. But even after the best inspection, sometimes good is not good enough. One evening, I watched the walls around me as my eyelids grew heavier and heavier. I fell asleep and woke up the next morning with fang marks on the side of my neck. The spider bite blistered through the night. Horrified, I jumped out of bed, found that, after the bite, I, in my sleep, rolled over and killed the spider. That moment—that second—I developed a phobia of spiders. There I was, pregnant and asleep while this eight-legged arachnid fed from my neck. Every night from that time on, I sprayed my room as my father looked on and shook his head in disbelief. I wrapped my neck with a scarf and slept with a skullcap on for the rest of my stay. It seemed unreasonable to Daddy, but between the spiders and Uncle Booker, who suffered from Alzheimer's, life was a bit much.

Uncle Booker was our eighty-year-old uncle. Since he had no children of his own, Mama, by selfless choice, was his caregiver. He occasionally and conveniently lost himself, walking out of the house and throwing Mama into a panic. She would find him in the woods or wondering along the country road, heading in the opposite direction of the house. My father called my uncle's illness

Some Timers rather than Alzheimer's, because he selectively remembered things. Uncle Booker disliked my daddy; perhaps it was because of my father complaining about his prolonged stay or Daddy's constant yelling at him for his forgetfulness. Uncle Booker might have had a limited grasp on reality, but he knew enough to grind my father's gears. Daddy, every morning, would find his shoes full of urine and would angrily stutter, hitting his leg to get his curse words out. In frustration, he wanted to know why Uncle Booker never mistook his own shoes as a urinal. And if that wasn't enough pandemonium, there was Uncle Teddy, Daddy's brother, who was seventy and suffered from paranoia schizophrenia. He lived in an asylum in New York before coming to stay with my parents. Teddy begged them for a place to stay upon his release from the nuthouse. Needless to say, my father did not want him to come. The house was already strained with Uncle Booker and my pregnant self, but Mama could never turn anyone away—especially someone who had nowhere else to go. She told Teddy to come on down. When we came home from caring for the elderly, Mama pampered Uncle Booker and Uncle Teddy, causing them both to vie for her affection. She consistently pointed out they were still human and deserved love and respect. She also said that even though I was afraid out of my wits, Teddy was perfectly harmless.

Uncle Teddy thought the mafia was after him, and, to complicate matters, he thought I was *the sleeper cell*, planted in my parent's home to take him out. I would wake up in the middle of the night and find him standing over my bed, ranting that he had been listening to me plot with Cleve (AKA Steve) to kill him. He reminded me that I should be careful, because he was going to take me out first. I shook with fear. All the while, my mother assured me, "Your uncle Teddy is harmless, baby." It was a madhouse for sure. However, looking back, that three-ring circus was probably the best thing to heal my wounds. I was so scared of the spiders and Uncle Teddy, I had no time to lament over my circumstances. Uncle Booker and Uncle Teddy knew that Mama was the one who said yes to their residence in our home, so they fought like kids for her loving care and attention, slapping at each other like teenagers. Mama would calmly tell them to stop and give them both a hug.

When my Father heard that Uncle Teddy was in my room, threatening me at night, he took off work and put a wooden latch on my door so Teddy could not get in. With his Lucky Strike cigarette in the corner of his mouth, Daddy stuttered, "Teddy don't let me catch you near this room again!" A curious thing about Uncle Teddy was that he never pushed buttons with Daddy or displayed symptoms of schizophrenia. Most of the time, he acted perfectly normal when Daddy was around. It was only when Daddy was gone or asleep that Uncle Teddy let loose. I believe he understood how fascinated my father was with the baby inside my womb. Uncle Teddy understood that if anyone had to go because of bad behavior, it would be him. I can't really explain the connections of babies and my father, but he loved my child long before it was born. I was so happy that I was carrying something in my stomach that he loved. It made my stay livable and allowed for good conversations with Daddy. Somewhere along the way, I even quit smoking. With Uncle Teddy hovering around me at night, I was more than tense, but I managed to kick the habit I picked up in the army.

The Baby's Coming!

While living with Mom and trying to heal my wounds from my marriage to Steve, I wondered what was to become of me. Of all the things he did—the women, the lies, the pictures—the worst was that he never called to check on the baby and me. I knew I would never see him again. Though not officially divorced, I felt the disconnection. He was dead to me. I took all the secrets from our relationship, pushed them into my secret closet, and moved on.

I wrote my army friend, Ray, in Germany, telling him about the pictures I found of Steve. He quickly responded by writing me long letters, sometimes reaching several pages in length. Our friendship quickly turned into something more. He began calling me every few weeks. I was worried about the future, and the thought of having a fatherless child scared me to death. After a few months, Ray convinced me to commit my love to him and wait for him to come home. He reassured me that he wanted to be with my child and me. It was too fast, but I thought that Ray was different. I didn't want to be a single mom living at Mama and Daddy's house in Marianna. Deep down, I feared that my baby and I would be trapped. Ray asked me to wait for him. In a few months, he would come and move us back to Detroit. Once again I attempted to fill the empty void inside, and, without really knowing Ray, I did as he asked. I waited for him.

November sixteenth came, and the doctor induced labor while my mother sat at my side. The nurses gave me instructions on how to safely deliver my child. "Right now we need you to just relax and allow nature to take its course, Wanda." Mom sat quietly, listening to their instructions. The second they left, she jumped out her chair and said, "Forget everything you just heard and listen to me only! I've had eleven babies, and nine of them lived. I know how to give birth. Keep your eyes on me and listen to what I tell you to do!"

Pulling through a mild contraction, I said, "Mom, times have changed."

She shot back quickly, "I don't care how much time has changed and how much folks think they know. Push!"

The nurses came back, found me pushing, and reprimanded me for putting the cart before the horse. They warned me that I could damage my baby by pushing too early.

They'd leave again, and Mama would say, "Bull hockey, push." For thirteen long, painful hours, I labored between "Push Wanda, push!" and "Stop pushing."

A mountain of pressure built, and voices drowned in the straining of my muscles. The pain reached monumental levels. They say that a woman comes closest to death right before she pushes the baby through. For a brief second, I thought I was going to die. After a long struggle that was too painful to remember, my baby boy came head first into the world.

* * * *

He was so tiny and beautiful. When I looked down at his glowing face, I saw the life that I had carried inside me. The minute I saw him, I thought about the abortion. I felt his little lungs expand and contract with his first breaths of life. Looking into his eyes, the desire to protect him grew even stronger. Nothing would come between my baby boy and me. We named him Brian Joseph Wolfe. My mother, my friend—in spite of all her crazy birth advice—helped me bring him into this world. Our bond grew deeper. After three days in the hospital, they let me take little Brian home.

* * * *

As I brought a new life into the world, my old life would come back to haunt me. The grapevine spread the news through the town like a wildfire. It didn't take long for Sam to hear about the birth of my son. One day a knock came at the door. It was Sam. He pushed right past me, came into the house, and looked into the bassinette at Brian . He scolded me for choosing to kill his baby and give birth to some other man's child. I cried as I scooped my son up and held on tight. I was speechless.

"How could you do this to me, Wanda? How? So this is your baby? So you went and did that, huh? You killed my baby, but you went and did that? How could you do this to me? Huh? How?"

I stood there silent, holding my baby and expecting Sam to hit me.

He ranted until he realized time had changed me. After a few minutes, he stormed out and slammed the door. I watched him get into the same old car, in the same old angry shuffle, and drive down the same old road that he had driven so many times before.

When Mama came home from work, she looked in my eyes and knew. She asked, "Has that boy been here?" I told her what Sam had said. Her eyes squinted so small I could barely see the white. She got back in her car and drove into town. The same grapevine brought the news back to me. I heard that Mama went to Mr. Wells's job and threatened to kill him and his son if Sam ever came near my baby and me again. Whatever she said, it was effective, because Sam disappeared. It would be ten years before I saw him again.

Who Will Help Me Raise this Child?

Ray continued to write me, reaffirming his promise to come and get us both the second he left the army. It would be five long months before he got out. While we waited, Mama offered to help in caring for my newborn. I was nervous about her help. There were things in the past that I remembered, and did not want my baby to go through. When I was little, Mama and Daddy used to give us the most bizarre remedies to make us well. They used to give us a teaspoon of sugar saturated in turpentine whenever we had a stomachache. It never helped. Castor oil was my Daddy's favorite treatment for colds. The only effect it caused was immediate diarrhea. Today, they use castor beans to make chemical weapons. Quinine, also used for colds, came straight from the pits of hell, in a clear bottle with three black sixes on the label. The medicine itself was a yellowish, gold liquid that tasted like pure hell. It was so bitter it made me gag on contact. Daddy would tightly hold our noses and force spoonfuls of that and castor oil down all of our throats. He loved the sadistic element of seeing us gag as we tried to swallow. Their remedies were just a step above bloodletting. I was cautious and suspicious.

Mama wanted to help keep Brian healthy. Referring back to a folk remedy, she convinced me of the therapeutic value of hives. There was something on the inside of the baby, she said, that needed to come out. Hives were a good sign in the old days. Mama told me to place sulfur on my breast as he fed. I followed her suggestions, and Brian sucked from my breast for almost a week before he became gravely ill. I took him to the clinic and learned that I was poisoning my son to death. The doctor's news confirmed my suspicions. Devastated by the diagnosis, I was angry with Mama.

I asked Kay to take me back to ASU until Ray came to save us. After a few terse conversations, Mama agreed that it was best that I leave. I told my mother that my child could have died because of her oldwives remedies. She sat quietly as I explained the doctor's prognosis. I explained out my reasons for leaving. There would be no more poisons, no more backwoods medical philosophy around my child, I told her. I could sense her hurt, but at that same time, all I could think of was the possible death of my little boy. My mother was doing the best she knew. I saw her shoulders shrink down in dismay and tears come to her eyes, but she never said a word. I went back to ASU and waited.

When Ray finally arrived, I put my running shoes on and got ready for the distance. He picked us up and prepared to go to the place I abhorred: Detroit. Before we left Arkansas, I took him back to Marianna to meet my parents.

The thing about running is that you're moving so fast you inevitably miss important things—the things that really matter. The difference in this journey was that I now had a child, a young boy that I inadvertently involved in my insanity. I did the same thing over and over again expecting a different outcome. When we were alone, Ray seemed like such a nice man. He treated me like a princess. He did all the little things women want. He opened doors for me and held my hand. He kept his arms around me to let me know he was always right there.

Mama said, "He *seems* like a nice person," and then with her sixth sense, seeing-the-future-type of way said, "Ray, I think you will do just fine as long as no one upsets you. There is something in your eyes that tells me you will explode if someone makes you angry." Ray smiled and kept his cool. When we left, they bid us farewell, but before we walked out, Mama whispered in my ear, "You always got a place to come back to, baby. You always got a home." We jumped in Ray's rental car and drove away while Mama, Uncle Booker, Teddy, and Daddy waved good-bye from the tiny porch. As I looked back, my heart dropped. It was sad to leave them behind, but I felt blessed leaving Marianna with my new baby.

Motor City: Round Two

We arrived in Detroit during the winter months, with snow up to our knees. Ray introduced me to his sister, Carolyn, who allowed us to rent a room in her home. Immediately we clashed like two rams on a mountain. She did not like my child or me, and quite frankly, I did not like her. She saw me as *Ms. Goody-two-shoes*, and I saw her as brass, disrespectful, and missing her front teeth. They were false and no one knew. She would shout down the stairs how much she hated me. Young and immature, I would remind her that I could not understand a word she was saying with her teeth out.

The truth is that Carolyn put in a good word for me at Blue Cross Blue Shield and helped me to get a job in the mailroom. I didn't know at that time in my life how to be grateful for kind gestures, but this woman went out on a limb and helped me gain employment. She had her own issues, but she cared enough to help me find a job. It was my very first job outside of the army.

At 5:00 a.m., I got up daily, dressed Brian, and lugged him through the ice and snow, catching the city bus to get him to daycare. It was grueling. Each time I stepped outside in the bitter cold, I became angry, because Ray chose not to provide transportation. Working for Ford Motor Company and having a pretty sizable savings upon his exit from the armed forces, he was more than capable of purchasing a car, but he chose to make us walk. Every morning as I prepared myself for work, I cringed at the thought of my face freezing and ice covering my ankles while carrying my child through the dark streets of Detroit.

Eventually, Carolyn introduced me to a young woman, named Lynn, who lived close by. I paid her to catch a ride to work. That was much better. Lynn and I listened to George Benson all the way to Blue Cross and then all the way home. As soon as we dropped Brian off at daycare, she would pull back out a joint. I looked forward to the morning drive to work as an escape from reality.

One day, I got into her car and expressed my exhaustion of mothering, and she gave me a small pill. She instructed me to take half of it, because a whole pill would prove to be too much for me. I broke the pill in half, popped it in my mouth, and a few minutes later, I thought I was losing my mind. Everything in life sped up to ninety miles an hour. My work at Blue Cross was erratic. Lynn, who worked beside me, warned me to pull myself together. That day, I found out that drugs and Wanda didn't mix. I made it through the day and even made it home, where Ray took one look at me and said, "You've been doing speed!"

I answered, "I don't know what you're talking about." And believe or not, that was the truth. I was just trying to stay awake in the midst of caring for a baby, living in Carolyn's house, and tending to his needs as a man. That was my last day riding to work with Lynn. And the last time I let anyone talk me into popping pills.

I had no idea what Detroit's city life was about. I'm sure that only by the grace of God am I still here to tell the story. I often wonder, *What was the difference between me and the average person being turned on to drugs such as crack cocaine or meth? Why was that the first and last day I did speed?* I will never understand the line that separates addicts from others. When Lynn came and approached me later about using, it was not up for discussion. At nineteen, there was a willpower within me to firmly say "No!" It was as if that day never happened. Meanwhile, Ray and I continued to smoke marijuana on a constant basis, but even that proved to wax thin.

Once in Detroit, after rekindling his relationship with Harold, a lifelong friend, Ray's personality changed. They shared secrets and did everything together. Harold was very protective of Ray. Every negative event involving Ray and me was a cataclysmic affair in Harold's eyes. He hated me and wondered why Ray had chosen to bring me to Detroit. The question continued to surface why I had not gotten on welfare to help support my *illegitimate* son. My answer was always the same: "Welfare is out of the question."

His response would always be: "Welfare, food stamps, do something, Wanda! You are wearing Ray down, especially with Brian not being his son."

Each visit would end in a meticulous chipping away at my already poor self-esteem. If someone paid me a compliment about my beauty and grace, before I could digest it, Harold and his sisters would respond, "Yes, she is so beautiful, just like a centerpiece on a table—she just sits there and does nothing but look beautiful. And just like a centerpiece, she has no specific purpose in life except to look pretty." I was saddened and disappointed that Ray allowed them to talk so badly toward me.

After three months, we moved out of the house with Carolyn to a place of our own. Harold made the suggestion that I make a better effort in taking care of Ray by staying at home and dedicating my time to cooking and cleaning. He felt that I was doing a horrible job as a mate. Ray validated everything that came out of his mouth with a squeamish "I agree with you."

One day, Harold, Ray, and I were sitting at the table, and Harold said to me the first kind words I had ever heard him speak to me. "Wanda you have the most beautiful smile I have ever seen." I immediately responded, "Thank you, Harold." He then said, "Has anyone ever told you that your smile makes you look easy?" Before I could catch the tears to hold them back, they came. They didn't just fall, they rushed past my eyelids as fast and furious as Niagara Falls empties herself back into mother earth, and they wouldn't stop. They completely saturated my face as I sat there, embarrassed.

Harold then went on to say, "Don't get so upset about it. You just may want to curb your smile a little bit, because it makes you look like an easy lay. I'm sure that every man you come in contact with feels the same as I do—you just look easy. Not a big deal."

I asked, "Are you saying you could take me to bed if you wanted to?"

He responded, "Yes, if I wanted to, but I don't want to. That's out of the question. I just wanted you to be aware that you look easy. Doesn't she, Ray?"

Ray cowardly answered, "Yeah, you do look kind of easy."

I don't think even Harold realized Ray would agree with him, for years later, he told me of his disappointment in Ray for not standing up for me. It was insanity once again. I silently got up from the table, picked Brian up out of his high chair, went upstairs, and slid down into my secret closet. I held my child close to me and promised to protect him as long as I lived. After Harold left, Ray came up and apologized, but it was much too late. The damage was already done.

Ray's Troubled Past

Ray was not the man I fell in love with, nor who he portrayed himself to be in his letters. His past was colored with cold, harsh, miscalculated strokes. Ray's mother, Penny Lang, was an alcoholic. When Ray was eight, his mother took him and his brother to the hospital for a TB incubation. She never came back to get them. The boys were left to fend for themselves. For days, they asked the doctors and nurses when their mama was coming back. No one knew what to tell them. Eventually the children were separated, becoming wards of the state.

Ray's formative years were a string of unmonitored foster homes, filled with mental, physical, and even sexual abuse. He frequently talked of the scar over his right eye as being a result of his refusal to continue performing oral sex on one of his male foster parents. In the middle of the act, he stopped and refused to go any further. The man took a blunt object and slammed it up against his head. He blacked out and couldn't remember the rest. There was so much sexual abuse perpetrated against him while being shuffled from house to house that he often closed his eyes in the middle of his memories and cried like a baby. When Ray turned fourteen, he felt he was old enough to seek his biological mother. He shouldn't have gone to find her.

Strained after reuniting, the relationship between Ray and his mother turned out to not be as happy as he had expected. He did not understand why Penny abandoned him, his brother and two other sisters yet chose to keep his other four siblings. Ray would find himself caught up in the mystery and horror of his mother, Penny Lang. The abuse that he experienced turned into repressed anger that he never dealt with until his relationship with me.

Ray declared me his property. He wanted to take control of my life so that no one would ever leave him again. Legally, I was still married to Steve, so Ray and I had some obstacles to climb. We contacted a slick, backwoods attorney in my hometown and after some legal wrangling, the marriage between Steve and I was dissolved. Not long after, Ray and I were married in Harold's mother's backyard. I felt a vast emptiness. Even though my life with Ray was just beginning, I felt the end was just around the corner. I was not clear why the hollow feeling was so overwhelming, but it was.

Ray's first rule for me was to stay in the house unless he was with me. Detroit was too dangerous, Ray implored, and murders were committed every day. Outside of the house, he wouldn't be there to protect me. He constantly reminded me of the evil just beyond the door. I lost myself in our small, two-bedroom apartment, just off the freeway in a rundown area of Detroit. It wasn't that we had to live that way, but Ray chose this way of life for us while I quietly participated. He got up early in the morning to go to work at Ford

Motor Company, and most of the time, he doubled over onto the next shift for overtime and would not return until the wee hours of the night. Because I didn't know how to drive, my eight hours inside would turn into sixteen. Before I knew it, the hours turned into weeks, then into months. Ray usually came home when it was dark while the rest of the world was asleep. When his off days rolled around, he would ask if I wanted to go outside. I had no desire. Darkness was everywhere. Void, lost, and believing what he said about the dangers that lurked on the outside, I became a prisoner in my own home.

One day, Ray convinced me to go to the neighborhood mall. Reluctantly, with my eyes squinting and hurting from the sunlight, I got in the car. Once there, I noticed there was a live symphony orchestra on the main floor. I stopped in my tracks. *Music!* I stood still and listened intently to the orchestra. *O' so glorious!* Music was a part of me. In high school, I studied the lives of Mozart, Johann Sebastian Bach, and Beethoven. Mesmerized by the sound, I stood frozen for so long Ray left me holding Brian's hand. The strings and horns enveloped me and took me far away from my troubles—away from the sadness, away from the horrible darkness. It was soothing to my soul. All of a sudden, the music stopped and, before long, every musician's attention fell on an older Caucasian man, slumped over his cello. Another musician moved him from his chair, laying him flat on his back. I watched as his lips turned purplish blue. Soon afterwards, paramedics arrived, pronounced him dead, placed him on the stretcher, and covered his face. There, right before my eyes, I saw the man die!

I had seen more dead people than one could imagine as a child. My father, along with all of us, slept in the room adjoined to the embalming room. Many times after school, I sat in that very room, waiting hours for him to finish his work and take me home. I saw the body of my classmate after he drowned at Bear Creek Lake. I saw my friend's brother's mangled body after his car and body had been torn to pieces by an oncoming train. As a child, I saw the dead too frequently, but never had I seen the process of death.

The Dark Times

The one thing that stuck firm in my mind was the cellists gasping for breath—a few seconds of long, labored exhalations—and the awkward way he held his left arm as he slumped over his instrument. I kept thinking about the process of death. The moment he clutched his left arm, I gasped for breath and held my left arm. I could feel my muscles tightening. I pulled Brian through the mall as I ran to find Ray. My breathing was getting shorter and shorter. The pain was increasing in my shoulder. When I found Ray, I said, "I think I'm having a heart attack! Get me to the hospital!" Ray raced me to the car and drove me to the emergency room. I sat, gasping for air as he told them about the pains in my chest and shoulder. They checked my vital signs and gave me a brown paper bag to breathe in. They told him I was hyperventilating and sent me home.

There would be dozens of trips like this one for the next two years. That day at the mall was the last day that I went out of the apartment, except when I went to the hospital. For over two years, I stayed inside with my son. I did not see the sunlight, rain, sleet, or snow. I was afraid to go anywhere, even in the company of Ray. His words "bad things happen" rang in my ears. When he left for work I was in bed; when he returned, I was still in bed. The years rolled away.

The Nightmare

The nightmare came as I slept with Brian in my arms. It was always the same dream. A man with an army poncho would enter into the apartment. He looked in every room. I put my arms tightly around BJ to keep him from moving. I'd whisper to him, "Shh... shh... Don't move, baby. If he thinks we're asleep, he may not kill us. He may let us live." In the dream, the man, after checking each room, peered into the bedroom where we were sleeping. He'd walk away from the room, then, without reason he'd double back, come inside, and lean over our bed with a huge knife. I could feel the cold blade from the knife against my neck. Each time in the dream, I would struggle to move, but I couldn't. My arms were locked. My heart raced as I tried to get the words out, "Kill me, but don't kill my son." Each time he would remove the knife from my throat, walk toward the doorway, and stare at the two of us lying there. I would try to move my legs but couldn't. My body was paralyzed until the nightmare released me. When I awoke, BJ was lying next to me in a peaceful slumber. The dream came so often I feared being asleep almost as much as I feared being awake. There was no solace in my life, not even while I was asleep.

I developed a series of medical issues. Phantom pains coursed through my body. There were inexplicable eye twitches, flickering throughout the day. I winced, massaged, and tried to blink the twitch away. Pounding headaches hit so hard I felt my head was going to explode. The pain was so intense they tested me for brain tumors. They ran brain scans and EEGs to find a medical reason for my mysterious ailments. I was diagnosed with having petite-mal seizures and prescribed phenobarbital to abate the symptoms. One night, after having an EEG, I lost control of my bladder and wet the bed.

Ray thought as well that I should self-medicate. To lessen my agony, he brought home more marijuana. I found myself trying to smoke the pain and sadness away. Early in the morning, I broke up small amounts of weed and twisted it into joints. After smoking, paranoia always set in, bringing the sensation of a heart attack. I contemplated the musician dying and relived the experience of shortness of breath repeatedly. I thought about all the secrets in my little closet. They were all so humiliating. Images from my past flashed through my mind—the horrible abortion, the beatings, and the absence of my father's love.

*   *   *   *

In December of 1980, I went to a specialist for breathing trouble. They could not find anything wrong with me. After returning home, I pulled the blinds tight and didn't leave the house again for another seven months. The only sunshine I saw was on TV. I was a shut-in, barricaded from the outside. I stayed inside and shook with fear at the thought of going outside.

One day, while watching TV, I saw a commercial about a doctor who diagnosed and treated depression. The possibility of depression never crossed my mind, even though traumatic events toppled one after another. After each cataclysmic episode, I picked myself up the best way I knew and moved on. The only certainty in my life was the fragility of constant sadness, a sadness that was as much a part of me as the fingers attached to my hands. To have operated in any other manner besides a state of misery was foreign to me. I woke up sad, made breakfast for Brian with tears in my eyes, made lunch and dinner with my head down, and took a bath, washing the tears off my face. Everything I did was from a place of gloom. Hidden away in that little apartment, I felt disconnected from the world. Mama was my only connection with the outside world. She would call most every day to check on me. She could hear the sadness in my voice. I saw myself as a loser, a failure, yet, I never entertained the possibility of depression.

Many times in the bathtub, I thought about slashing my wrist but couldn't bring myself to that place, because I didn't want Brian to have to live with such a legacy. I still wanted my son to see me as a strong black woman who was capable of standing the test of time, come what may. Yet the harder I tried to fill the role of a strong mother, the weaker I became. My life was an endless hole, so black and deep—there seemed to be no way out. I could see myself going further and further down. My back was wedged tightly into the grooves of the wall. I felt as if I had no other choice but to make my way to a trained mental health professional, so I made an appointment to see the doctor.

When I stepped outside the apartment to get into the car, the light was blinding. Ray waited on the driver's side as I tried to pull myself together. I squinted my eyes and covered them with my hands to protect them from the glaring sun. *I find this to be one of the hardest subjects for me to write about. I think it is because I was so far gone.* When I think of mere daylight being such a monumental foe, it causes me to shift uncomfortably in my chair. I am here today, but I am humbled to know that agoraphobia had me so disconnected from the outside world that I couldn't stand the light in my eyes. For two years I lived in that little apartment, cut off from the world. My eyes welled up with tears as I closed them and waited for the drive to be over.

That day I was tested and diagnosed as *severely depressed*. The doctor prescribed medication and set weekly therapeutic sessions. While antidepressants were prescribed, my doctor was a strong advocate of the patient working to solve his or her own puzzle. He told me that he could not help unless I was involved. He wasn't there to fix my problems. Only I could do that. After I told him my stories, he ordered me to go home and visit my parents. I followed his advice and went home more often. With much hard work and counseling sessions, I started to leave the house. Instead of shutting myself in Detroit, I left the state and went home as often as I could. I spent more days in rural Arkansas than in Detroit.

A Ceros Moment

One day, while lying on my parents' couch in Arkansas, my mother and I got into a heated conversation. I told her that many times, as a child, when she whipped me, I simply needed her to hug me and make me feel safe. Mama replied, "Baby, I wasn't thinking about hugging anyone. I was trying to put food on the table." I broke down and told Mama that I wanted to die—that I didn't want to be on this earth, I didn't believe that God existed. But if by chance He did exist, He was a cruel and unjust God. Finally I said, "I hate God, so don't come in my face with anything about Him, because if He was real or even a loving God, He would not have allowed all these things to happen to me." I cried uncontrollably as she walked away from me and went into her bedroom. A few minutes later, she returned with a photo in her hand. It was an eighth grade school picture of me, taken right after the hair loss disaster. I had on the dreaded Afro wig; I looked sad and lost.

With tears flowing Mama said, "Every day I look at this picture. You said the doctor diagnosed you as being depressed. At first when I heard it, I did not believe it, but one day I was searching through the drawer for something and ran across this picture of you and saw the tears in your eyes and said to myself, 'Lord have mercy on my child. She's been sad all her life.'" Mama then said, "I'm so sorry. I tried to be a good mother. I thought if I just provided food and a roof over your head that would be all you needed. But I've learned so much about being a mother through watching how you hug and kiss BJ. I truly wish I had hugged you more often."

That day I cried *with* my mother. She apologized for everything. It was a huge apology and the most genuine that I can ever remember. She held the eighth grade picture in her hands as she spoke. That was the year all the pain began. I had lost my hair, and it was the beginning of my end. Looking at the picture, I remembered the moment the photographer snapped the shutter. I was about to cry as I knew that my massive, fake Afro wig— the source of so much humiliation and pain—was about to be memorialized for eternity. In the photo, tears rested on the edge of my eyelids. There was a giant pimple on my nose, and I looked so miserable. This photo was in Mama's drawer all those years, and there she stood, holding it in her hand. She wanted me to see the depression for myself. When I looked into the eyes of my photo, it brought back all the pain. I could see the sadness. The picture was taken even before Sam. All I could think about was, *I can't get back the years.* It was too late to get it back! Looking into my eyes, I could see the depression on my face. I was in a little purple dress, with a soft, pink chiffon blouse underneath, thinking about how to kill myself.

I held the photo as Mama told me she was sorry. I think she blamed herself. She repeated to me, "Fay, I just didn't know how to hug you. I am sorry, and I wish I could take it all back." Those hours with the picture from my past and this endearing time with Mama changed my life and our relationship forever. A ceros moment is a "defining moment, the instance of certainty when you just know that something big has happened and is going to last forever." This was our ceros moment, sealing our friendship for life.

A genuine apology is a rare event. With her expression of sorrow and guilt, Mama too, took up residence deep within my heart. She became the *one true thing* in my life, and from that point on, I tried to treat her with great honor and respect. The relationship grew more solid as time passed. I always loved my mother, but that apology transformed our relationship from mother and daughter to best friends. Our bond was deep and genuine. We spoke every single day for the rest of her life.

Mama opened up to me about her journey. She was not the type of person to talk about others. Never a gossiper, there were things that she held on to so tightly that no one knew about. She told me secrets about things that only best friends would discuss. The bullet resting in my father's back hip—the one that we all touched as he regaled us with the story from World War II—well, he didn't get that on the beaches of France fighting against Nazi tyranny amidst German Panzers in a hail of machine gunfire.

Not at all. He took a bullet in the ass as he bailed out a window of some other man's house after jumping out of bed with his mistress. Daddy didn't go to the hospital, rather, he limped back to Mama, crawled in bed, and carried the bullet with him for the rest of his life. For years, Daddy would tell his war story with such pride. Mama would stare into space, still as a statue, never saying a word. She carried that secret with her, untold, until she shared it with me.

Mama told me about the mistakes she made in her life. When she was younger, she was offered a recording contract to sing the blues. She turned it down because she wanted to sing gospel only. She regretted not pursuing a gospel singing career. It would have taken some of the control out of my father's hands.

Three decades of her life were totally controlled by my father. She depended on him for transportation and was almost fifty before she learned to drive. If Daddy was gone, and she needed to get to work, she had to walk or wait on someone to pick her up. Any time she needed groceries, she had to walk. I realized that a major reason why I never left the apartment in Detroit was because of my lack of transportation. With encouragement from Mama, I went back to Detroit, determined to get my driver's license.

The second BJ and I returned from Arkansas, the tiny apartment felt claustrophobic. Bit by bit, I challenged myself to see the outside world. At twenty-four, I studied for the driver's exam and after a month of studying, I passed the written exam with excellence. The next step was to convince Ray to teach me to drive.

Ray, with reservation, took me to a mall parking lot and told me to switch seats. The first I sat in the driver's seat, I held the wheel so tightly that my hand went numb. I was scared to death. If I had driven as a teen, I would not have been afraid. As an adult, however, my mind was filled with images of disaster. That hardest part of the test, parallel parking, was impossible. Ray tried to show me how to parallel park for weeks, but I never got it down. Frustrated, I went and took the exam anyway. Much to my surprise, the instructor never made me parallel park, and I passed the test! To this day, I don't know how to parallel park.

I called Mama and told her that I had my driver's license, and she said very calmly, "Oh, I knew with all my heart you were going to do it. I talked to God this morning about you, and I was not worried one bit." She then challenged me to tell Ray it was not a good idea to leave me in the house with no transportation. When faced with this challenge, Ray fought back—hard and for many weeks—but eventually gave in to my demands. He agreed to let me have the car a couple of days a week. That was better than nothing. I had nowhere to go and no one to see, but each day I had possession of the car, I drove like Forrest Gump ran.

Things Fall Apart

In 1981, I found myself pregnant again with my second child. BJ was three years old. While I wanted him to have a playmate, I was worried that my depression would cause problems. Lethargic from antidepression drugs, for nine months, I carried my baby with no appetite. Forcing myself to eat, I tried to help the fetus survive, but at seven-and-a-half months, my normal pregnancy was changed to high-risk, and I was watched a lot closer by the obstetrician.

After eight months of carrying my child, I went into premature labor. The doctor was able to stop the contractions and delay the birth. He sent me back home for bed rest. I closed my eyes and slept for two weeks, waiting for my due date.

On May 22, 1982, I noticed that I had not felt my baby kick for at least six hours. I called Ray at work and asked him to come home and take me to the hospital. The nurses put a fetal monitor on me and discovered that I was having small contractions, but at each one, the baby's heartbeat grew weaker. The hospital staff placed a small, thin rod inside me, pricking the amniotic sack, forcing my water to break. The contractions started to come, but with every tightening came distress with the baby's heartbeat. The medical staff warned me that my child's heart might not be able to withstand a normal delivery. I watched the beating of my baby's little heart on the monitor next to my bed. As my stomach muscles tightened and pulled, the contractions, only a few seconds long at first, grew longer and longer. Each time I felt the tightness return, I looked at the monitor. As my pain increased, the beeping of my baby's heart grew fainter and fainter.

The doctor eventually came in and told me the fetus was probably not going to make it. He warned that I needed to act. The baby would not live through a natural birth. Dr. Yen, an Asian man in his forties, handed me a clipboard with papers and a pen. Rushed, he told me to grant permission to remove the baby by cesarean section. I signed the document, and a team of nurses rushed me down the hall to the operating room. A myriad of hands grabbed my shoulders and rolled me into a ball. I felt a long needle slide into my spine. The nerve endings exploded so sharply it felt like shock. I tried to tense my muscles, but the numbness washed over them all in a matter of seconds.

Dr. Yen grabbed the knife, cut me open and pulled out a beautiful baby boy. The nurse said he was a healthy baby, but before they placed him in my arms, something changed. While cleaning the mucous away, our baby stopped breathing and went into seizures. They raced him out of the delivery room. My body was numb from the medication but not my heart. I wanted to get up and run to my child, but all I could do was lie helplessly on the hospital bed.

I began to cry. I asked Ray what was wrong. He didn't answer. I think he was as stunned as I was. As they rolled me back into the recovery room, I begged for answers. The nurse was silent with a grave look of distress on her face. After she left, I turned my face to the white walls of my room and cried silently. Ray and I waited for hours with no answers. We didn't speak; we just cried.

Eventually Dr. Yen came and grabbed my hand. "Wanda," he said, "the child will likely die. He has stopped breathing several times and has had more seizures." I couldn't look in his eyes, or maybe it was he who couldn't look into mine. I stared blankly into space and said, "I want to see my baby. Please let me see my child!" With compassion, he told me he would see what he could do. The poor child was nameless, and somehow that made it worse. Dr. Yen said he would make a way for me to be wheeled into pediatric intensive care, but that I should prepare myself for death. "Too much trauma has happened to this baby," he said. After a few hours, the staff took me to the ICU to see my child. They were amazed; he was still holding on. Refusing to give up, my child was a fighter.

There was a clear, plastic tepee on top of a steel baby cart. My baby's tiny body was under an oxygen tent, with tubes running through him. The tubes were more visible than the baby was. After running extensive tests, the doctors found that some of my blood was mixed with his. They wanted to investigate whether my child had bled into me or if I had bled into him. One scenario was more dangerous than the other. I tried to wrap my mind around that thought. My body gave the child life, but my blood could possibly kill him.

Kay called from Texas and said she had come up with the ideal name: Jason. I thought of the mythical Jason, who fought along side the Argonauts to find the magical healing fleece. Without reservation, I said, "That name sounds perfect to me. What do you think, Ray?" He agreed. Jason was fighting hard for his life.

While in ICU, I noticed the little baby hat on Jason's tiny head, almost covering his tiny, sleepy face. His fists were clenched as if he was ready to fight the world. His light brown skin was red all over. Hanging on for dear life, the doctors gave me bleak statistics for his future. They determined that, because of the seizures and the fact that he stopped breathing several times, there was a seventy-five percent chance of mental retardation and at least a fifty percent chance of cerebral palsy. They even said there was a strong possibility that he could be blind, because of the high level of oxygen he'd received. I was shaken. After a week of recovery, I was released from the hospital while Jason stayed behind.

My mother and younger sister, Rosa, arrived to help us adjust to the new baby. Each day, Ray, Mama, and I would go back to intensive care to bond with Jason. He had so many issues. The doctors did not understand why his blood platelets were down. Each day they worked hard to stabilize his health, yet it seemed to be one thing after another.

One day while mom and I were in pediatrics intensive care, she asked to sit and rock the baby. I handed Jason to her and walked around the rocking chair as she started to sing to him. She stopped in the middle of her song and said to me, "I don't care what the doctors have told you, this baby is fine. When you handed him to me, his little eyes followed you when you released him to me. Don't you worry. He's a healthy baby, and he knows that you are his mother already." Mama was right. His tiny eyes followed me everywhere I went. After three weeks in intensive care, the doctors allowed us to bring Jason home on phenobarbital for his seizures. I was grateful to introduce Brian to his new brother. The moment he caught sight of the new baby, he screamed, "Take him back!" This, I think, was my first realization that I had *two* little boys that needed a good mother. I smiled and gave Brian a big hug and said, "Your brother is here to stay, BJ."

By the time Jason went in for his first check-up with our family pediatrician, he was almost two months old. Dr. Natalie Tanner, tearfully deemed him our miracle baby. Fighting to hold her tears back, she said, "His reflexes and vitals are good. After all the trauma—the loss of blood, oxygen, and low blood platelets—I cannot find one thing wrong with him." Dr. Tanner then said something that would ultimately change Jason's life forever. She told us if we treated him normal and included him in on every family activity, he would have a fighting chance of being a healthy normal individual. Even though the hospital said there was a seventy-five percent chance that he would be mentally impaired, she told us to treat him like any other kid. She instructed us to change whatever plans we had for that day, go to the beach, and put his feet in the water. Ray and I, in response to her counsel, went home, packed a picnic basket and took Jason and BJ to Belle Isle beach. After spreading our blanket out in the sand, I carefully removed Jason's shoes and placed his tiny feet in the warm, summer water.

* * * *

Today, Jason is twenty-nine. He is a staff sergeant in the U.S. Army. He has served in the military for over eleven years, doing one tour in Afghanistan and one in Iraq. He is working as an army recruiter and is as healthy as the next person. He never had a seizure after leaving the hospital. When I look back, I can see the evidence of God working in my life. Even though I did not acknowledge Him, He was still merciful. He kept me through my terrifying nightmares of depression. He kept my unborn baby in my unhealthy womb. He allowed Jason to be weaned off the seizure medicine within the first twelve months of his life. The Creator held onto me tight while I was ignorant and oblivious of His faithfulness. I think we all have, at times, walked on water without knowing it. The birth and life of my son, Jason, has been nothing short of miraculous.

* * * *

One day, I was driving in my car with my sons, listening to Dr. Sonya Friedman, a talk show host. There was a middle-aged woman on her program, talking about how she faced depression. The woman said it had taken her years to look at life and find the humor in it. She talked about how some people lived their lives from a *sad* point of view, and that a genuine, deep, belly laugh or laughing out loud was a foreign element for many folks. The words of Dr. Freidman's guest speaker cut wide and deep. They were talking about me. I pulled over on the side of the freeway and cried. It wasn't like I didn't want to be happy and see the funny side of life. I wanted to laugh, but it would not come. On the side of the highway, the cars whooshed past as I struggled to remember when I had found something funny or when I had laughed out loud. I cried even harder. I couldn't remember. So many things had happened to cause me to be absent and somber. So, on the side of the road, on the west side of Detroit, I promised myself that instant, I would work on the *inner me*.

After Jason was born, I talked Ray into looking for a house. The apartment was too small, and we needed more room. After much pushing and nudging of the mule, he agreed to get out and look. We settled on the first house we viewed. We had no idea what to do or how to do it, but we closed the deal on a small home on Church Street in Oak Park, Michigan. I took a part-time job at Burlington Coat Factory to supplement Ray's income.

Though void during this time, I fully understood that Ray saw me as a liability. His friend, Harold, helped to color and distort every facet of our lives. There was no intimacy in our relationship, just an occasional touch and go. I was alone, but did not disturb him. And even though Ray had a big family, they made it perfectly clear that I was not welcome in their lives. They all felt I was snobbish and stuck up. Although we both came from poverty, Ray's family was vastly different from mine.

The first time Ray's mother, Penny, met BJ, she referred to him as a little bastard. Although young and innocent, his feelings were hurt. At three years old, Brian was very vocal about Penny's poorly kept, roach-infested home. On our first visit, he quickly built a poor rapport with her, by screaming, "Ugh, your house is nasty. You got a lot of roaches. My mommy and daddy don't have roaches." Penny never forgot or forgave him for his big mouth. Full of contempt for Brian, each time Penny saw him, she grabbed him by his ears and cursed at him. That was how every meeting began. I wanted Ray to make peace with his mother, for after a few years of counseling, I knew what damage a strained relationship with a parent could cause. Yet every encounter with Penny was a disaster.

Penny Lang was a six-foot atomic bomb—boasting giant, sharp, pointed breasts that looked like torpedoes. Her face was long and twisted into a permanent scowl. Each gathering was filled with drunken rages. If her guest didn't see things the way she saw them, Penny threatened to kill them. And the drugs—there were enough drugs to spare for everyone. She scared me to death, yet we never said anything past hello to each other. Even if she did something I didn't like, I never addressed the issue; I took it up with Ray later. I guess that made her hate me even more.

* * * *

Knowing that he had control over my life, Ray was not concerned about whether I was comfortable or not. He basked in the knowledge that my happiness totally depended upon him. His world swallowed me up. God did not exist in our lives. As the years passed, the relationship between us became even more pressed. Ray's taste for pornography grew. He kept magazines and x-rated movies in the house. To make matters worse, there were whispers among his family members that Ray was gay and had been hiding his relationship with Harold all his life. Ray doted over Harold's well-being much more than he did with the boys and me. Questions began to surface about his sexual preference.

One day in the fall, Harold's eighteen-year-old niece, Aubrey, came home from college to see me. While Ray was at work, we sat on the patio, drinking lemonade and talking about life, college, and friendships. Our conversation carried over into the evening. When I told her that Ray was coming home, she became agitated and wanted to leave. I didn't understand, because Aubrey's family was so close to Ray she referred to him as *Uncle Ray*. Confused by her odd behavior, I continued to press her about her sudden distaste for spending time with him. After a few minutes, Aubrey emptied herself of her concerns. She began to talk about my husband's unusual behavior and about how uncomfortable she felt when he was around. "It isn't a new feeling," she said. "it is something that I have felt since I was a child." Aubrey desperately wanted to leave before Ray returned home. With my composure shattered, I asked her to stay with me for a while longer. She conceded but begged me to stay with her while Ray was around. I told her not to worry and that I was right there. I spent the rest of my time with Aubrey reasoning with her and creating scenarios where maybe she might have misunderstood Ray's intentions. My heart was broken. I didn't want to believe her, but deep down, I knew something was wrong.

Ray and I had been together for six years. In my heart, I wanted us to make it, but this information shook my very foundation. Aubrey told me that her mother explained to her what a safe hug was. She said there were things that Ray would say about her breasts and make other comments that she felt were inappropriate. She shivered at the thought of Ray coming home and being left on the patio with him. She pressed me about the time he was supposed to arrive. She wanted to be gone before he made it back from work.

My husband had dealt with Aubrey since she was in diapers. In fact, he changed her diapers—many times! My heart bled, but I remained objective. I asked her why she was so scared. With tears in her eyes, she said, "I don't want to talk about it, but please if you love, or care anything about me, don't leave me alone with him." I continued to reassure her that she had nothing to worry about; I would not leave her alone.

In the middle of the discussion, Ray walked out on the patio. With tension written all over her face, Aubrey stood, straightened her clothes in a nervous sweep, and said she had to leave. Ray looked at me, then at Aubrey, and back at me before he spoke. Looking away and avoiding his eyes, I felt like the biggest betrayer of the year. Ray asked Aubrey to stay and chat, but she refused in a terse voice. She gave me a quick hug, then walked through the house and left. I never saw her again.

After a few days, I approached Ray about Aubrey. He blew it off as a simple misunderstanding. "She just got it wrong," he said. "She misinterpreted my intentions."

God gives us intuition that we call gut feelings. If we listened to our hearts, we could probably avoid many pit falls. I wanted to believe Ray, but there was an unsettling in my heart. Most of all, I wanted us to have a good life with our sons. Yet there was this feeling of trouble and disaster looming. Ray and I were growing further apart every day.

Weekly counseling was beginning to open my eyes. My therapist asked questions about my life. He made me evaluate the fairness of my life. *What did I want in life? How did Ray treat me?* Though my counselor never made a single judgment about my marriage or about Ray, I began to see the sadness of my existence. The inequality and lack of freedom—even with the car two days a week—was too much to bear.

Just as Ray and I were growing further apart, I became pregnant. This time I made myself a promise to watch every detail of my pregnancy. After two children, I knew what I had to do. I ate better, carefully scrutinizing everything that went into my body; the pregnancy went perfect.

The delivery, however, did not go well. One of the doctors that had seen me throughout my pregnancy was rumored to have a cocaine addiction. I prayed that of the four listed in the practice Dr. Grimes would not be the one to take me through my second cesarean. I was not so lucky.

On May 20, 1985, I went to the hospital to give birth. After a quick examination, they prepared me for the C-section. The anesthesiologist asked his usual standard questions. Just like with my second child, the doctor instructed me to roll into a ball while he injected the anesthetics into my spine. I felt the electric sizzle of the needle, then a warm wash of pain medication, wave across my body. After waiting a while, they allowed Ray to come into the delivery room. Just like before, my legs were numb. As I lay on my back, staring up at the lights, Dr. Grimes got into position to begin the operation. Something was wrong!

I felt the tip of the scalpel touch my stomach. It was cold; I could feel the temperature of the blade. *I shouldn't feel that*, I thought, *something is not right.* When I signed the papers, I read that the medication didn't always work. Every once in a while, they warned, someone would be awake and able to feel the pain of surgery. *But that is rare*, I thought, *too rare to happen to me.*

I felt the cold blade move. I gasped for breath as Dr. Grimes slid the knife across my belly. I felt its razor sharp blade slice through my abdomen. My mind pounded with sensations of pain. The doctor began to cut away through layers of my skin. I'm not sure on what day, what year, or what moment I stopped screaming when I was in pain. I must have stopped when I was a young girl. I turned my head from side-to-side with tears streaming down my cheeks. I squeezed Ray's hand tightly and whispered to him, "Tell them to stop. I can feel the knife! Oh, God, help me!" Dr. Grimes continued to slice through my abdomen. Ray told the medical staff, "She said she can feel the cutting."

The doctor responded, "No she can't. She's numb."

Ray whispered back to me, "Wanda, the doctor said you can't feel anything."

I never said another word after this exchange... Tears soaked my face, neck, and hospital gown as the doctor cut away at my stomach and then moved my organs around to retrieve the baby. I could feel him shifting my bladder and liver. The pain, the fear, the horror of it all was unimaginable. It was medieval pain, something from another age when the persecuted used to have their intestines ripped out in front of cheering crowds. The pain twisted with the strange sensation of fingers clawing through my insides. Some people cringe when they hear fingernails on the chalkboard, or a dentist's drill, but imagine that feeling combined with the sensation of a hand digging through your organs. And by the time, my *Oh Gods* had become audible, a nurse told the doctor that my blood pressure was spiking. I heard someone else say something about Valium. Then, after all the pain, everything went black.

* * * *

I woke up in the recovery room with Mama by my side and no movement in my legs. There was a hot, searing pain over the wound across my stomach. Something had gone wrong with the anesthetics. I lay there, horrified, not even caring about the sex or name of my child. I could not believe the horror that I had gone through. *Was that even possible*, I thought, *to be numb, where you could not move your legs but feel the blade as I did on my abdomen?* Later on, I found out, it was very possible—a mishap—but very possible. I lay there as my mother told me that I had baby boy. It was to be the last pregnancy, because I had asked that, after the delivery, the doctors tie my tubes. I was done with having children. I found myself so angry with Ray. I had needed him to help me, to protect me, to fight for me, to believe me when I said, "I can feel them cutting me." He chose not to be my voice.

I never uttered a word about it, but that was my breaking point. I stopped loving Ray that day.

Making Wallets

We named the new baby, Bradley Sean. He was a good baby boy, and I wanted to be there for him, but I felt something inside me after he was born. It was a sensation as painful as the doctor digging around inside my womb. It was a sinking feeling that pulled every thought into the darkness. I sunk so far into depression that it felt as if there was no going back. I was sure that a nervous breakdown was inevitable. I had been depressed before, but this was different. Intense thoughts of suicide and anger flashed through my mind. I began to rationalize my death and create reasons why I needed to die. I loved my children, and because I loved them so much, I needed to kill myself. If they saw me growing up as a depressed woman, it would ruin their lives.

On the other hand, I wanted to die, but couldn't leave them. My three boys—I wanted them to be happy, and they would be devastated if I killed myself. Behind this obsession with death came thoughts of my traumatic past. The painful cutting away at my womb and no one caring to listen, consumed my days. I couldn't believe that I was so insignificant, that my voice was that inconsequential, of no value. Like so many people said when I was a kid, I was a nobody. Why shouldn't I simply go ahead and get it over with and die?

There was a woman named Kimmy who lived ten minutes from my house. Tiny in stature, she was a Vietnamese woman, stuck in Detroit since the Vietnam War and a friend of the family. Years before our relationship began, Kimmy's husband died of a massive heart attack, leaving her to care for their two beautiful children. I saw her every weekend. When I first met her, she was shy. At get-togethers, she sat in the corner by herself. In the beginning, we didn't talk all. But Kimmy and I had something in common. She was also plagued by demons of suicide. When she did talk, she admitted that she wasn't doing well. When she really opened up, she shared with me that she wanted to die. Passionately, Kimmy told me repeatedly that she did not want to live. You could see the pain in her face as she said it time and time again. I told her I felt the same way, that I had similar thoughts. Several friends pulled me aside and told me that Kimmy was full of it; that she would never kill herself. She always talked about it. In fact, she spent ten years talking about it. Friends told me to ignore her and let it go.

After a while, I unintentionally became like a therapist for Kimmy. She sought me out at each gathering. I did not realize I was finding my reason to live through my telling her to try to stay alive for her children's sake. I said so many many times, "Your children need you, Kimmy! Stay alive for them." She would respond almost in an unsalvageable state of mind, "Oh no, I can't live without my husband. I jus' wanna be with him. I don't wanna live. I cannot live anymore."

I would shoot back, "Oh, Kimmy, live for me. I am your friend. I don't know what I would do without you. What will I do without you, Kimmy?" With each encounter, I ran to the kitchen where other friends were preparing our Saturday meal and said, "Guys, Kimmy is going to do it this time! We have to help her!" Their response was always, "Right. She's been killing herself for years. She needs to get over it."

One day, while Kimmy's children were at school, she went down into the basement of her house, put a gun in her mouth and blew her brains out. Her little girl found her when she got home. Her daughter told the story of how she walked through the doors, calling for her mommy. When Kimmy didn't answer, Lee Lee, who was only twelve, ran to the basement where she usually played after school. She couldn't stop crying over the memories of seeing her mother's brains splattered on the walls of their game room. As hard and painful as it was for me to admit, Kimmy helped to save my life. I watched as her children tried to salvage their lives though the rubble. She was too far gone in her mind to even care about the aftermath. Lives were ripped apart by this selfish and violent act. The day I heard the news of her death, I searched for treatment. I was not going to kill myself, and my sons were not going to find me on my kitchen floor.

I frantically searched for a doctor. I felt I needed the best that General Motors Company and Blue Cross could afford. Many people in the field of psychology recommended a Korean man, named Dr. Hun. He was a tiny man who believed in nipping problems in the bud. The questions he asked were few. I went to several sessions with him, and he told me if I wanted to save my life, I would have to admit myself into the hospital. Only then, he warned, would I receive adequate and proper care. "You're at wit's end, Wanda. Make a choice. Live or die."

He recommended no less than a month's stay at Ardmore Acres. I agreed. I was so emotionally spent that I saw no other way out. When Ray was given this recommendation, his first question was, "Who will take care of the children?" Dr. Hun's response was, "If you care anything about your wife, you will make arrangements for a caregiver."

During my years in Detroit, I saw doctor after doctor, but there was something different about this man. He explained the pros and cons of antidepressants and helped me to understand how these drugs served their purpose when intermingled with counseling. He wanted to analyze me and understand what was eating at me; what was tearing me apart. He prescribed medication, but our sessions were the focus of his treatment. I, alone, searched and found a sitter for the children and checked myself into the hospital.

There were group sessions with young people who had attempted suicide. There was a circle of chairs of people with bandaged wrists and broken hearts. I thanked God that I had not gone that far. Some were schizophrenic or manic-depressive. Each individual suffered from a painful, dysfunctional past. I only knew that I wanted desperately to grow and recover, to understand why I was so melancholy. I had hidden so many things that I'd forgotten what door they were behind. After one week of therapy, I realized my life could have been much worse. There were so many hurting people in the world—hopeless souls, standing on the brink of insanity and suicide. Most of the patients were wealthy, white children, trying to cope with the pains of growing up. Most had tried to commit suicide already and were looking for the chance to do it again. After spending time amongst those hollow-eyed kids,

I began to see that I was blessed. Angels had somehow guarded and protected my sanity.

Entering into Ardmore Acres Hospital was one of the healthiest choices I ever made. Being there taught me to not take life too seriously. Moreover, as selfish as it sounds, my stay there was centered on me. I was learning to take some time for myself. The hospital compound was on thirty acres of sprawling land. There were manicured lawns and red brick walkways that wound through gardens with flowers of all types. The psychiatrists designed exercises that sent me outside to examine the flowers. They would give me an hour or two with nature, then ask me what I found and thought about a specific flower. Sometimes they would ask me to locate a particular kind of leaf and bring it back. After I came back inside, the doctor asked how the leaf made me feel. I grew up in the country, but I never thought about beauty. There was too much pain to detach myself from the troubles of the world. Ardmore Acres opened my eyes. Beauty was everywhere; all I had to do was reach out and grab it.

There was one exercise where we were all required to choose leather pattern pieces to create a wallet, purse, or a belt. Most of the patients worked on purses or belts, I chose to do a wallet for Ray. Stitch by stitch, I put his wallet together in leather. Because he loved football, I engraved a helmet and football on the front with the name *Ray* on the back. I found out through this exercise that pleasing him was the most important thing to me. In making the wallet, I wanted to show Ray that I was worth something; that I could accomplish a goal. I labored for almost two weeks to complete this task. While I was making his wallet, I got a message from Dr. Hun that my time at Ardmore was coming to an end.

In the middle of my stay, Ray called Dr. Hun and demanded that I come home. He felt that while he was working hard, it was unfair that I was horseback riding in the country and playing volleyball. Dr. Hun continued to insist that I needed this therapy to save my life. He even challenged me to fight. "You must stand up and fight for your right as an individual to stay, Wanda," Dr. Hun warned. "You must stay here. You must get well." After a long conversation with Dr. Hun, I refused to go against my husband's wishes and went home to care for the children.

Ray drove out the next day and picked me up. He was there at eight in the morning with my three boys. I knew I shouldn't leave; I wasn't ready to leave. But I bowed my head, followed him outside, and got in the car. I gave him the wallet that I made him. He thanked me and put it on the dashboard. "Wow," he said in a hushed tone... "Wow...." The billfold sat there as we rode home. Inside, I was very angry. I never uttered a word about my contempt. Life moved along. I didn't see that wallet again for twenty years. Ray never used it.

Change Is Going to Come

During the summer of 1986, Kay came to Detroit to visit me. She was focused on one thing. She knew of the depression I was struggling with and wanted to help me move forward in life. She inundated me with questions about my stay in Detroit. After evaluating the endless string of menial jobs, Kay determined that my life was headed in the wrong direction. She wanted me to find gainful employment to provide me with independence.

Kay was a Rehabilitation Counselor for the State of Texas. Her job was helping people get back on their feet. She questioned me as if I was one of her clients. Initially, she asked me if I wanted to work in an office. I told her that any type of clerical work was out of the question. I couldn't type, and I didn't like talking on the phone. She then asked, "What do you like to do?"

I responded, "The only things I like to do are cook and watch the response on my family's face after they've tasted my creation."

Kay reminded me that in the Wolfe family, education was a must. There was no way around it; I had to get an education. She told me that if I loved cooking, we needed to find a college or university with a curriculum for culinary arts. I promised her that I would look into it the minute she left. But Kay was adamant and demanded, "No, we will get on this right *now*! If you are to cook, you must put education behind your food." Before she left Michigan, she helped me to enroll in Oakland Community College's Food Science Program. Ray was upset. He disdained my new independence, but I did not waiver. I was determined to go forward with my education, and before I knew it, I was deep into culinary science.

* * * *

From thirteen years old to twenty-six, I teetered on the edge of destruction. I even told myself that I would never live to see age twenty-five. Yet, here I was, in school with people—potential friends—with similar ambitions. They wanted to talk about food, roux's: blondes and browns. We were all obsessed with mire poix, stocks, soups, desserts, and food competitions. I was enthralled. For the first time in my life, I felt like I was moving forward. It was a different universe, and I was a part of it.

The instructors moved the students to an industrial kitchen. They showed us the tools: pots, pans, ovens, and utensils. I found small pieces of myself in a pot of fish stock. The art of food became my world; finally, something I was good at! I made friends and set goals. Creations of food helped fuel a competitive fire in me that I did not know existed. There were several competitions ahead, but the chief one was the Michigan Culinary Olympics.

I quickly found an ally in a girl named Jody. We prepared for the Culinary Olympics together. While we worked and planned for competition, older students told Jodie and me not to even bother. A gold medal, especially the first time around, was impossible. Everyone's first competition was for experience only, they said. We smiled at each other and set out to conquer the Olympics. We wanted to upset the status quo. Jody and I entered the competition separately, but we worked together on creating new trends in cake artistry.

We pushed each other to attempt a complex icing called rolled fondant and Australian Lace work. While we worked diligently on our project, an older culinary student, intimidated by what she saw, told me that everything on my entry had to be edible, even the pillars to hold the cake up. Without a second thought, I created edible pillars for my tiered creation. I had no idea that this student was lying to me to create roadblocks. To make our creations even more uniquely different, Jodie and I devised a plan of using pastillage to create an illusion of art against the mirror when reflecting our Australian lace work.

After the long ride to the competition site, I removed the cake from the van and took it inside. I was amazed. As far as the eye could see, there were cakes and petite pastries everywhere in the arena. Jodie and I located our names amidst the hundreds of entries. She sat her cake up as I did repair work on mine, quickly trying to fix the pieces of lace work that had broken off from the ride there. After some minor repairs, Jody and I walked away, believing we had created culinary masterpieces. But… *what would the judges think?*

Exhausted from the grueling work, I went back home and slept while the judges scored all the entries. In the middle of the night, Jodie called and said, "I've got some good news, and I've got some bad news." With my eyelids still shut from sleep, I told her to give me both. Softly she said, "The good news is, I got a gold medal." And then she screamed, "The bad news is, you got a gold medal too!"

I hushed a tiny scream so I wouldn't wake my sons. I could not believe that I had actually found myself in the art of foods. It was a unique form of pride. The power that I felt within was unbelievable. I created a masterpiece with my own hands. When I arrived at Cobo Hall and found my entry, my heart beat ninety miles a minute as I read the judges' comments. One judge wrote on the comment card that my roses looked lifelike. Another master chef wrote that my edible pillars were beautiful. He wrote to be mindful of the width of my pillars. They were a bit heavy, but all was well, because the trap that the older student was trying to set up for me turned out to be one of the things the judges looked at to consider me for a gold medal.

Afterward, an offer came only a few days following the competition. Charlie's Crab, a premier restaurant in Michigan, picked me up to work as the assistant to the well-known Michigan Pastry Chef, Carmen Vilican. My life started to take shape as Ray struggled to connect with the changes around him.

The Loss of an Angel

It was the summer of 1987. I had a dream that Aunt Sophie died. I was a little girl the last time I saw or talked with her. The haunting, lost charm bracelet consumed me for nearly fourteen years. My failure to keep it safe, I'm sure, was one of the major catalysts that helped to transport me into that deep, black self-loathing hole. I needed to see her and face the demons of my past. I wanted to hold her, and I desperately needed her to put her arms around me and tell me it was okay. Most importantly, I had three beautiful sons, and I wanted them to have the privilege of meeting Aunt Sophie.

I talked with Ray and convinced him to take me to New York. It was an incredible challenge for me, because I dreaded the question "Where is the bracelet?" I cringed even more at the thought of never seeing her again. And so, with few words spoken between Ray and I, we made the long drive from Detroit, Michigan, to Laurelton, New York.

Aunt Sophie met me at the door. Age had added a frailty to her frame, but her beauty still radiated through. She welcomed my family and me into her home by wrapping her tiny arms around us one by one. She took my face and kissed my forehead and both my cheeks just as she had done when I was a child. While she talked of her excitement, she motioned with her tiny hands, directing us to sit at the kitchen table. As I was about to sit down, she took my hand and, looking at my wrist, asked, "Where is it?"

I stared into the blankness of space as I tried to find the right words. She also wanted to know why I failed to call her all those years. With my heart racing and pounding away, I told her the story of how I went to sleep and woke up to a bare arm. I asked her to forgive me for allowing the bracelet to be taken from my wrist. I explained to her the fear and anguish that I felt for fourteen years: that the missing bracelet kept me from calling, because I was so afraid of what she would say.

Aunt Sophie immediately grabbed my hands and said, "What a shame! The bracelet was special to me, but you are my flesh and blood, and I love you so much. You have always been important to me." She went on to say that she knew who took the bracelet but to let bygones be bygones. She got up from the table, gave me a tight hug, and told me to let it go—that I had punished myself long enough.

That week in New York was one of the best weeks of my life. I, along with my husband and sons, went to revisit the Statue of Liberty on Ellis Island and Madison Square Garden. When I was a child, Aunt Sophie accompanied Kay and me to Ellis Island, but she was much too frail now. Her days on earth were coming to an end.

Aunt Sophie told me she was suffering from lung cancer. Somehow, she still found the strength to get out of bed to groom herself, put on makeup, and create the glowing beauty that was her trademark. She was to be a complete diva to the end. It wasn't just the makeup that made her beautiful. She was one of those rare women that could wear a burlap sack and still look like a supermodel. She had a personality that caused her to shine. She was such a brilliant figure.

After a wonderful day in the Big Apple, I returned to her home. That night I went to her room. As she lay sleeping, I sat on the side of her bed, beating myself up for taking so long. *Why had I waited all those years to connect with one of the few people that loved, believed, and saw the good in me? What was wrong with me?* I mean, I knew Aunt Sophie loved me. *Why had I been so selfish in not calling and keeping in contact with her?* It was complete absurdity. And just as I was giving myself the lashing of a lifetime, she woke up out of her sleep and peered into my sad eyes. She quickly read what was on the inside of my heart and told me once again to let the past go. She told me that the only thing that mattered was the moment at hand; that the past could not be undone, but the future was wide open to set things straight and get it right. *Wow!*

She instructed me to look in her nightstand and pull her jewelry box out. I pulled the small box out and laid it beside her on the bed. She calmly looked inside. She pulled out of the box and placed in my hand a beautiful gold chain with a single pearl and a pendant in the shape of a golden bird attached to it. I sat speechless as she went on to tell me how dear I was to her.

Each encounter with Aunt Sophie was life altering. We stayed with her one week. Some of the time, she was up and moving around as if she was perfectly fine. Other times she was so weak that she could barely lift her spoon to feed herself. While I sat with her, I felt as if I was the luckiest of all my parent's children. I was smart enough to seize the opportunity to spend time with Aunt Sophie. When our vacation ended, I tearfully said my good-byes and made my way back to Detroit.

A few months later, I got a call from Mama saying that Aunt Sophie had passed. I promptly packed my bags again and waited for Buddy and Daddy to pick me up. They were driving from Tennessee. The last trip to New York had proven to be a bit much for Ray, so he volunteered to stay at home with the children while I paid my respects. I said my final good-byes to my closest aunt.

Aunt Sophie taught me how to be a proper woman. She showed me that there was more to the world than our little town in Arkansas had to offer. Her love transcended all boundaries of time and space. All the things she told me, I repeated to my children. She was one of the greatest women I had ever known.

Upon returning from my aunt's funeral, I decided that I no longer wanted to struggle with Ray. I wanted my own car and subsequent freedom. After many arguments, he conceded, and I purchased my own automobile.

I also purchased—against Ray's will—a second pair of dress shoes. He was angry, because he could not understand why anyone would need more than one pair of shoes. With good money coming from my new job and the freedom provided by my new vehicle, I continued to buy more shoes and clothes. I hid the gifts for myself from Ray. I would race in while he was at work and shove my purchases under the bed. Before long, I created a real wardrobe. I hid everything I bought, knowing what he would say. It would be years, well after my divorce from Ray, before I stopped hiding things after purchasing them. I simply did not feel right treating myself well.

After about a year of working at Charley's Crab, the executive pastry chef took a leave of absence, because of her struggle with lymphoma. I took on the role of pastry chef, running with my dessert menu and studying hard to attain my degree. Outside of the Michigan Restaurant Association's Culinary Olympics, Oakland Community College held their yearly competition. I moved into the last phase of culinary training. This complex phase was the fine dining competition of elite cuisine. I prepared pates, galantines, and pate en croute. In this competition, I not only got a Gold Medal, but also the *Auggie*, which represents *Best of Show*. Jodie took home a silver medal, and our relationship waxed thin after that, but never had my self-esteem been so boosted. I remember being quiet, because I didn't want anyone to notice that I was a winner. I wanted people to continue to like me, and I thought that my success would create resentment among my classmates. I treated this major success gingerly. The culinary field is extremely competitive. Chefs are not judged collectively; rather they are pitted against other chefs. Injured pride and resentment are often the result of a meritocracy. I was ready to cook, but I was not ready for the backstabbing and envy that existed. To compound matters, males mainly dominated the industry. I found culinary arts not for the faint of heart.

My pastry instructor, Chef Bender, warned me not to take my gold medals too seriously, because I, like all my other competitors, took two weeks to work on each project. What is really important," he said, "is the amount of cakes you can do in one hour. Clients don't wait two weeks for one cake!" From that point on, I made a vow never to compete again; I determined that my focus would always be centered on becoming good and fast in my profession.

With three children, a new pastry chef position, full-time classes, and a home to manage, my plate was overflowing. In the midst of my already stretched fabric, Coco, Ray's niece, ran away from home and asked to stay with us. After talking with her mother, Ray and I agreed that we would try to help her. Coco was Ray's brother's daughter and he, on demonstrating what a strong man should look like, was a terrific hot mess. He had spent most of his life in jail and on drugs and had little to do with his daughter. Although Coco was only fifteen, she was well-endowed like her grandmother, Penny, and looked to be in her early twenties.

The first days of her stay were quiet, but after about a week, she began to act out. With lots of prodding and convincing her that she could trust me, she finally poured her heart out. Coco was scared to confide in me for fear that I would hate her. I assured her that I would not judge her. I had some big secrets in my life, a lifetime of painful memories that I struggled every day to face. I gave her my word that I would believe her.

And Coco opened the door to her secret closet.

She said, "In the middle of the night, Uncle Ray comes and gets in bed with me. He puts his hands in my underwear and touches my breasts. Every night he goes further and further. Auntie, he puts his tongue in my mouth and forces me to kiss him."

I sat, numb and shaken to my core. I am ashamed of what I said next. In distress I responded, "Coco, why are you lying on my husband?" I started crying along with her.

She replied, "I knew it was a mistake to tell you. I knew you wouldn't believe me. Please don't tell Uncle Ray. I'm begging you not to tell him. He will kill me. Please don't tell him."

I said, "Coco, I don't understand why you are saying these things."

We both sat crying.

She went to her room and sobbed on her pillow as I waited quietly in my bedroom for Ray to come home from work.

At 1:00 a.m., he arrived, and I told him about Coco's accusation. Without uttering one single word, Ray got up, pulled his leather belt off, went to Coco's room, and dragged her out of her bed by her arm, through the hallway, through the living room, through the kitchen, and down the basement stairs. As she screamed and I tearfully protested, Ray beat her viciously and called her names. I sat, crying, at the top of the stairs. The noise awakened the children. Brian shouted, "Why is Daddy doing that? What's wrong, Mommy?"

I grabbed him up in my arms and went to shield Jason and Sean from the violence. We sat in my bedroom. All of a sudden, the screaming stopped, and we heard a door slam.

Ray came into the room with sweat pouring from his face. Out of breath, he said, "She's gone. She ran out into the streets."

I cried, "No Ray! You can't leave her alone in the dark. We have to go find her."

He said, "I'm not going anywhere. You can go out, but I'm done with her."

In the middle of the night, I got in my car and searched and searched. Coco was gone. She disappeared. Something was horribly wrong. I had never felt an emptiness like that before. And in my heart, I was so disappointed in myself. I dishonored this child. I wasn't sure what I should have done, but I knew, deeply, what I did was wrong. After hours of searching, I drove back home, pulled up into the driveway, and cried.

The next day, I went to Carolyn's house. She sat quietly as I told her the story. Her eyes filled with tears as she said, "I believe Coco. I believe that Ray molested her just like uncle Clem molested me. No one believed me. Why is that so hard for people to believe? I don't understand. You should have believed her!"

Carolyn cried for a while, then she looked far off and began to tell *her* story. "Uncle Clem was the only one of Mommy's brothers who was a financial success. Everyone respected him and wanted to be like him. When I was a child, he had sex with me. When he died, everyone cried except me. I spat on his grave. Coco did not lie to you. She went out on a limb and told you the truth, but you couldn't handle it. I don't understand how you could protect Ray in that way! You are worse than him because you know that something is not right!"

I told Carolyn that I wanted to talk to Coco and apologize. "Do you know where she is?" I asked.

She said, "I know where she is. She is safe, but Ray beat her so bad she has horrible bruises all over her body. I don't think this is a good time for you to see her." She went on to say, "You and I have never been close. I believe that the reason is because of Harold and Ray's relationship. I have always felt that they were lovers. You can't see it because you don't want to see it. I don't think you are a bad person, but you are naïve and misguided. Everyone in our family believes that they sleep together. When you came to Detroit, you and I were developing a sisterhood and friendship, but Ray's relationship with Harold overshadowed everything. Harold controls Ray, and you allow it. What do you really know about my brother? I mean, he was sexually abused when he was a child. Why is it far-fetched to believe that he would perpetrate the same crime? He never went to any type of counseling that I know of to deal with his issues. Uncle Clem had sex with me until I was eighteen. The wounds I have from his sadistic behavior left me so bitter. I deal with men, but I don't trust them. I can't tell you what to believe, but I believe that Coco told the truth."

I sat there in silence as Carolyn talked of her painful past. I didn't know what to say, but she was right. Ray came and went as he pleased. In the eight years we'd been married, I had never questioned him about anything. His relationship with Harold was extremely secretive, and I never challenged him in regards to it. I apologized to Carolyn for my participation in the prior night's events. I hugged her and asked her if we could be friends. She solemnly looked away and replied, "We can try," but in our hearts, we both knew that we would not. Too much damage had already been done. That was the last time I saw or spoke to her.

There was a fire on the inside of me as I drove home. It is impossible to go forward in life until you've made peace with your past. I did not have the guts to confront Ray, so I took all the information from my conversation with Carolyn and tried to shove it into my secret closet. By now, I had to pile and stack feelings of hurt and disappointment on top of each other. There was so much trash hidden away, there was no way to keep it from spewing over and under the door. By the time I made it home, I had forced that imaginary door shut, and Ray and I never discussed the events of Coco again. It was as if the night before never happened.

I held onto the secrets, and every time I looked at Ray, I burned with anger.

Seldom was there any intimacy between Ray and me. We could go months without touching each other, and it was fine with both of us. We went on with our lives, pretending to the outside world that we were *the happy couple*. We were both very good at hiding the truth and skillful at creating the illusion that we were in love. When people saw us they would say, "Oh, Wanda, we just love seeing you and Ray! You all are so loving! You two are so happy! Honey, look at how Ray treats his wife! They had no idea we were teetering on the brink of divorce.

It shocked the hell out of everyone that I was leaving him. The rumor throughout my family was that I was leaving him for another man.

When the story broke, my family members went after it like ravenous wolves go after raw, bloodied meat. Ray called each sibling and trashed my name. It became a mystery to them as to why I would leave such a kind, gentle, caring, and tolerant man. And when Ray pushed me down the stairs and fractured my tailbone, one of my siblings responded, "He should have broken more than her tailbone. I would have done much more than push her down the stairs." Another brother said, "He gave her food to eat and a place to stay, what more could she want?"

I learned a valuable lesson about my family during these times. One of the biggest things was that no one cared about the next person. We shared the same parents, but that was all! It quickly became crystal clear that I was on my own during my divorce. Ray, in response to my leaving, seized complete control of our money, even though we both contributed to our checking and savings accounts. He informed my mother that he was going to smoke me out as a hunter would smoke out a fox. My mother, my only friend, informed him, "She's not a fox… she's a Wolfe. She'll survive." In a panic, I called one very wealthy brother and asked him to help me leave the city of Detroit. After clearing his throat ten times in discontent, he reluctantly told me he could wire me one hundred dollars, but that fourteen dollars would be subtracted for the cost of the wire. I bit my lip and accepted the $86.00.

My family never stopped talking about me after that. My *irrational actions*, as they would call it, would be discussed during family reunions and get-togethers for years to come. I was the rebel who did the opposite of what I was expected. I became the rumor, *the great big lie* that everyone told to garner attention. Sophie Mae, in particular, sent me fifty dollars in the mail, telling me that *God* had laid it on her heart to send the money, but *God* also instructed her to tell me that I didn't have to sell my body to men to survive. It was insane. Someone in our family had spread a very hurtful rumor that I was a prostitute. Sophie Mae, who was also extremely well off, cautioned me to take the fifty dollars and use it wisely. "Thank you," I told her, "I won't spend it all in one place." The lies about me were coming quickly. The rumor mill was spitting out new tales each week. I didn't know what to think, but the lie about prostitution cut me to the core. I didn't understand how someone in my family could be so cold-hearted and calloused to spread such horribly fallacious words.

While everything else was falling apart, my mother and I grew even closer. Mama told me of an incident that happened with Ray during her visit for the birth of Sean. She asked Ray to take her out to get groceries. While he was driving, she said, he acted strange. Mom said she became very uncomfortable as Ray drove out of our nice neighborhood in Oak Park and into a rundown section of Detroit, parking in an alley behind a Burger King. Instead of going inside to use the restroom, Ray got out of the car, turned his back partially to her, pulled out his business, and urinated right in front of her. After finishing, he got back in the car as if nothing happened and took her to the grocery store.

Mama began to watch his actions closer after this incident. Another time when Mom came to Detroit, she brought my niece and nephew, Meeky and Bobby, with her. She listened more attentively as Ray talked about how beautiful ten-year-old Meeky was and how he wanted to spend time alone with her. Mama noticed that Ray was always trying to get Meeky by herself. He wanted to take her to the store, to the park, or on a walk—just the two of them. He never wanted to take little Bobby. Each time when he had an errand to run, he asked Meeky to go with him. Innocently, Meeky would get excited about going, but Mama would tell her no.

My mother was the only person happy over my leaving Ray and the city of Detroit. I took BJ, Jason, and Sean to my parent's house, and they, along with their cousins, Bobby and Meeky, went to school in Arkansas while I searched for employment in Atlanta. I found a job as the assistant pastry chef at the Double Tree Hotel. After getting an apartment and settling in, I was excited about building a new life for me and my children.

One morning at about four, my mother woke me up and told me that Ray and a strange man came in their house in the middle of the night and snatched the children out of their beds. I called into Doubletree Hotel where I worked and informed them that I had to go out of town on an emergency. My children were all I had. I was nothing without them. Frantic and angry, I drove into the black of night, back to Detroit.

Detroit to Atlanta is a long drive. All the way there, I thought about my boys. I knew about Ray's past, and I was scared about the future. *How was I going to get them back? What was I going to say? Ray had already filed for divorce, but legally we were still married. What would I do when I saw him? What if... what if...*

After twelve hours in the car, I reached Detroit. I shuddered at the thought of a run-in with Ray. The moment I pulled into the driveway, I raced out the car up to the house and knocked on the door. Alicia, the babysitter, answered but refused to let me in. I pleaded and begged her, but even though she was like a daughter to me, she shook her head at the glass window between us. She and her parents lived directly across from us and were friends of ours until Ray and I split. Alicia called them for support. They came outside and told me to leave. Before I could think, I lost my head and put my fist through the glass door, shattering the window and severely injuring my hand and arm. I grabbed my children with blood all over my clothes as someone called EMS. All I could think about was getting to my boys.

I didn't care about the blood, nor did I even feel the pain of the huge cut on my arm that exposed tissue and nerve endings from the tear. No one would take my children away from me! EMS raced me away to the hospital as I protested, leaving my kids behind. They stitched and bandaged me up as I contemplated an exit route. Stranded at the hospital, I had no way of getting home. My mother called Ray and begged him to pick me up from the hospital. He obliged but made me promise to stay home with the children, cook for him, and never work again outside the home. I knew I had no other choice. I had to lie to him. The truth would have been too ugly. I promised my loyalty. He was relieved, but I could tell that inside his heart, he knew it was over.

When I was a child, there was a nursery rhyme that went, "What's gone is gone." That was an apt description of my feelings toward Ray. He knew I cared about how people perceived us. However, eight years of abuse was enough. I no longer cared what anyone thought. I don't know what he was thinking. I can only tell you where I was.

I was gone.

The day I talked to his sister, Carolyn, about Coco, I was gone. Many times within our marriage, I asked Ray to participate in marriage counseling. He always refused. Our problems grew. And little by little, I left mentally, long before my physical exodus.

My left arm was bandaged and immobile with extensive nerve damage, but Ray said, "I don't care if you got two fingers, a nub for a hand, and one arm to work with, this house better be cleaned and food better be prepared by the time I get home from work. He took the keys to my car to work with him as I lay in bed quietly. All day long, I kept the children close beside me. That evening, I cooked spaghetti with garlic bread. It was Ray's favorite meal. He held onto my car keys. The next day, I made pork chops and rice. That was his second favorite meal. He came home, boasting about how his fellow workers at Ford Motor company had commended him for taking control of his household. One of his friends said, "If you had kept her barefoot and pregnant, none of this would have happened in the first place. After dinner, he handed me back my car keys. He had no idea that this would be his last supper. On the third day, after Ray went to work, with partial use of my right arm and hand, I put my children and a minimal amount of clothing for them in my car and left Detroit for good.

The next day Ray probably ate Ramen noodles, his least favorite meal.

Rumors would always fly about me leaving Ray for another man. That person that my family was talking about was Eddie Fritts. In my mind, Eddie was a tag along boy who sometimes, when it was convenient, wanted to be a man. And even though he shadowed me wherever I went, he was far from the reason why I left the abusive lifestyle that consumed my life for over a decade.

Atlanta

If we could take mistakes and measure them on a Richter scale as they do earthquakes, the relationship with Eddie would register a ten. Eddie was the destroyer of worlds. Wherever I went, he came along. Atlanta was no exception.

Oh, Eddie…there is such a thing as a boy trapped in a man's body. The boy gets a chance to do all the things that a man would do, with the exception of accepting responsibility. A part of me desires to neglect to tell of this nine-year period in my life. Yet, I realize that if I give in to this urge, it will be like serving an entrée without a veggie and starch. Just as the meal would be incomplete, so would the story of my life.

My son Brian, his wife Kelsy and Grandbaby Ripley.

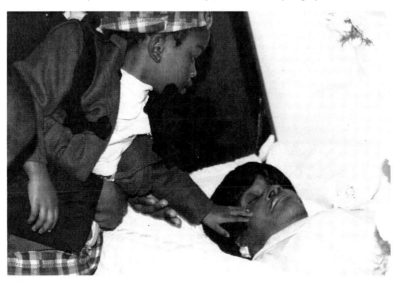

Saying Good-bye to Mama.

Jason, me and Brian(My sons and I were extremely close.)

One of my Mad Hatter creations

Cha**Chat** **Wash**ington

Search

Jason Williams's Photos - Profile Pictures

Photo 3 of 3   Back to Album · Jason's Photos · Jason's Profile

Added November 23, 2009 · Like · Comment

 Wanda Wolfe Jason, I just realized that this is General Petraeus.
Congratulations again,Son!!!! I am so incredibly proud of you...I
could not have asked for a better friend and son. I love you so very
much!!!!!!

October 3 at 4:32pm · Like

Jason and General Petraeus

Me, Jason and Brian visiting Buddy

Mama in her favorite space(the piano) with Daddy.

I love this picture of me and Daddy.

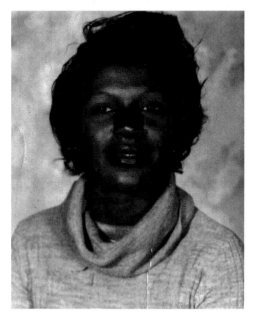

Me at 18. I was pregnant and didn't know it.

Aunt Sophie and me.

After the Gold!

Mama and Daddy.

Loan Officer; Cecil Epperly, his wife Cathy and me right
before Wanda's Cake Gallery opened in Tulsa

Visiting with onlookers about my Gold Medal cake.

Jason, me and Brian

Me, Brian, Jason, Blu and Poncho

My father may not have been close to me but he loved my babies.

My truck was totaled in the car accident.

Brian, Sean and Jason during their stay with Mama.

Me at Denise LaSalle's home with famed R&B artist, Ann Peebles

Buddy and artist, Janet Jackson.

Me, 30 years after H.S. with my mentors, Coach
James Coleman and wife Katherine.

Me, 2nd from the right. I was a company Squad Leader.

Me and Vice President, Al Gore.

Me in Germany.

My Gold Medal.

Graduating high school.

US

-ts? Please call
ttor Christina Rook.

ditor Melissa Birks.

ditor Gregg Parker,

nty 1-800-372-3922.

LOCAL

Monday, January 1, 1996   PAGE 3A

Presidential get ready to race
This week, the men running for the
Republican presidential nomination will
step up the TV ads they've aired so far,
bombing Iowa and New Hampshire
viewers with their ideas. Page 8A

► MORE

Across West Tennessee	4A
World	5A
Deaths	6A
Nation	8A

Concert marked by joy, tragedy

om
OHS

ear of
ation

» Year!
here do we
ere? For
County the
'e go
future at a
t allow time
rflecting.
crest of the
nd it'sall we
ny on it.
xcited to be-
e. These are
metro,
ple effects
oughout West
communities
e
n are facing,
look forward

e us

ve been close
times:
nsance"
ed an old,
lustral city
erially split
a cost of
Canada's
oufty

■ The mother of
concert organizer
James 'Super' Wolfe
dies during a spiritually
emotional concert.

By THOMAS CLOUSE
The Jackson Sun

A Sunday evening concert at
the Jackson Civic Center was
marked by first joy and then
sadness when the organizer's
mother collapsed on stage and
later died of an apparent heart
attack.

Melinda Wolfe, 65, was performing "One Day at a Time
Sweet Jesus" when she fell to
the Civic Centre stage floor.
Paramedics spent about 40
minutes trying to resuscitate
her backstage before transporting her to Jackson-Madison
County General Hospital,
where she was pronounced
dead, said her son, James
"Super" Wolfe, who owns local
radio station KIX-96.

The show, sponsored by
Wolfe Park Productions, had
attracted a capacity crowd and
continued even after Mrs.
Wolfe's collapse. It included
performances from other
groups like The Lighthouse

Singers of Baton Rouge, La.
and the Greater St. Luke Mass
Choir. The show was headlined
by the Mississippi Mass Choir.

The show attracted an enthu-
siastic capacity crowd to the
Civic Center with only a few
empty seats left by show time.
The audience was caught up in
the emotion from the beginning, clapping and singing in
time with the performers.

Mrs. Wolfe lived in Marianna,
Ark., and had traveled from Atlanta for the show. She collapsed a few minutes before it
p.m., only moments after her
son had introduced her performance. Wolfe and his mother talked on stage about her

putting nine children through
college and of the symbolism of
the family's pot-belly stove.

"The introduction he did for
her was beautiful," said former
Jackson City Councilwoman
Anna Parks-Covington. "James
said when he was a child, he
thought that they chopped
wood every day just for the
stove. But she said that was
where the family prayed to
Jesus

"She said the problem with
children today is that people
are leaving Jesus out – that
the pot-belly stove is just there
for heat."

After Mrs. Wolfe was taken to
the hospital, her son addressed

the crowd and told them he was
going to be near his mother

People gathered around the
paramedics and watched with
concern. One woman knelt onto
the concrete floor backstage
and prayed. A chant of "Jesus,
Jesus" filtered through the
crowd

Wolfe was visibly shaken

"It's like a nightmare I
watched her die on stage. I had
just told her how much I loved
her," he said, tears streaming
down his face.

Wolfe's father passed away in
September. "His grave wasn't
even cold yet," he said. "It's all
like a bad dream."

A BEDROOM FOR BIRDS

■ Crows have made a
roost on North
Highland Avenue near
Super Valu Foods.

By PATRICK RICE
The Jackson Sun

A t dusk, when Mike
Uselton looks out the
window of Jackson
Fire Station No. 5 and
sees hundreds of crows
circling, macabre images come

4.5 ounces, was born at 12:13 a.m. on New Year's Day at Jackson-Madison County General Hospital. Peete arrived seven days early to be the first Madison County baby born in 1996.

▶ Local, Page 3A

'Super' Wolfe listed in stable condition

James "Super" Wolfe was admitted to Jackson-Madison County General Hospital on Monday, a day after his mother died of a heart attack while singing in a gospel concert.

Wolfe, 45, was admitted to the hospital around 11 a.m.,

Wolfe

he said from a hospital bed. He was rushed there by private vehicle after complaining of chest pains.

"I'm just under so much pressure after my mother passed," he said. "It's just hard."

His mother collapsed onstage moments after he introduced her performance. The two had talked onstage about her raising nine children.

Wolfe, whose father died in September, was listed in stable condition late Monday.

Clinton, Congress take budget breather

WASHINGTON — Congressional leaders and President Clinton took a one-day break Monday after three consecutive days of White House negotiations on a seven-year balanced budget. The stalemate has left the government partially closed since Dec. 15.

▶Federal workers begin new year with frustration. 6A.

— From Sun and wire reports

Please call
Christine Rook,
Melissa Birks,
Gregg Parker,
500-372-3922

Cold wave kills 80 in Mexico

Snow, ice and freezing temperatures have killed more than 80 people in Mexico, particularly among peasants in the northern state of Chihuahua. Page 2A

Community joins Wolfe in mourning loss of mother

■ James 'Super' Wolfe urges the 150 people at his mother's memorial service to 'be ready when the roll is called.'

By HENRY GOOLSBY
The Jackson Sun

Last Sunday, Ora Hobson went to the Jackson Civic Center to witness one of the biggest gospel concerts of the year. But tragedy struck that night, and on Thursday, Hobson was expressing her sympathy.

Hobson joined more than 150 family and friends saying good-bye to the mother of Jackson businessman James "Super" Wolfe.

Malinda Wolfe, 65, of Marianna, Ark., collapsed Sunday night while singing "One Day at a Time, Sweet Jesus" before a crowd of about 1,200. She was later pronounced dead of a heart attack.

"It was startling," Hobson said. "It's something that will stay with you for ever and ever."

Choir members at Mother Liberty CME sang while ministers prayed. Members of the Wolfe family spoke about how they remembered their mother.

James Wolfe, owner of local radio station KIX 96, said the incident was tragic but also uplifting. People, he said, should use the passing of his mother as a learning experience.

"The main message is to be ready when the roll is called," he said. "I don't care how big you are in stature — God is in control. When he wants you, he can come and get you."

Wolfe's father, James Wolfe Sr., died four months prior to Mrs. Wolfe's death. On Monday, a day after his mother's death, Wolfe was admitted to Jackson-Madison County General Hospital with chest pains. He was released Wednesday.

The elder Wolfe and his wife combined to form the family singing group "The Wolfe Family Singers," which consisted of their nine children.

CHRIS STANFIELD/The Jackson Sun

James 'Super' Wolfe, sitting with his wife, Denise LaSaile, wipes tears from his eye Thursday during a memorial service for his mother, Malinda Smith Wolfe, at Mother Liberty CME Church. Her funeral service is Saturday in Arkansas.

Panel approves leasing building

■ Long-range Planning Committee will recommend that the County

WHAT'S NEXT

The Madison County

Daddy is the little boy on the far left; with aunt Effie, Aunt Sophie, Uncle Teddy, Uncle Clarence (who disappeared) and Grandpa Tobias.

One of my creations.

ARTS

• TULSA WORLD •

Five arrested in alleged
Posh Spice kidnap plot
PAGE 5

Food

LIVING
[SECTION D]
WEDNESDAY, NOVEMBER 6, 2002

Also **D-2** COMICS AND MORE **D-10-11**

www.tulsaworld.com

Wolfe uses plastic gloves so she won't smudge the delicate folds on this rose.

Photo by MICHAEL WYKE/Tulsa World

Wanda Wolfe arranges fondant flowers on a small wedding cake that will sit in the window of her shop. Wanda's Cake Gallery is at the Farm Shopping Center, 51st Street and Sheridan Road.

Icing on the cake

Local pastry chef shares tricks of the trade

BY ASHLEY PARRISH / WORLD STAFF WRITER

In the kitchen, behind the elaborate wedding cake with the fountain of ribbons, a pair of bakers work in companionable silence. The only sound comes from Ella Fitzgerald, who's crooning from invisible speakers somewhere in the antique-filled shop.

Every few minutes, one starts a sentence. And the other finishes it. Then they collapse into giggles over pans of bubbling vanilla pastry cream and mounds of snow-white fondant.

In this little bakery at the Farm Shopping Center, everything is filled with warmth. There are homey corners with stacks of cooking magazines. And there are flowers — on the cushions and on the walls.

And, in big glass cases, there are cakes and tarts and cheesecakes festooned with white chocolate shavings so

elaborate they drape like silk.

Those are in addition to the wedding cakes of every shape and size.

That same warmth extends into the kitchen, where Wanda Wolfe and her son create frilly works of art. Twirls of frosting. Delicate roses and calla lilies with perfect petals and tiny gold tears with pastel icing.

But spend a few minutes with the pair at Wanda's Cake Gallery, and they quickly stomp out any notions of primness.

"I am not a frou-frou person at all," Wolfe says, although her impeccable, bright-red lipstick, tiny braids and fancy chef's hat belie the statement. "I know how to get down and dirty, and I know how to clean up well."

She loves to see the expressions on people's faces when they hear about the catfish she likes to catch on Sundays, the day her baking smock is replaced with rubber waders.

Or the fact, that in the middle of this spun-sugar world, she and her sons

can't stand to eat sweets.

It's understandable, she says, because her three sons grew up using pastry bags with technicolor frostings instead of crayons.

But Brim reminds his mother that her coconut cream pie tempts even him.

That's when he goes and gets a dream of a dessert. It's pale pastry cream studded with coconut. And light, vanilla-tinged whipped cream with curls of white chocolate. All enveloped in a thick, flaky tart crust. Amazingly, it's not cloying. There's only a whisper of elegant sweetness.

And that pretty much describes everything in this shop.

Open less than a month, already the door chimes all day long.

One after another, customers come in asking for the woman who does fondant icing — that perfect, porcelain finish on wedding cakes. The kind that adorns every Martha Stewart cake and is the toast of every bridal magazine story.

But there aren't many people who

want to deal with the frosting that's rolled out like pie crust before it's draped and shaped over cake layers.

"People are afraid of this like it's a monster," she says while picking up a big piece of white dough then slapping it against her stainless-steel table.

"It's fussy, yes. Tear it, and you'll have to start over. No smoothing out the imperfections, because it's not forgiving like buttercream.

"But then buttercream has never looked like crushed velvet. And it's never been molded into precise pearls and fragile flowers with gently curving petals.

Fondant is just corn syrup, sugar, vanilla, glycerine and shortening and it tastes like vanilla-scented candy when done well.

Wolfe doesn't do it any other way.

"It's something a home cook could learn but probably wouldn't try enough to get good at."

SEE **CAKE** D-5

THIS & THAT

Easy as candy pie

Easy no-bake desserts are a nice way to get kids interested in cooking, so when the editors of a national cooking magazine came across Shellie Hansen's candy-bar pie recipe, they took notice.

The Tulsan likes this recipe because it's easy to remember and can be thrown together quickly. Her only tip: "I freeze the candy bars and use a rolling pin to make crushing them easier."

— Taste of

Home's Quick Cooking is available on magazine stands now, and Hanson's recipe is in the "Kids in the Kitchen" section.

Candy Bar Pie
Makes 6 to 8 servings
1 8-ounce package cream cheese, softened
1 8-ounce carton frozen whipped topping, thawed
4 2.1-ounce Butterfinger candy bars
1 9-inch prepared graham cracker crust

In a small mixing bowl, beat the cream cheese until smooth. Fold in whipped topping. Crush the candy bars, fold 1 cup into cream cheese mixture. Spoon into crust. Sprinkle with remaining candy bar crumbs. Refrigerate for 2 to 4 hours before slicing.

Giving thanks

The BamaPie Kitchen wants to know why you're most thankful this year.

The first-place winner in the Thanksgiving contest gets a smoked turkey and two gourmet pies — just in time for the holiday.

To enter: Tell us "Thanksgiving Contest." The BamaPie Kitchen, P.O. Box 4829, Tulsa, OK, 74159 or call (877) 566-0905.

For more information about the contest or Bama pies, you can go to:
www.bamapie.com

Smokin'!

And an Oklahoma barbecue team brought home a prize from the recent Jack Daniel's World Championship Invitational Barbecue in Lynchburg, Tenn.

Billsaster's Taco Oke Smokin Crew became this year's Reserve Grand Champion and won $1,500.

The team won last year's grand championship.

FOOD TIPS

Power of steam works in microwave

To clean your microwave, heat a bowl of water on high power for 5 to 10 minutes. Keep the oven closed for several more minutes to allow the steam to do its magic.

Using oven mitts, carefully remove the bowl of water. Then wipe the walls of the oven — almost effortlessly.

Put out the fire with milk produce

You thought that was a bell pepper but it was a chili pepper and now your mouth is on fire?

To ease the burning sensation, reach not for water or alcohol but for a dairy product (such as milk, yogurt or ice cream) or starchy foods (including rice, tortillas or bread).

Fast foam fast, no pumping required

To obtain fast foam for a latte or cappuccino, the Aerolatte (about $20) is the perfect battery-powered frother. No pumping is required. Simply place a small amount of cold or warm, skim or whole milk in the bottom of a coffee cup. Slide the switch into the "on" position.

In 20 seconds the job is beautifully done. There are no parts to attach or lose. It's small and easy to store in a drawer. Or, proudly display your Aerolatte suspended from a handy stand (sold separately).

The well-tempered egg

When recipes, such as custards, involve blending uncooked eggs into hot mixtures, "tempering" will prevent the uncooked eggs from scrambling or curdling.

To temper eggs, whisk beaten eggs in a medium bowl; whisk in a small amount of the hot liquid from the custard or sauce. Continue adding hot liquid by spoonfuls until the egg mixture warms. The tempered eggs are now ready to be smoothly whisked into hot liquid.

For singles, only

To make a single portion of lasagna or other pasta dish, substitute egg roll wrappers for lasagna sheets. The egg roll wrappers are easier to work with and cook in boiling salted water in less than a minute.

Don't treat ginger root gingerly

To peel ginger root, rather than using a knife and cutting away much of the usable ginger with the peel, try a spoon.

Place the edge of a metal spoon against the tip of the chunk of ginger root. Exert firm pressure and move the spoon downward along the root. The edge of the spoon will remove the peel but none of the underlying ginger.

It's the pits

To easily pit a large number of olives for a recipe, place the olives on a cutting board and, using the flat side of a large knife, squash each olive until it splits. Then use the tip of the knife or your fingers to extract the pit.

Food for thought

Bring on the clams, chicken wings and fish sticks. More people, apparently, are taking pleasure in frying in oil.

According to the research group NPD Houseworld, in the category of "Kitchen Electrics," retail dollar sales of deep fryers grew at double-digit rates in the last 12-month period, compared to the same time period last year.

From wire reports

MICHAEL WYKE / Tulsa World

Wanda Wolfe, owner of Wanda's Cake Gallery, works with rolled fondant while and her son, Brian, rolls tart dough in the kitchen of their new store, 6562 E. 51st St.

CAKE:

Her only secret is the chocolate.

FROM **B-1**

But there are other techniques and recipes she's willing to share. Like how to make a fantastic white chocolate pie. (See recipes below).

And the baking ingredients to splurge on.

She thinks Nestle white chocolate and Land O' Lakes unsalted butter are good, economical choices. But buy Tahitian or Madagascar vanilla "if you really want to please someone."

She lists five things every baker needs in the kitchen — a French tapered rolling pin, a Kitchen-Aid stand mixer, a Cuisinart food processor, a good wire whip and her favorite tool, a cheap plastic dough scraper. It's how she smooths and cuts dough and gets every speck of batter from her mixing bowls.

And decorating doesn't need to be anything more than good silk flowers, she says. Or roses.

Or ribbon.

It's something that she uses on almost every cake she makes. Buy good-quality fabric ribbon when it's on sale, and you create any color combination without pulling out food coloring. Just wrap a piece of ribbon around a cake, and secure the ends with a dab of frosting. Or tie a bow. Or let streamers of it flow from the top of the cake.

All are tips she shares willingly.

Her only secret is the chocolate. Her trademark.

All she'll say about it is that she was playing around one day with chocolate and a bench scraper. That's when she figured out how to make those wide, elaborate curls that look like draped fabric on top of a cake.

Already, she's had inquiries about classes, and she's thinking about teaching some on baking and decorating.

Like how to make the fruit tarts her son is assembling for a party.

With that thick tart shell, pastry cream, strawberries and mandarin oranges.

It's nothing like those gorgeous desserts in shop windows that are all tease but taste like a 59-cent box of pudding.

"It's great when you can make it look good," she remembers a cooking instructor telling her once, "but you have to make it taste good, too."

So her advice to home cooks is to concentrate on the recipes and perfect a repertoire. A good pastry cream. A good crust and a good chocolate cake. And a favorite — maybe an Italian cream or a red velvet.

Because no matter how fancy you dress up a bad cake, it's still a bad cake.

Her own recipes have come from everywhere, even customers who try something and want to pass it along.

It's all part of her philosophy.

"When people eat cake and sweets, it makes them laugh and it makes them happy," she says with a big smile. Who could pick a better business to be in?

"If you love desserts, there's a connection between you and I," she says.

Ashley Parrish, World staff writer, can be reached at 581-8318 or via e-mail at ashley.parrish@tulsaworld.com.

GRAND OPENING

The official grand opening of Wanda's Cake Gallery, 6562 E. 51st St., will be Friday at 1 p.m.

The ribbon-cutting ceremony will include free samples.

RECIPES

White Chocolate Pie

12 ounces white chocolate, chopped
3 tablespoons unsalted butter
⅓ cup heavy cream
3 tablespoons creme de cacao
1½ teaspoons vanilla
¼ teaspoon almond extract
1⅔ cups heavy cream
2 egg whites
2 tablespoons sugar
1 cup raspberries
1 almond pie crust, recipe follows

1. Melt chocolate, butter and ⅓ cup cream together in double-boiler. Once melted, remove from heat and allow mixture to cool. It should have the consistency of a paste. Blend in liqueur, vanilla and almond extract.
2. Beat 1⅔ cups cream until stiff peaks form. Add to chocolate mixture.
3. Beat egg whites until soft peaks form. Add sugar and beat whites until stiff. Avoid overbeating. Fold this mixture into chocolate mixture. Pour into pie shell. Freeze pie until firm.
4. Garnish with raspberries and whipped cream.

Almond Pie Crust

Makes 9-inch crust
1¾ cups blanched almonds, toasted
3½ tablespoons unsalted butter, melted
2 tablespoons white corn syrup

Coarsely chop almonds and stir in melted butter. Add corn syrup. Press into a greased pie plate.

Raspberry Mousse with Chambord Cream

4 cups raspberry puree (fresh or frozen)
6 cups heavy cream
¾ cup cold water
1 ounce gelatin
Chambord cream: 1 quart cream
½ cup powdered sugar
⅓ cup Chambord liqueur

1. Have the puree ready.
2. Whip and set aside 6 cups heavy cream.
3. Put ¾ cup cold water in a stainless-steel bowl and sprinkle the gelatin over it. The gelatin will absorb the liquid (this is called "blooming the gelatin." When gelatin is bloomed, set it over hot water to dissolve. Do not stir! Let it melt.
4. Ladle 2 ounces of puree into clear melted gelatin (to temper it), then add all gelatin to the puree.
5. Fold cream into gelatin-puree mixture, not the other way around. Mousse will be loose. Set it up in the refrigerator for 15 to 20 minutes before piping into glassware.
6. For the Chambord cream, whip together 1 quart cream, powdered sugar and Chambord. Pipe cream with star tip onto mousse.

Wanda's Cake Gallery

HOT TUB COVERS
Better Design, Better Materials
838-1560

BuySell
World Classifieds
advertise 583-2121

Eddie

I met Eddie while working in Detroit for Charlie's Crab. He was a prep cook. He, much like the spotted, cleaning shrimp, hovered around me, forging on my insecurities. Pretending to be something he was not, Eddie attached himself to me with presumptuous lies, appearing to clean the filth of my past by listening to my pain. When he heard I, along with three other employees, were leaving Detroit for Atlanta, Eddie expressed his desire to go also. The city of Atlanta boasted a diverse community. People were in search of a more stable and safer environment. African Americans all over the United States were leaving their homes to get to this progressive city. I became a means of escape for Eddie from a neighborhood racked with poverty and crime. We all got in our cars and caravanned to our promise land. The day I left Detroit was the day the level of my independence changed. For the first time in my life, I was on my own. Once out, I readily accepted the responsibility of taking care of myself.

From the time I began dating, I never caught a break. There was no time for reflection in between relationships, no weekends to gather my thoughts, grieve, or recover. After two weeks of being in Atlanta, Eddie asked to share an apartment with me to lighten the load on both of us. Without much conversation, Eddie moved his things into my apartment and bonded with Brian, Jason, and Sean. Whatever video games and systems were out, the four of them discussed enthusiastically. Things like the rent and utilities were left for me to figure out alone. He neglected the responsibility of being a man, and my boys were growing up without a father. In sheer ignorance and desperation, I succumbed to a relationship with him.

Handsome, with a pensive face and a muscular build, Eddie had the curiosity of a child. When I took the position as the assistant pastry chef at the Hyatt Ravinia, Eddie stuck out his chest as though he was the one who gained new employment. He tried vicariously to live a successful life through me. He never understood what my expectations were of him, and he didn't care. The complexities of a relationship were beyond him. When Ray refused to pay child support, Eddie shrugged it off. When Ray said, "Go outside, cut some shrubbery down, and put lights on it," because we didn't have money to purchase a Christmas tree, Eddie laughed. He provided no emotional support and always laughed at our misfortunes.

Good friends like Barb and Rochelle screamed, "You can do much better!" Rochelle asked the question often, "Why do beautiful black women always go for the trash around them? If there are two black men, one who is meek and yet responsible, the other who is muscular, but foul, the average black woman will go for the foul one who is going to use and abuse her. What's wrong with the black woman?" With no child support from Ray, nor assistance from Eddie, many times I went to the closet and drawers to scrape for pennies to make ends meet.

I lost faith in people in those days, yet, when I thought about my helpless children, the will to survive became even stronger. Every negative thought was replaced with the *Mother Bird Survival Kit*. Determined to lessen the sting of the blow of my leaving Ray, I worked hard to give my sons a better life. With meticulous calculation, I chose middle class neighborhoods, integrated with other races, to give them a fighting chance. My children didn't know it, but they were pushing me to succeed. Thinking of them drove me to excel at work. Even in tough times, my life began to turn around. The hard work paid off.

After struggling in Atlanta for several years, I got a promotion.

California Dreamin'

The Ravinia promoted me to executive pastry chef and transferred me to the Hyatt Grand Champion. They gave me a small raise and shipped me off to sunny Indian Wells, California. Eddie quit his job and dug his tentacles even deeper. We never talked about him coming, but then the host never talks to the parasite attached to it. It carries the bloodsucking freeloader around on its back, depleted of energy. I drove the U-Haul past the Grand Canyon, watching in my rearview mirror as Eddie followed behind me in his red hatchback, clinging to my gills as we headed west. I tried not to think about it too much, for California promised to be a dream world.

I'd never been there and was excited to see it. I wanted to take the kids to the beach, learn how to ride the waves, and teach my kids to surf. I imagined a world of palm trees year round with seventy-degree weather. The excitement of the move was short-lived. We ended up one hundred fifty miles from Los Angeles. Desert and sand storms swallowed us up. With no rain, it was hot enough to fry an egg on the sidewalk. And even though my apartment in Bermuda Dunes was beautiful, the cost of living positioned us right below the poverty level.

Money problems continued to drag me down. Affording only the bare necessities, I needed a second income just to survive. We were often only able to purchase just enough chicken and vegetables to last us for the week. We clipped coupons, bought store brands, and purchased cheap bulk food. Ramen noodles, bananas, potatoes, and crackers were our usual fare. Yet for the first few months, Eddie sat on the couch, played video games, and rubbed his forehead.

Much of the desert, especially the poverty, reminded me of Marianna. I witnessed the abuse of the forbidden welfare system. My sons and I looked on in discontent while other shoppers bought steak and prime rib with food stamps. It was commonplace to see people purchase two hundred dollars in first class meat with stamps, then buy cigarettes and alcohol with her pocket cash. Welfare, from my perspective, was more of an enabler than a sustainer.

After working eight months for Hyatt Grand Champion, a white sous-chef working under me bragged about his forty-thousand-dollar salary. He didn't understand how my position was higher than his yet my salary was not. I attempted to renegotiate better pay, but the Hyatt swore their hands were tied. Executive chef, Theresa, admitted they treated me unfairly, but she was instructed by Chef Tom in Atlanta to start me out on a low salary. This was a horrible blow, because I worked late nights, closing down the kitchen and getting up at five o'clock to begin the day again.

With three kids to feed (four, counting Eddie), $900 a month rent, and checks so small that I went into more debt every month just to get by, California didn't seem so special. After only nine months, I loaded the kids up and headed back to Atlanta. I left the Hyatt altogether and took a job at Emory University as their pastry chef. To help Eddie once again, I hired him on as my head baker.

Turning to God

With all of the moving, job shifting, and instability, I turned to God and began searching for a church. The result was a church organization headed by a husband and wife team. With the parasite in tow, the kids and I joined a massive mega church in Atlanta.

This preacher led his church with strict guidelines. Past visitors and former members had compared the church to a cult. One of the pastor's messages, which challenged me, made me stay. The words "I can tell you anything, and you will believe it, because black people don't like to read," struck a cord with me. He preached an entire sermon on the importance of reading and knowing the Word of God for oneself. From that point on, I read the Bible daily and applied the words to everyday living. My relationship with the creator began to blossom.

One day in church, the pastor talked about sex outside of marriage. He preached about the sin of sex when not bound by the institution. He spoke about women allowing men into their household and allowing them to come and go as they pleased. These women, he warned, gave up their virtue by lying down with a man and not asking anything in return. His words hit home. I informed the parasite that his days of nipping at my side were over. Our living arrangement was not acceptable. Eventually, Eddie moved out and into his own place, but not for long.

Three weeks later, he came over with a ring and asked me to marry him. I, like a complete fool, accepted. I made up excuses for why he had not played a positive role in my son's lives, paid bills, or held a steady job. I told myself all kinds of lies about the future Eddie. I made up excuses for his lack of responsibility—this man didn't even know how to balance a checkbook. I thought I could change him. He was six years younger than I was. Perhaps, I could use my maturity and experience to counter balance his childishness. I lied to myself and said, "God will take care of it." I buried myself in reading the Word of God and prayed for God to bless my mess.

Eddie and I went through premarital counseling. The minister questioned him about fatherhood. He asked Eddie if he understood the huge task and responsibility that he was embarking upon by marrying a woman with three young males. Eddie nodded. In March of 1993, Eddie and I planned to take our vows. For the first time in my life, I understood the significance of the oath of marriage. Previously, I'd said "I do" without understanding the sacred implications of this commitment. This time I knew fully the responsibilities of a wife.

I asked my sister Rosa to stand as my matron of honor. She said yes, but right before our wedding changed her mind because I refused to give my oldest son to her and her husband, Tyrone. The previous summer I'd allowed Brian to go and visit them in Oklahoma for two weeks. After his stay came to an end, they failed to put him on a plane. I called, wanting to know what the problem was. Tyrone told me that they felt that it would be better for all concerned if I allowed Brian to live with them. They were childless at that time and became very upset when I told them to send my son home promptly. Rosa and Tyrone had not understood why I said no. They accused me of being insensitive. On my wedding day, I was hurt because Rosa was missing. Yes, she was spoiled. Yes, she was self-centered, but I cannot tell you how much I loved her. Since she was a child, I had tried to be all that she needed in a big sister, but giving away one of my children was not up for discussion.

My mother, father, and older brother Buddy came to witness our vows. They watched Eddie and I as we went to our knees in submission to God while the minister prayed over our union. After the wedding, we zipped away on a cruise to the Bahamas that I paid for. One week later, we returned to work at Emory.

Emory University

Emory University for me was a wealth of experience. I came into the job as their pastry chef earning twenty-four thousand dollars a year. I inherited two old gentlemen, who informed me that they had worked at Emory for as long as the college existed. They consistently reminded me that there were two dressing rooms, two sets of bathrooms, even two water fountains. I probably worked at Emory two years before I inquired why such a redundant layout.

Mr. Browning, who insisted the best way to ice a cake was to let the crumbs show through, challenged me to take a tour of Emory. He escorted me upstairs and showed me a small space in the back. He pointed and said, "This is where the blacks used to eat." Shifting and looking in the opposite direction, Mr. Browning continued, "The white people ate in that nice dining room over there." We walked back downstairs, and he explained why there were two sets of everything! "This big dressing room was for whites only, and this small one was for blacks. Pointing to the fountains, he said, "I can remember as clear as if it was yesterday when the *White Only* sign hung over this water fountain." It looked to me like Emory University would have removed all evidence of such blatant racial residual, but everything was still intact—everything except the *White Only* signs. That day I bowed my head in respect to Mr. Browning and all the other ol' timers who paved the way for me to obtain a position like executive pastry chef.

When I took the job, I saw these ol' timers as stubborn old men, unwilling to change. After taking this life-altering tour of Emory, I found a way to work my magic around the crumbs showing through the icing. Together we were able to turn a bakeshop that had operated for years in the red into a serious profit entity. Blessed with my position, I learned to survive in the midst of a male-dominated industry. Just as I improved the pastry kitchen, the people in the kitchen shed a new perspective on my life.

While Mr. Browning and crew made me appreciate what I had, old habits die hard. Even when the ol' timers were upset at Emory's office management team, they remained quiet and subdued, never saying a word. One year, our payday fell the day after Christmas and Emory's kitchen management informed everyone that checks would be issued after the Christmas holiday. With three boys at home and gifts still to buy, waiting to be paid was unacceptable. Frustrated, I spoke to my bakery crew. "This is unbelievable," I told them, "we have to do something."

In total submission, Mr. Browning said calmly, "That's just the way things are. There aint nothing' we can do about it." I could not believe their docile response. I marched up to the manager's office and told him that I needed to buy gifts for my kids. They cut me and everyone else in the kitchen a check that very day. There was no big fight, no disagreement. We were all paid and able to celebrate Christmas like everyone else.

After four years of supervising a crew of six, including the parasite, I decided to move on. I had prepared desserts for former President Jimmy Carter, Bishop Desmond Tutu, Charles Dutton, and many more, yet I knew the only way I would be able to experience liberation in the culinary field was to open my own business.

There were many cake shops in Atlanta. Everyone said I was crazy to try it. Only a few people considered it a viable endeavor. Rochelle and Barb pushed me forward with positive reinforcement. With much prayer, persistence, and a focus on creating an avenue to provide for my sons, I located a space, and in 1994, I launched my first business, Wanda's Patisserie. The drive to succeed held a greater value than the painful memories of my past. I also focused on service to God.

My Church

My business ambitions grew because of my faith in God. I went to church three times a week, serving in the choir, intercessory prayer, and children's church. My pastor was everywhere: on cable TV, on nationally broadcast shows, radio, billboards. Money! Money! Money! It was always about the money! He couldn't preach a sermon without throwing in damning words about ten percent of my earnings. And oh, such an eloquent speaker who could move a crowd; he knew just what to say to make the congregation empty their last into the offering plate. As I began to uncover the truth beneath his words, I saw the lies in his message.

Hilarious and very intelligent, the pastor and his posse were always into pulling inappropriate tithing stunts. On one occasion, his head staff went before the church and announced if you were not a tithing member you would not be eligible for prayer or any other services that the church would ordinarily perform. I watched Eddie's sister, with no money in her pocket, put her jewelry in the collection basket. Yet, when she petitioned the church for help, having no place to stay, they refused. My mother came to visit and, after going to church with me one time, referred to the leadership as scoundrels and scoffers in the temple. She respectfully told me if I wanted to do some good for my life, I should find a church that truly cared about the well-being of its people. I didn't listen to Mama. I stayed allied and loyal to *my* church.

The pastor criticized the so-called laziness of black people and our inability as a race to stay on point and work hard for the things we wanted in our lives. We kept going—Eddie, my sons, and I.

I joined this church with a sincere desire to serve God. I had been skeptical about the new church as a whole and even though Eddie, the sponge, was enamored with the leadership, I intentionally focused on my readings, my personal quiet time with God, and expository search of Sunday morning's sermons. I listened carefully to the words spoken from the pulpit to make sure they were in line and biblically correct. It was clear to me that, from the pastor's perspective, tithing was much more important than living right.

One day the pastor made a point of saying that, just like health club members had to pay a fee to belong, so did a member of his ministry. He warned all members present that if they were not tithing members, they would not be entitled to counseling, getting married, nor would the church bury their dead. Although I tithed and supported his ministry financially, I was sickened with outrage.

The pastor thundered away at the congregation, demanding people give their required one-tenth. Every gain or loss was attributed to money. If your marriage was going wrong, it was because you didn't give. If your car broke down, it was because you didn't give. You all are going to *not give* your way straight into hell! I was appalled at what I saw beyond the veil. It was organized deception. It was my first glimpse at the hypocrisy that exists, many times, in the church.

One Sunday morning, while standing in a congregation of five thousand, the praise and worship team got up with lifted hands. The crowd stood in ebullient anticipation. At this point, usually church members would be shouting and screaming as the bodyguards escorted him down the aisle. The flock had grown so big the pastor felt he needed the added protection upon entering the sanctuary. This time, the congregation waited in great suspense for the pastor's arrival. He did not come. It became so silent you could hear random people cough and shift while they stood. All of a sudden, Assistant Minister Henry got up and announced that the pastor would not be coming to the pulpit today. Not only was he not coming today, he went on to say, but the pastoral staff had been up with him all night long, trying to convince him to not quit permanently. He was sad to say, but they were unsuccessful. The pastor made up his mind. It was over, because the people did not give with all of their hearts. He simply could not take it anymore.

While the church screamed and begged for forgiveness, Rev. Henry said, "Maybe the pastor will consider giving you one last chance if you give from the depths of your soul, but if we do not raise twenty-five thousand dollars, this congregation will never see him again." The copastor went on to tell the people to submit themselves and speak in tongues, their heavenly language. The people went wild with wailing, crying, and incomprehensible words as they emptied their purses into the offering baskets.

After tallying the tithe, Minister Henry came back and announced to the congregation that over thirty-thousand dollars had been raised. Before he could finish his statement, the pastor walked in with his bodyguards. People responded as if God himself had arrived. The crowd was in disarray. He went to the pulpit and preached as if the earlier events never took place. That was my last Sunday. I never went back again.

After three years of service in this ministry, I followed Mama's advice and left. Even though my experience at this church ended up being a negative one, there were some positive aspects. For instance, the pastor's challenge to read my Bible proved to be one of the most valuable assets of my life. I learned to seek the Lord for everything. I developed a very personal relationship with Him. God became a friend that I listened to and spoke with every single day.

I poured my heart into Wanda's Patisserie, and, little by little, the business began to improve. Eddie, instead of staying at Emory University to cushion the business, came home one day and said, "I quit my job. I'm coming to work with you. My desire," he said while pushing his shoulders back, "is to be a businessman, carrying a brief case."

Excuse me, I thought, *carrying a brief case?* I was in so much trouble. Whatever adolescent fantasy he had, I did not want him to fulfill them at my expense. I needed him to work as head baker of Emory until the business could stand on its own. Like a child, he made the decision to put all of the pressure on me to support us financially. Despite my protests, Eddie came to work with me anyway.

Every morning I set the alarm for Eddie to get up. Not only did I set it, but when it rang, I had to talk him out of bed. While my diligent parasite held on for dear life, I worked even harder to get Wanda's Patisserie off the ground. I heard the maxim about starting a new business. Many people told me that the vast majority of new businesses fail in the first year. Undaunted, I kept at it every day, twelve hours a day. After a few months, I got my first break.

* * * *

Holiday Inn Crowne Plaza bought out The Hyatt Regency Ravinia, where I served as assistant pastry chef a few years before I started my company. They replaced Chef Tom, who manipulated my salary at Grand Champion, with a young chef named Donna. The new chef eliminated all in-house baking, creating a need for an outside vendor to perform the task. Yen Tan, The Crowne Plaza's purchasing director recommended me for the job. He suggested that the chef meet with me to see if I was open to possibly providing desserts for their hotel. We hit it off, and she decided Wanda's Patisserie would be perfect for the job. Chef Donna's guarantee saved the life of my company.

With sixty and seventy cakes at a time, Wanda's Patisserie grew wings and was ready to fly. I worked night and day to accommodate this huge responsibility while Eddie found supermarket parking lots where he could sleep in the car. My will to survive never allowed me to give up, even though I was going at it alone. I had no time for emotions. There was too much to do to spend time thinking about other things. Pleasing my clients consumed me. I felt that I had made so many bad decisions in life, it was about time for some good ones. The business was an excellent choice.

Working for eighteen hours each day, sometimes halfway through the night, just to meet orders, our kitchen was hot and frantic. Yet each grueling moment was worth it. To assert myself as an African American businesswoman meant so much to me. Each day I arose to meet difficult challenges. And oh, how the challenges came...

On one dreadful occasion, I was given the task of delivering a wedding cake to the Crowne Plaza. As simple as this sounds, the day would be filled with the perfect ministorm to stop my delivery. I worked for hours on my wedding cake. Yes, I said, *my wedding cake*, for when I am in the midst of such a project, I become very possessive, taking ownership as if it was my own nuptial. In the middle of decorating the last tier, I discovered that I was out of gold luster dust. I asked Eddie to go around the corner to the store and locate the accent for my cake and a few other things needed to complete the day. After pulling the cash he needed, he jumped in the van and left.

Hours passed. We waited for Eddie to return. I was sure something dreadful—perhaps a car accident—had happened. I tried not to think negatively as I worked to complete dozens of other cakes alongside the responsibility of the bridal cake. My heart began to pound as time raced by. The deadline to get the project done was quickly approaching, and I was without a delivery vehicle and the material to finish the cake. My head began to ache.

Wedding cakes, especially big ones for special clients, can make or break a small pastry shop. I took quick, short breaths as I looked around at the stainless steel tables in my bakeshop. The kitchen was filled with small cakes that needed to be finished. It was all left up to me! I scrambled to complete the orders. Eddie was not competent enough to decorate, nor was he conscientious enough to deliver the wedding cake. I zipped through the shop as my sons watched from the sidelines.

The bakery became school outside of school for them. They watched very carefully as I maneuvered through the chaos to make a living for our household. They watched as I lifted fifty pound bags of sugar and even heavier kitchen equipment. They observed as I got on my knees alone, laying commercial tile on the bare floor of the bakeshop, assembling huge display cabinets and any other thing a man would be expected to do. They were getting a life lesson on *how not to treat a woman*. They were young and in their impressionable years. No one ever told them that they should honor me as their mother. No one ever said that I had a fragile side to me just like every other woman. They watched me wake Eddie up in the morning, and after he arose, they peered in to see him wait for me to make decisions of how the day would go. There was nothing special about me; I was a man in their eyes. The distorted gender roles the boys witnessed when they were younger would affect our relationships in the years to come.

A few minutes before my delivery, Eddie came back to the shop and said he accidentally fell asleep in a Kroger grocery store parking lot. I was horrified but had no time to argue because there was a cake waiting to be delivered. I begged him to help me lift the tiered cake into the delivery van. He shoved me out of the way and said that he could carry the cake by himself. I was angry yet relieved, exhausted from the frenzied pace of the day. I watched as he lifted the cake and walked outside to the van. I waited inside, putting finishing touches on the other cakes. He eventually came back and told me that the cake was safely inside the van and ready for delivery.

I was shocked when I opened the door to the van to find my wedding cake smashed up against the seat. Instead of sitting the cake on the back floorboard of the van, he sat it on the angled seat. I grabbed the cake out and cried like a baby as I attempted to repair the damage. With one entire side crushed, all the hours of delicate lacing work, the tiny subtleties I'd fawned over lay wasted. I ran the cake inside and did what I could to save face. After fussing over the repair work, I delivered the cake without the Crown Plaza ever knowing of the chaotic events of my day.

*   *   *   *

It was one thing after another with Eddie. One day, he left fifty-four chocolate mousse cakes out on the table overnight, causing them to split in the center while he came home to sleep. Simple measurements escaped him as he put one gallon of grated carrots in a sixty-cake recipe that called for fifteen gallons. My friend Barbara and I could not believe it when we walked in the shop and found Eddie asleep next to the twenty-quart mixing bowl as whipped cream splashed on his face and the walls of the shop. He was standing, leaning against the mixer while the gear was in high speed. Barbara walked over and tapped him on the shoulder to wake him up. His ashy, black body was covered in white cream.

Years later, during counseling, Eddie confessed that he wanted to wreck the business. He knew that the contract I had with Chef Donna was the lifeline of Wanda's Patisserie. He also knew that Chef Donna was gay. He was tired of being stressed with all the orders—even though he didn't do much. He started doing things to sabotage the account. Whenever he delivered cakes to the Crowne Plaza, Eddie made horrible remarks about Donna's sexual preference. She called my shop, telling me how much his words hurt her. She reinforced her concerns, "I love your bakery. You have the best cakes in town, but your husband is a bastard, and if you don't get control of this situation, he is going to be your downfall!" Donna warned he would destroy the contract. That night in bed, I said to him, "Eddie, I'm upset. This cannot continue." His response was, "Yeah, you're always upset, what's new?"

A Father's Love

One day, in the fall of 1995, a telephone call came, altering my life. Daddy was in Crittenden Memorial Hospital in West Memphis, Arkansas on life support. Mom admonished all of the children to come and be by his side. Leaving the shop in Eddie's hands, I immediately flew to be next to Daddy. When I arrived, I found Mama sitting in a chair in the corner of his hospital room. She was in a stupor as she looked absently into space.

Daddy smoked two packs of non-filtered Lucky Strike cigarettes a day. I never saw him without a cigarette in his hand. Ignoring the doctor's advice, when he was diagnosed with lung cancer, he continued to smoke for years. Mama warned, "All this stuff you're doing, James, is going to come back on you. God's going to teach you a lesson before this is all over!" It was a horrible illness to battle. By the time Daddy reached his end, he was a vegetable, unable to walk alone. Mama had to lift him out of bed and put him in his chair. When I visited them from Atlanta, I assisted her by helping to move his iron lungs with him as he gasped for air and tried to walk. Emotions swept over me as I tried to reconcile with the stillness of his hospital room.

My father, always full of life, lay in bed, a fragile man. There were tubes running through his nose and down his throat. Death was looming at the mortician's bed. I looked in his face and found hollow eyes. Once he caught a glimpse of me, one tear fell from the corner of his eye as he slammed his hand on the bed. Because of his stutter, my father always slammed his hand on his leg in frustration when he was getting ready to lie or when he was facing an impossible situation. He would drag his words for miles, trying to get his point across.

He was trying to tell me something. From the motioning of his hand, I found that he wanted to write me a note. I grabbed a pencil and pad as he scribbled, "Fay, I'm sorry. I love you." Weeping uncontrollably, I removed this term of endearment from his weak hand and thought as I held the note close to my heart, *My daddy loves me.* He motioned for more paper. He then wrote, "I'm ready to go home. Please help me." He struggled to breathe with the tube in his throat.

When my older sister arrived, we all discussed the pain dad was in. Sophie Mae, who worked with dying patients, explained to my mother that life support was one of the most horrific ways to die. "With the tube shoved down in your throat," she said, "you cannot breath, cannot swallow, and cannot speak. All the while, you are conscious of the pain." Daddy's eyes were wide open and filled with suffering. He wanted to go, but Mama was not ready to let him. After Sophie Mae explained how inhumane life support was, Mama agreed to release the love of her life to the death angel. We informed the medical staff that she was ready. The room was quiet when the doctors came and removed the tubes.

We all sat in the room, watching as our father peacefully closed his eyes. The labored breathing produced by the life support tubes disappeared and were replaced with calm, sporadic, shallow pants. The end was fast approaching.

My mother, while sitting over in the corner, started to sing my father's favorite song, *The Storm Is Passing Over*. Everybody sang, except me. There was a deep void inside of me. For the first time in my life, he'd said he loved me. Well... he didn't actually say it, but he wrote it, and that was good enough. I didn't understand why God had to take him at this moment. I needed more time. *Why had he waited until he was on his deathbed to say he loved me?*

I needed my father to pick me up and hug me when I fell; to show me what a good man looked like, but, most of all, I desperately needed him to be proud of me. *Why had he waited until he was dying to ask forgiveness? Was he only sorry because he was dying?* I was thirty-five years old; there had been plenty of time to apologize, but he chose the last day of his life to set things right. And then the thought of him personally knowing that he had mistreated me; *how could he have lived with himself all those years?* Knowing that he was going to meet his maker, I believe he was making his peace with God more so than me.

I did not feel like singing, so I lay my face on his. A cold dampness hit my ear as I listened to his breathing. It was the closest that I'd ever been to my father. His respiration was faint. *Don't stop breathing*, I thought as I pressed my face even closer to his. *He was so cold*. Even the moisture from his breath felt cool. Thoughts screamed through my head. "Stay with me...please don't leave me." I pleaded...even bargained, with God. "Let him stay a little while longer. I'll do whatever you want me to do. Just don't take him right now!" Daddy's breathing became shallower and more distant. Small currents of air drifted off until they were barely audible. The space between exhalations grew wider and wider.

Then there was nothing.

And just like that, in the middle of my quiet ranting, Daddy, who was never there for me, became even more distant and absent in my life. For thirty-five years, my father abhorred the ground I walked on. For thirty minutes, he was my world.

At that moment, I felt like something in me died as well. The need to be loved by my father did not dissipate upon his death; it simply became unfinished business in my heart. The moment he took his last breath, I scooped all my hurts and pains up and threw them into my already cluttered secret closet. No one in my family knew that I took his death hard; they thought that because he didn't love me, I probably didn't love him. They were wrong!

Death is one of those things that, no matter how prepared you think you are, is a major surprise. The moment I realized Daddy stopped breathing, I started to hit his chest to get my family's attention. I was so shaken, I never thought of shouting it out. They were still singing when I beat harder on his chest in tears, motioning that he was gone. It took a minute for them to understand what I was trying to say. Once they did… arms flew up, hands went wide, and the hospital room went in total disarray. While Mama sat in disbelief, my siblings lost their composure, pulling and tugging at Daddy's body in hopes that God would reverse his decision and make the Death Angel go away.

In the midst of the screaming, someone knocked Daddy's eyes open, and the conclusiveness of death became our reality. His hollow gaze told of a finality that could not be reversed. It was over. There was no movement; just stillness and a blank stare on our father's face. I squeezed in near him, amidst the panic-filled room, and kissed his forehead. My daddy was dead.

At Daddy's wake, people came and paid their respects. Someone said, "Oh, Mr. Wolfe was such a good man. Another said, "He was always smiling." Someone else said, "I can't think of one bad thing to say about this man. He was kind, loving, and cared about his family!" Their words were not out of the standard, considering where we were. People say good things about the dead, but Ms. Savannah Mulligan, a professional funeral goer, went to the microphone and surprised everyone. She said, "You all are lying. What's wrong with ya'll? Is ya'll crazy? She pointed into the casket and said, "ya'll is talking bout him! Mr. Wolfe knew he could dish out some dirt, and Mrs. Wolfe knew she sholl could take it! I caint believe this. What's wrong wit ya'll? Is ya'll talking bout the same man? Ms. Wolfe took all kinds a dirt from this here man." Although shocked at Ms. Savannah's words, Mama sat quietly and listened. Ms. Savannah continued in a loud voice, "What's wrong wit ya'll? Mr. Wolfe was low-down, and he treated his own kids like dirt. Mrs. Wolfe is the one who did everything. She took care of those children all by herself with no help from this man. What's wrong wit ya'll? He was evil. What's wrong wit ya'll?"

Ms. Savannah went off the deep end so bad, we were all taken aback, but everyone knew she was right. Mama said in her usual quiet, controlled voice, "I didn't want her to say that about James, but let's just let it go!" Nevertheless, if Mama could have had a private hour where no one could see or hear, she would have whipped Daddy out of the casket and onto the floor, because right before he died, Daddy cashed in his burial insurance policy. He gave a large sum to one of my siblings. He took a lump sum and went to Tunica, Mississippi, to gamble one last time. When he came back, he purchased Mama a vacuum cleaner. He left no burial money to put him away.

My mother stood, looking into Daddy's casket with a stoned face. As she walked away, she said, "If I could pull him out of that casket, I would. That's the lowest thing he could have done. He can't even speak for himself. That's a low down person!" Mama was angry. We all reached deep into our pockets to help our mother bury Daddy.

After the wake, we prepared him for burial and moved on with our lives, each of us grieving the best we knew how. My siblings went home to Texas, Tennessee, Oklahoma, and Arkansas. I headed back to Atlanta.

I searched for the note my father had written. In those two sentences, he acknowledged his shortcomings. Those two sentences did not make up for a lifetime of coldness. However, they represented the last communication that Daddy and I had. Like so many other treasured mementos, someone had removed it from my coat pocket. And like Aunt Sophie's bracelet, I had to rely on my memory of the moment to get me through.

I went back to my shop in Atlanta. With Eddie and my three boys to care for, I had no outlet for my grief. As an entrepreneur who needed to sell cakes to survive, I put on a stoic facade. Internally, however, the brief reconciliation with my father troubled my thoughts. One night, I fell asleep and dreamed that Daddy was holding me in his arms and wiping the tears away from my eyes. In my dream he said, "It's okay! Daddy loves you. Go ahead and cry. I'm here." I woke up sobbing, yet I felt at peace. My father was dead, yet he put his arms around me. I wondered if he had visited my mom in the same way.

My brother Gary and his wife agreed to stay with Mama for a while, until she adjusted to living without Daddy. As a family, I think we failed to see the fragile woman inside of her. We lost our father, but she lost the only man that she ever loved. Yet we saw her as a tower of strength, larger than life. We expected her to live a hundred years or more. Gary was the only one of our siblings that made the sacrifice to stay close to Mama. He moved his family from Pine Bluff, Arkansas, into the same small shack we all previously lived in as children.

Not much had changed. The road was barely graveled with potholes everywhere. It was amazing to think that each one of us lived relatively successful lives, yet our parents continued to live in dire poverty. While married to Ray, I suggested that we all come together to build them a decent place to live. It was the least we could do. This proposal never materialized into anything more than a good idea. Mama and Daddy would both die in the poverty they lived in all their lives.

A Mother's Pride

Every day, regardless of how busy the shop was, I found the time to call my mother. Sometimes, we spoke for just a few minutes. Sometimes conversations would roll an hour or more. I could tell that she was trying to be the rock the family expected, but her tone and breathing told a different story. Many times during our conversations, she almost sounded angry about Daddy leaving her. I didn't know what to say, for his leaving had left me broken as well. If I initiated a conversation about Daddy, she would change the subject to how proud she was of me. "You did it, baby, I am so happy for you." I would follow her lead and tell her how many orders we were getting and how Eddie had determined *we were too busy.*

Eddie felt that running a business was too much work for him. Who would have ever thought it? Too much business—all small businesses wish for such luck. My mother consistently urged me to push forward and not to succumb to his way of thinking. She reminded me how blessed I was to be a successful African American businesswoman. Most of all, her voice reminded me of my youth in Marianna; of how far I had come from the poverty of those sheets speckled with embalming fluid and blood.

About three months after Dad's death, Mom decided to go on a road trip to visit all of her children. In early December, she traveled by bus to Austin, Texas, to spend time with Sophie Mae and Kay. She stayed one week with them. Her plan after leaving Austin was to go to Oklahoma to visit with Rosa and Tyrone. In the middle of her trip, she changed her mind and decided to bypass Oklahoma and come to Atlanta instead. Her decision would prove to be a point of contention between Rosa and me for the duration of our relationship. Neither of us understood the change in plans, and I was not about to question Mama. I eagerly welcomed her into my domain, my patisserie, and my dysfunctional life. Her stay with me would be two weeks, much longer than her visit in Texas.

Mom was quiet and different in spirit as if she was another person. She was full of questions and wanted answers. "Why have you not called your sister Kay? Did you know that she had a serious bronchial infection?" And she had responses before I could answer. She said, "I'm ashamed of you!" I stood at the foot of my bed, challenging her. My mother and I were used to going toe-to-toe on issues. Throughout our lives, after Mom and I disagreed, we always ended with a hug. This time was different.

She asked each question as if she was not a part of the equation, as if she was viewing me from afar. This disconnection irritated me. In retaliation, I questioned her about why she bypassed Oklahoma and neglected to see Rosa through her colonoscopy. She responded through clenched teeth, "Rosa is a spoiled child. She only cares about her and Tyrone's well-being. That's my child, but sometimes I don't recognize her. When your father and I went to Oklahoma, they made us wash and sanitize our hands before we were allowed to touch their baby girl. I came to see you. I knew what I was doing when I came here. You needed me right here at this time!"

I shot back at her, "No, Rosa needed you more."

Mom burst into tears, which was completely unlike her, and said, "Baby, you don't understand, you needed me more."

As I walked away from her, I saw her face. Her anger was genuine and intense. But so was her unalloyed love. I was discombobulated, shaken. She didn't hug me. I didn't hug her. *What in the heck was wrong with us?*

She then proceeded to wash every piece of dirty clothing in my house. With a broken dryer, clothing was everywhere: over the doorways, on the railing of the beds, and on the stairway rails. The clothes she washed dried in record timing. After everything was clean in the house, Mama came and sat at the foot of my bed with tears streaming down her face and said, "I'm sorry, baby. I didn't mean to make you cry!"

I got up out of the bed, sat next to her, and said, "Oh Mom, I'm sorry too. I didn't mean to make you cry either."

She interjected before I could say another word. "I always want you to be happy, and I can tell that there are some things going on here. Eddie's not taking care of you, and you know that I can tell when you are worried, because your skin turns darker and is not as pretty as it usually is. There's gonna come a time when I won't be here to help you through this, so you have to learn to stand up for yourself. And in regards to your sisters and brothers, you have got to learn to forgive them and let it be." We put our arms around each other and held on tight.

The next morning, while I was making breakfast, my mother got up out of bed, walked in the kitchen, went directly to the pot, picked up rice with her fingers, and shoved a fist-full into her mouth. She had a far-off look on her face as grains fell from her half-open jaw. Such sloppiness and disregard was uncharacteristic of Mama. Something was terribly wrong!

A few days later, in the front of the cake shop, she laid her head on the dessert counter and fell asleep while standing up. And she slept right there, in an extremely awkward position, right in front of one of my favorite customers, Mary McCarthy. I asked my mother to wake up and go to the back of the shop. I gingerly explained to her that it was offensive and inappropriate to sleep in front of customers. Mary politely stopped me as I tried to correct the problem. She said, "I'm not offended. Your mother is tired. With all that she's been through, she should be able to lay her head wherever she wants." My mother laid her head back on the counter and fell back asleep. Her strange behavior at the shop was followed by odd requests. Mom asked me to cut our dish towels in half, for they were just too much for her to lift. The towels weighed no more than a washcloth. It was an unusual request but after the Mary McCarthy episode, I obliged.

One afternoon, near the end of Mom's stay, my friend, Barb, and her husband Walter came over to meet Mama. For dinner, I ordered rotisserie chicken. Before the table was set, my mother, who was known for being Ms. Prim and Proper her entire life, tore into the chicken with her bare hands and shoved the meat in her mouth. She stumbled to sit down as part of the meat fell back to the table. Embarrassed, I stopped her as she tore at another piece of meat. I said gently, "I'm nearly done, and the food is almost ready. Mama, do you think you want to wait until the table is set?" She ignored me, got up, and walked away. The next day Brian found bones from the chicken in the bathtub. "Grandma is acting strange," he said.

On the morning of December 31, while I was in my personal prayer closet, my mother opened the door abruptly and then apologized for interrupting my quiet time. She then started to talk about my father and his journey. She told me that I needed to forgive him for all that he had done. She said, "Your daddy's list of offenses against you are too long to examine but you must forgive him. In order for you to go forward, you have to make peace with the past. She said, "Baby, I do not know why your father was so cold to you, but I tried to make up for how he treated you. Your father has made his peace with God, and it is important that you do the same. Someday you will have to travel that same road he traveled. No one can escape Judgment Day."

Then in a cryptic voice Mama whispered, "Even I have to travel that road. You must forgive him. He is in heaven. I was worried about you, but I'm not worried anymore. You are a strong woman. Just don't let Eddie wear you down. He's lazy and lets you work like a man. Just be careful about that."

I got up off my knees, and we embraced. "I love you. I'm so sorry about us arguing," I told her.

I held onto her tight, and she replied, "I know that you're having a hard time over your father. But you've got to forgive him so that you can have a good, peaceful life. You were always the child that needed lots of hugs. It didn't occur to me that I needed to drop the belt and hug you until you grabbed it one day while I was whipping you. *You forced* me to put my arms around you. When I think about it, you even forced your daddy to hug you."

I said to her, "Well, he really didn't hug me. It was always more like a pat on the back." We both laughed, and Mama gave me the longest hug of my life. One final time, she said, "I'm so so proud of you!"

We moved into the shop kitchen, waiting for Eddie to carry Mama's luggage to the van and then to the airport. Mama had never flown in her life. She wasn't going far, so we thought it odd that she chose to take a plane to Memphis rather than ride the bus. As she prepared to leave, she took the time to tell the boys to take care of me, that it was their duty to make sure I was okay. After Eddie came in and grabbed her bags, she reached out to give me one final hug. This time when she hugged me, we held on for dear life as she said in a deep, somber, almost unrecognizable voice, "Ahhhh, this hug is the best Christmas gift you could have ever given me."

When you are intimate with God, He will open up mysteries to you. When my mother's arm went around my neck, a voice too distinct to be my own said, "You're never gonna see your mother alive again." I stopped in my tracks and pleaded, "No, Mama! Please don't go!" But she said in her natural voice, "Baby, I gotta go before I miss my plane. I love you! But I got a plane to catch!" and she and Eddie walked out of the door.

I could not stop thinking about the feeling I got when I hugged Mama. I heard the voice and felt her pass. If you have ever heard the voice of God, it is a powerful thing. The thought that Mama was going to die rattled me to my core. *It would be wrong*, I thought, *for God to take my mom*. She was the only person I trusted in life.

I completed and delivered my wedding cake by six. Before Mama left, I described to her what the finished product would look like. She became so excited about the possibilities. Later on in the afternoon, she called and told me that she had made it to Larry's house. She questioned me about my cake. I told her how beautiful it was. "The luster dust on the ribbon made it look like edible silver." I said. She was disappointed that she didn't get a chance to see it. Mama went on to tell me that she cooked Larry's favorite dish: a huge pot of collard greens and that later in the evening he would be driving her to Jackson to see Buddy.

Later that night, after I had gone to bed, Kay called to let me know that it was probably nothing to worry about but Mama had collapsed on stage in the middle of her song. She had not even mentioned to me she was going to be singing. Kay said that Buddy, for his annual New Year's Eve program had just introduced her to a packed house of twelve hundred people as "My beloved mother."

"She probably fainted," Kay said.

I lay in bed rocking back and forth with an assurance that God was not so cruel. I was confident of His care for me. The second call came. It was my sister-in-law Mary, and she said, "They are still working on Mama. It's probably going to be okay." At that point, I sat up in bed as Eddie watched me talk aloud to God. "God, you are tripping," I said. "But I refuse to trip with you! Hurry up and do what You need to do to bring her out of this situation! I am not even worried, because this simply is not your nature. As a matter of fact, I am going to lie down and go back to sleep while You rise up for battle.!" I slumped back down into the bed and pretended to close my eyes. I needed the phone to ring with news that Mama was awake and recovering in the hospital.

Gary was playing the keyboard for Mama while she was singing. Buddy had put the entire program together at Carl Perkins Convention Center. Larry was there also to see the show.

They all saw her collapse on stage. *What kind of God would allow this to happen in front of her sons? Not my God; not the Lord that I love and respect.*

The third call came. I don't remember who delivered the news, but the voice on the other end of the phone said, "Mama's dead... Mama's gone.!" I screamed! I was not sure where I was. The tears came so fast that it felt as if I was drowning. I stumbled out of bed, fell on the floor, and crawled to the kids' room. I could not see, for the water in my eyes. I hit my head up against Eddie's weight bench, crawled like a wild animal a little further toward the stairs, and blacked out there in the darkness.

By the time I came to, I was rocking in a corner while Eddie and my three sons looked on. My mother was gone. I begged God to bring her back. Then my pleas turned into anger. I pointed my finger up toward the ceiling of my apartment and showered a stream of hateful words toward him. "I hate you, I hate you!" I felt He personally attacked me. God did not answer back. I felt he did not love me. My mother's unconditional love was gone. She was all I had.

On Monday, January 1, 1996, the Jackson Sun newspaper ran an article titled "Concert Marked by Joy, Tragedy." It described the eventful night of my mother's passing. The newspaper article said Buddy introduced Mama to a packed house then proudly talked about how she put nine children through college and the significance of our family's potbelly stove. Mama told the audience that this was where we went to pray. She said that the problem with today's family is that people are leaving Jesus out and using their stoves for just heat. Only minutes after Mama began performing "One Day at a Time Sweet Jesus" she fell to the Civic Center stage floor. Paramedics spent over forty minutes backstage trying to resuscitate my mother before transporting her to Jackson General Hospital. (To

read complete article see: jacksonsun.com.) It was just like
Mama and typical of her. She wasn't going to wait until
New Year's Day. She made her early entrance into heaven
the night before. I, along with the rest of my nine siblings,
traveled back to Marianna to prepare for Mama's funeral.

It was too much grief for all involved. To compound matters,
no one knew how to grieve. We all were hurt and angry. With
tensions running high and no one to blame, we lashed out at each
other. There was more contempt and fear amongst my siblings
than at any point in my life. It was shameful to see a room full
of sorrowful relatives and not a single hug or pat on the back
among us. Any display of mourning was viewed as competition—
you don't hurt as much as me!—and contempt. The environment
was an awful display, and I was as much a part of it as any of my
siblings. Externally, I pretended my mother's passing did not hurt
me, yet internally I was a wreck.

Most of my siblings stayed at Mama's house in Marianna. There
was not much room and there was even less talking. We looked
around at the trinkets that our parents had collected throughout
their lives. All of us knew when we left; the house and everything
left in it would be gone forever.

The day of Mama's funeral started out warm and clear. By
midday, it was a biting cold. Piercing winds lashed at exposed
cheeks and whipped between dresses and coats. It was a dreary
day, and all nine siblings were angry. None of us knew why. Some
of us, including me, attempted to make up reasons why there
was so much resentment and bitterness. We all sat, numb, void,
and irritated through Mama's funeral, then piled quietly into the
vehicles as we followed the hearse to lay her to rest.

The moment we arrived at the cemetery and got out of the limos
to finalize her burial, a great wind came, colder than anything that
I had felt in my life. Hats tumbled off heads and obituaries tore out
of hands. It roared with a fury as the preacher tried unsuccessfully

to commit our mother to the ground. His words were inaudible because of the great rush of wind. Snowflakes, out of nowhere, flew through mourners as the preacher tried to overcome the weather. The wind was so great it was impossible to stand around our mother's grave. It was as if she was saying in anger to us "Get away from my grave with your foolishness. You are not welcome here. I am ashamed of your petty bickering."

The wind and snow ended the funeral service before it started. I don't think the preacher said more than ten words. Everyone raced back to his or her vehicle. Our mother had the last word. All of us now believe that Mom was watching from a distance as we quarreled over petty things. When she was alive, she always fought against division within the ranks. Any fire that ignited a family squabble was always promptly extinguished. Her kind words had assuaged tensions for half a century. When she was gone, there was no one to keep the peace.

Before leaving Marianna, Eddie, with help, packed Mama's piano in the van. On the way back home to Atlanta, I thought about the harsh reality of Mama and Daddy living and dying in poverty. It didn't have to be that way, but it just was. Every sibling was educated and living relatively good lives, but the world around us was colored cold. It was much too painful to think about. More than anything, I rehearsed the odd things Mama did in my home prior to her death. She was actually dying during her stay with me. Mom was cognizant of her time coming to an end and came to Atlanta to try to help me deal with the death of my father. There were things that she wanted me to understand. Our friendship was that strong. Watching my mother during her final hours, I learned *living and dying is a process.* Life was not to be taken for granted.

Once back in Atlanta, I became less tolerant of dealing with Eddie's immaturity. I was concerned about the things my mother said about him before she passed. She warned me about him freeloading and sabotaging the business because of his distaste for my success. Eddie was dissatisfied with our business and to make matters worse, I heard from some of my clients that he was having an affair with another woman. One day, I was at the grocery store with Eddie and the kids in the checkout line, waiting for the cashier to ring up our groceries. The second the young lady saw Eddie had a wife and kids, she went ballistic, screaming obscenities about how he was a liar and a cheater and how he needed to man up about his responsibilities. Eddie didn't say a word. He just lowered his head as she questioned him.

"Why are you not saying anything," she demanded. "You were full of words the other night! What are you going to say now?"

Ready to move on, I was not fazed. My mother had prepared me for this moment. Mentally and physically exhausted I offered him a way out: a clean break, where we both could move on with our lives. But parasites don't leave on request; they only flee after the host is dead, and there is nothing else to gain. Eddie dug his tentacles deeper than ever.

My Black Pearls Journal

Just after the New Year, in 1996, my dear friend, Rochelle, gave me the most priceless gift I had ever received. It was a small, leather-bound book, filled with blank pages. She suggested that I use the book to sort through my grief and organize my thoughts. I held the book in my hand, tossing it up lightly to feel its weight. Turning the book over, I stared down its spine as a hunter might look down the barrel of a gun. The hurt and pain had to go somewhere, or I would die.

Back in high school I'd dabbled in writing and found the process cathartic and enjoyable. There is a mystical transition that happens when thoughts and feelings are put onto paper. Writing offers structure to emotions; like you can pick them up and examine them from all angles. Sixteen days after the passing of my mother, I made my first entry. My marriage was loveless, the work was endless and I missed my parents. I felt like I was living in hell. The cryptic handwriting of my scrambled mind spilled out on to the pages. Journal entries trickled out at first. I talked about trivial matters, about life. About Eddie, but when I began to talk about my secret closet, pages spilled out of my mind like ash crashing out of Mount Vesuvius.

Sometimes my mind would outrace my hand, and my entries would degenerate into an incoherent ramble. Mostly, though, the journal helped me organize my thoughts. I sifted through my secret closet, pulling back layer upon layer of hurt, lies, and private insecurities. I'd write an entry and then reread it only a few days later. Reading back through the journal helped me. It would not be an exaggeration to say that my Black Pearls Journal saved my life.

Eddie did the very thing that my mother warned me about. Our chief client, responsible for more than half of our business, canceled the account. Donna was gay, and Eddie knew it. Every time he brought cakes and pastries over to the Crown Plaza, he made rude comments about her sexual orientation. I was ashamed.

The loss of business was devastating. We were making just enough to cover expenses and pay partial salaries. I knew that we needed another client to survive. If I did not find one—somehow, someway—the business was going under.

I had come to understand that even though Eddie never laid hands on me physically, he tormented me mentally. I blamed me and me alone for making such poor choices for my life. Even in the midst of his failure to take responsibility, I treated him with respect. I was angrier at me than him. I was thirty-five; he was twenty-nine and a stone wall. He lacked any semblance of empathy for my pain. Any attempts to explain my frustration were met with an apathy so powerful I felt three feet tall. He was untouchable emotionally. His irresponsibility fueled my fury. Desperate, I turned to self-help books to nurture the woman inside of me. Every day was a major challenge.

Others around me began to pick up on Eddie's ineptitude. The rent for the shop was late, so I sent Eddie to Mr. Pinkard, the landlord, to ask for more time. Eddie promised him we'd have the rent a few days after the due date, when in reality we wouldn't have it until weeks later.

I got the eviction notice in the middle of the month. Panicked, I rushed over to the landlord's office and told him the truth. I begged him to give us another week.

Mr. Pinkard was a tall, eighty-year-old white man, with a full mane of white hair. He pointed at me with a long finger and told me that I should have never sent a boy to do a man's job. He warned me that he did not want to see Eddie again as he was too immature to handle adult business. In the end, Mr. Pinkard was gracious enough to give me another week to get the rent paid.

One night in the middle of winter, on our way to work, Eddie and I ran out of gas. I sat quiet and dumbfounded because just yesterday I asked him to gas up the van. When I approached him about whether he remembered, he boorishly replied, "If I said I was going to put gas in the car, then I meant it. Let me handle it." He was annoyed at my questions, but there we were, shipwrecked. Nothing else needed to be said.

I sat quietly in the dark as he walked out into the pitch black in search of gas. Eventually he returned and emptied gasoline from a plastic jug into the tank. We sped off in a mad rush to get to the shop. A large Marriot order sat waiting on the table, and we were running late. Once we reached the shop, I raced inside and started to work. My mind drifted back and forth from baking to finishing to packaging then finally delivery. I was consumed from start to finish, so consumed that I ran to the oven and accidentally pulled a hot tray out without mittens. My hands were burning! Eddie stood watching as I shifted the tray from hand to hand. He never moved. He knew the pan was burning me but offered no help. It happened so fast I didn't think to drop it on the floor or maybe the Marriot's order was more important than my burning. Had I dropped the pan I would have destroyed my cakes. While Eddie stood frozen in time, I raced to the table and released the pan from my hands. That hurt badly.

To help alleviate some of the financial stress associated with our struggling business, Eddie and I found a cheaper month-to-month apartment to live in.

The day of the move, I walked into a dark apartment. Eddie chose to let the lights be turned off in the old apartment, seeing it was our last day. I, along with my sons, silently packed the boxes and loaded the truck in the dark. Afterwards Eddie drove us to our new home.

The moment I sat foot in the new apartment I contemplated my troubled past. As far back as I could remember I had carried the load of a man. I didn't feel like a woman. The apartment was so small and cramped, I felt like I had taken a step backward. I thought about my running. It felt like I didn't belong to anything or anyone. I didn't want to run anymore, but I didn't know how to stop myself. It was all I knew how to do.

Church Folk

Somewhere during this fragile period, a couple, named Mark and Lisa Patterson, came into our business out of the blue. They just happened by Wanda's Patisserie with no agenda. They told us *all* about themselves. "Our lives are open books," they boasted. One point of commonality was that they were members of the same *Mega Ministry* with the corrupt pastor that we previously belonged. Although Eddie and I had left the church, it opened doors for conversation.

They invited us to visit them at their home and even bring the kids along. Upon arrival, we were surprised to find that they lived in a gated community in Atlanta. After calling their house from the entrance of their community, we drove through a huge wrought iron gate and up a hill to a circular driveway. Beautiful shrubbery and Japanese Maples outlined their perfectly manicured lawn as their three-story mansion sat majestically at the top of the hill. The children were amazed, and Eddie was enamored with their wealth.

The Patterson's were giant people, both in weight and stature. Mark was morbidly obese. His beautiful light-skinned wife had long brown tresses hanging down her back, but she struggled with her weight as well. They boasted as they showed us around their house. Mark narrated our tour. "This bed is hand-carved out of mahogany. These elephant tusks came straight from Africa. Do you like French Provincial decorating, Wanda?" While Mark boasted about their possessions, Lisa added commentary. "You can have all this, Wanda," she urged. "All you have to do is speak it into existence." Everything in the house was big just like them.

The first visit ended with them leading a discussion about how hard it was to be a black entrepreneur. They set a date and invited us back a few days later.

On our second visit, they asked us to bring our best desserts. Eddie was ecstatic. "Possibly," he said, "they want to purchase our business." I remained silent and skeptical. Good things don't come easy. Nothing in life is handed to you on a silver platter; you have to work for it all. I was skeptical about their *help*.

With strong reservations, I prepared an apple tart, a chocolate raspberry cake enrobed in white chocolate, and a lemon Bavarian torte. We ate dinner, and afterward, the Patterson's sampled our desserts. Compliments followed each tasting. After dinner, the doorbell rang, and a young man walked in and was introduced as their attorney. He joined us at their massive dining room table.

Mark ate just as hard as he breathed. His jaws emitted the sound that a boot makes when stuck in mud. He spewed stories of his diabetes as he stuffed deserts in his mouth. "Delicious," Mark exclaimed, "I can't stop. They are just too delicious."

As he was eating, Mark initiated a no-strings-attached proposal. "Lisa and I were talking," he began with a mouthful of food, "and we decided we wanted to bless you, and my question to you is what amount of money would make things run smoothly in your business? I mean, you must be bogged down in bills. All new, small black businesses struggle, and Lisa and I just want to help you." I sat there even more suspicious and quiet. Lisa then addressed me and said, "Wanda, you're so quiet." My response was, "Forgive me, I just don't know what to say." I was concerned by this show of support from people I had just met. How did they know we were struggling and financially strapped?

I had not discussed the details of our financial battles with anyone. Lisa added, "I want to bless your boys. They are such nice kids. They should have whatever they want in life. Mark and I want to send them shopping for some new shoes and clothes."

I responded, "I don't know what to feel about that."

They then turned to Eddie and said, "What amount of money at this moment would make you complete right now?"

Eddie replied, "Wow, that's a hard one."

Mark said, "Make it simple on yourself. Throw out a figure." Eddie then said, "I don't know, maybe three thousand dollars or so.

Mark responded, Three thousand dollars, that's it? No more than that?"

Eddie's response was, "Three thousand dollars would clear up a lot of issues."

As the rest of us sat silently at the table, Mark got up and went into one of the rooms in the back of his house. He returned with a stack of twenties. He sat down and proceeded to count out $3000.00. He shoved them in my direction. I immediately shoved the money back toward him and said, "I can't accept that."

"It's a gift, Wanda, and when someone gives you a gift, you simply say, 'Thank you, I receive this in the name of Jesus.'" He pushed the money toward me again.

I promptly pushed it back. "I am so sorry, but I can't accept it."

He then said, "That's fine. Eddie, when a gift is given to you, you say, 'Thank you. I receive this in the name of Jesus.'" He pushed the money toward Eddie. After picking up the stack of bills, Eddie ran his fingers over the crisp money as if he was shuffling cards. "Thank you, I receive this in the name of Jesus."

Mark then said, "Great, that's how you receive a gift! Buy the boys some shoes. They need some new shoes."

When the night was over, I got into our van and told Eddie that something was not right and that he must return the money to them. Even though he rarely expressed his thoughts, he gave me a piece of his mind. He said, "That's fine if you didn't want any part of this gift, but I'm going shopping. Brian, Jason, and Sean, do you guys want to go shopping?"

They all screamed, "Yeah!"

That night I tossed and turned. I remembered my mother saying when I was a child, "You don't get something for nothing." I knew that whatever Mark and Lisa Patterson wanted, it had to do with Wanda's Patisserie.

Eddie slept soundly.

* * * *

A few days later, Eddie went on his shopping spree with the children. Shortly after that, Lisa called and asked us to meet them at their house. "This time," she said, "leave the kids at home." Eddie and I obliged. Upon our arrival, we were met by four, ferocious Dobermans in the kitchen. They growled and barked as if they were in attack mode. Mark quieted them down by telling them we were good people, that we meant them no harm. He then led them back into the garage, their living quarters. Even though the dogs were removed from the room, I could still hear them breathing against the door. He made light of how vicious they had responded to Eddie in particular. "Those dogs would have eaten you alive if I wasn't in this room, Eddie—tore you to bits."

Lisa asked questions about the money. While she was speaking, Mark left the room and came back and casually put a pistol on the table. "One can never be too careful," he said while looking wide-eyed at us. "I keep this around me just in case."

Mark talked about becoming a silent partner in Wanda's Patisserie. In so-called good faith, he laid a cashier's check for $1,500.00 on the kitchen counter next to him. Leaning across the table he said, "Lisa and I are just trying to help you all. You got bills coming out the wazoo and we can't stand seeing good black Christian folks struggle like you are struggling. So what is it going to be?" Mark waited for a response, but the room grew silent. Eddie looked dumbfounded and lost. Without uttering one word, while looking at the gun on the table, this time I picked the check up and left for home. Mark's actions, the subtle intimidation, the veiled threats, and Lisa's self-aggrandizing display of wealth and fake benevolence, reminded me of the church I'd left behind.

When we returned to our apartment, I took the check and placed it behind Mama's photo. From that night on, Eddie harassed me about depositing the check, "Did you put it in yet? Have you spoken to them? Where is it?" I always found my way out of the conversation. When I called Lisa, there was no answer. For two weeks, I tried to reach her unsuccessfully, until I threatened to tear the check to pieces. She then returned my call and said that she and Mark had been on vacation in London. "When are you going to deposit the check," she asked sternly.

"I felt I should talk to you first," I replied. "I noticed that you wrote in the memo section that this $1500.00 would secure 60 percent of our company. Wanda's Patisserie is not for sale!" My children and husband are enamored with your wealth, but something is not sitting well with my spirit. I believe that you and Mark are trying to take our company."

Lisa shot back, "Why would you think something like that? Mark and I have been so kind to you, but just last night he said *you* would probably be the one who would throw a monkey wrench in this deal!"

"I am not trying to cause problems, but this company is not for sale. What was the gun display about," I asked. "And what about the Dobermans? Were you all trying to intimidate us?"

After that question, Lisa changed the subject and started to do irrelevant small talk. Eventually we said good-bye, and I tore the check to pieces. We never spoke again. A month later, the Pattersons' attorney came in and told us that he had abandoned his contract with them and that they had been arrested on fraudulent attempts to illegally gain control of small, black-owned businesses. Even with all of Mark and Lisa's strong-arming and intimidation, God still hid me underneath the shadow of His wing.

Leaving the Past behind Yet Again

My sister, Rosa, called from Oklahoma in hopeless despair. Since the death of our parents, depression had settled on her life. In one conversation, she told me an elaborate story about contemplating suicide in her garage. Rosa needed me, and after all the commotion in Atlanta, I figured a change would be good for all of us. After much thought, I decided to move to Oklahoma, offering Eddie once again a way out. Yet again, he declined. "I can't live without you," he said in a perfunctory tone. "I love you, you are my wife, and I don't want to live without you."

My friend, Rochelle, and I were chatting about the complex insanity of my relationship with Eddie. She reminded me that even in bad relationships, most people bring something positive to the table, adding some value to your life, however minute or obscure. She then pointed out that every once in a great while, there comes a taker, a subtractor, a grim reaper, who takes, takes, and then takes some more, giving absolutely nothing back. Eddie was my grim reaper.

I had so many feelings about Wanda's Patisserie. Some were positive, but most were negative. I was working alone and received no help or support from Eddie. When I woke up in the morning I cried. When I went to bed at night depression set in even more. We had some of the most beautiful desserts in Atlanta, but each day I carried the weight of the business and our home on my back and I was exhausted from trying.

The day Eddie carelessly broke the gear handle on the twenty-quart mixer then pulled the mixer out from the wall and I fell and slammed my head on it I couldn't cry. My tears were all dried up. Blood raced down the side of my face as he looked on. As I struggled to stop the bleeding, he laughed and said, "Don't be such a baby. You can handle it." I felt no need in trying to keep the business open. I had nothing left to give.

The Road to Babylon

Each time I moved, I believed things would be different. While running, it never occurred to me that I was traveling with the heavy baggage of my past. I kept the weight of my pain far out of sight, packed away in my secret closet. With the hurt of a dysfunctional relationship strapped neatly around my neck, I was suffocating and didn't know it. Deep in my heart, I believed that living near Rosa would alleviate at least some of the pain. So, on July 1, 1996, I carried my issues from Atlanta to the great state of Oklahoma. We moved into a house that was next door to Rosa's pastor, Dr. Cirrus, and Michelle Smith. Rosa lived only a few doors down the street with her family. To settle into this small but elite town, I took a job as pastry chef, fifty miles away at Adam's Mark Hotel in Tulsa, while Eddie sat at home, watching TV and rubbing his forehead. Though discontent with him, I was happy to live down the street from Rosa.

Pastor Smith and his wife were self-consumed, a bit materialistic, and put their two children off on me. The moment I hit their small town, they exercised their free labor rights. Before I even consented to babysitting for the evening, Michelle would say, "We really appreciate you staying with the kids tonight," Dr. Smith was a talker and a thinker. Launching into long deliberations about life, he was always up for political and religious discussions Still, living next door to them was nice in the beginning. Life was sure to turn for the better.

On my way to Rosa's house, I often ran into Pastor Smith. We launched into long discussions about my life. He gravitated toward me and learned of Eddie's laziness, challenging him to find a job to provide for the children and me. I was in awe. No one had ever looked out for my well-being as he did. He demanded answers and wanted to know Eddie's plan to correct our financial issues. On one occasion, in my kitchen, Dr. Smith, who was huge in stature, lovingly lifted my sister, Rosa, up in the air and bounced her up and down, showing me they were intimately connected.

Once Rosa left the kitchen, he commented on the fact that I had no refrigerator. I was too embarrassed to discuss the drama. He then turned to Eddie's poor personal hygiene. "Why doesn't he put lotion on his legs? Look at those rusty knees. How disgusting. Why does his breath stink? That is no way to keep a woman." He suggested that we both come to see him for marriage counseling. The way he discussed my husband's appearance was cold and unusual; nonetheless, I agreed that counseling was necessary to make my marriage work. The following day Pastor Smith had a used but workable refrigerator and lots of frozen fish delivered to my home. I was so grateful and amazed at the veracity with which he attacked my problems. The man presented himself as a larger than life character.

Dr. Cirrus Smith, THDD, Min.

Cirrus was born in Colorado. The story he told from the pulpit was one of grace and nothing short of a miracle. As a teen, he and his girlfriend were parked on the crag of a cliff, making out in his '56 Chevy, when a car plowed into his vehicle from behind. Cirrus's face was almost cut off, but God saved him from death. This miraculous mountaintop experience caused him to change his life, and supposedly, the call to preach came the moment the car struck. Each time he shouted the story from the podium, Cirrus reflected, taking a long, deep breath, and pointing to the massive scar across the length of his nose. It was an out-of-body experience, according to him. God had reached into the clutches of death and picked him to deliver the message to the people. Due to this auspicious event, Cirrus always stayed one giant step ahead of his congregation, boasting disciples who wanted to be just like him.

In actuality, Dr. Cirrus Smith had a past like the average human being; there were no burning bushes that miraculously caught fire, nor dead, dry bones coming to life that caused him to turn his life over to God. No, he was human just like the rest of us. Cirrus went to college, failed, and liked many young people in transition, dropped out of school. He drove a commercial truck for a little while and, after becoming bored with that, went back to school, hoping to become a medical doctor. He finished his undergrad with a new focus. He was accepted, on a probationary status, at a medical school. During this time, he made mistakes, fathered children with unwed mothers, married, divorced, and married again as many people do. While in medical school, Cirrus squandered his time and, because of his probationary status, was not allowed to take core curriculum subjects. One adviser suggested that he leave med school, because it appeared to him that Cirrus was there to feed his ego. His heart was not in saving people's lives. The adviser suggested that he go to seminary. He did and found success in the industry of the church, becoming the doctor that he had always dreamed of being.

To Rosa, Cirrus was a demigod. Rosa and her husband's lives revolved around their pastor and his wife. They went with the pastor and his family on vacations and weekend getaways. The Simpletons spent breakfast, dinner, fish fries, and all their free time in the company of the Smiths. Cirrus often used his reprobate mind and lewd behavior to entertain his guests. The good pastor would lie on his basement floor like a large, beached whale with his right hand in his pants, fumbling with his private parts. Rosa, Tyrone, and Michelle disregarded him, moving on as if his behavior was perfectly normal.

My first Sunday attending Unionized Baptist Church was an enlightening experience. Dr. Smith, in spite of his shortcomings, had a gift for oration. He understood the Word of God. The voice he boomed from the pulpit was scholarly and moving. Cirrus's sermons were so powerful that I forgave him for other shortcomings. The first time I saw him, I sat in the front row. He stood above me, shouting and pounding his fist on the slanted wood like a judge calling a courtroom to order. Though the pastor thundered on for nearly a half hour, his eyes rarely left mine as he spoke.

That week, after witnessing the Sunday sermon, Eddie and I began our counseling. Dr. Smith's attention seemed to be more on me than my relationship with Eddie. He chastened Eddie for his shortcomings, and to be frank, I was so emotionally spent that I was not too offended about his reprimands as a pastor. The sessions began with Eddie and me together. Before I could blink my eyes, Eddie lost interest. He was out of a job and was not motivated to find one. He always followed my lead, so I went out and found him employment at the cafeteria of Phillips Petroleum Oil Company.

By Christmas time, Eddie had all but shut the door on his family. One day, out of the blue, he made the decision to discontinue marriage counseling. He began coming home from work later than normal and disappearing for hours with no explanation. At the Christmas parade, a young woman stared me down while I stood in the cold with Rosa and her child. I questioned Rosa about the woman. Rosa said her name was Anita and took me over to meet her. Before I could get my name out, she rudely said, "I know who you are. Eddie and I are friends!" I was shaken by the firmness of her words.

Later that night, I confronted Eddie. I asked him if they were sleeping together. He told me no, but that their conversations were of a serious nature, and that I should leave it alone. He then apologized for her behavior and said he would tell her to never let it happen again. Astonished by his words, I understood the situation perfectly. From that night on, I slept in the living room and did not ask any more questions. I told Pastor Smith about the incident. He suggested that I continue my counseling with him, alone. At this junction in my life, he explained, I needed to focus on my own issues. I agreed.

In our first session, Pastor Smith asked me to make a list of three ways my father wounded me. I wrote the list while he watched.

1) I was walking down the steps, getting smart with him, and he took a log from the wood stove, slammed it across my shoulder, knocking me to the ground.
2) He held me down with his feet and beat me until I peed on myself.
3) He made a big difference between Kay and me, even stealing my belongings and giving them to her so her

needs were met. He flat out refused to be a father to me by having nothing to do with me.

After I finished, Dr. Smith read them aloud. I was overwhelmed with grief. He then suggested that I journal over the week and bring my writings back for the next session. In my eagerness to get well, I informed him about my Black Pearls journal. That turned out to be one of the biggest mistakes of my life. He said that, within those pages, was likely the key to my healing. I didn't realize how vulnerable I was, nor did I understand that the words from my journal would transport me from my already dismal and misguided life into Babylon.

The next session, I brought him the journal and watched as he thumbed through the pages in haste. After reading a few entries, he decided he needed to change courses with me. I was a difficult case; there were many issues to work through. After that day, Pastor Smith saw me every day, no matter what.

At the same time, wealthy people in the community, heard that there was a pastry chef from Atlanta living in town. Those words spread like wildfire. Before long, eager clients helped me find a location to open a cake shop. After the space was located, I quit my job as pastry chef of Adam's Mark Hotel and opened Wanda's Cake Gallery.

Eddie eventually moved out and into an apartment of his own. With my husband out of the house, the good pastor was always at my breakfast table or on the exercise bike in the den.

Very Strange...

One day, Pastor Smith's wife, Michelle, came over and told me that she was so happy that Cirrus was spending time at my house. In a strange voice that was equal parts love and hate, she said that she could not stomach or stand the sight of him. The longer I kept him, the better off she was. She then put her hand on my shoulder and said, "You know, Cirrus and I agreed in the beginning that you were mine." I shifted my weight to offset the conversation. Feeling extremely awkward, I said, "Dr. Smith is just my counselor and nothing more. And what is that supposed to mean when you say that I am yours?"

She then said, "Cirrus has his and I have mine. We agreed that he would not mess with you." I stepped away from her and said that certainly there was a misunderstanding, because Dr. Smith was no more than my pastor. I was shocked at her disclosure and wondered if I heard her right.

The next day, I approached Dr. Smith about his wife's behavior. "I felt like she was coming on to me," I explained to him wearily. He laughed and said, "Yeah, stranger things have happened." I couldn't believe his response. He wasn't at all disturbed that his wife; the first lady made a pass at me. To further complicate matters, there were rumors going around church about another member.

Apparently, Dr. Smith had a female disciple named Suzanna, who also suffered from the Mary Syndrome, yet desired to become a minister. While she was studying under him, they became intimate. Cirrus and Suzanna became the talk of the town. Everyone hated Suzanna and swore on their mama's Bible that she was the one who led Cirrus down the road to sin. Some members said that she was bisexual and was in love with Cirrus but was also intimate with Michelle. This trio was the hot topic at church; everybody was talking! The members of the church found no fault in their esteemed pastor; rather, they went directly after Suzanna. After a few weeks of particularly slanderous gossip, the entire church turned their backs on the female disciple, eventually isolating Suzanna until she had nowhere to go.

The news troubled me, but Dr. Smith had yet to come on to me. Our counseling sessions remained professional. For the first time in my life, I started to feel as if I was finally receiving medicine for what ailed me. Dr. Smith had a gift with words. He could piece sentences together that would ring in my head for days. With a mesmerizing fatherly tone, Dr. Smith took my Black Pearls journal, and found his way into my secret closet. He systematically attacked each of my private pains. The fist that was squeezing my heart gradually loosened. After a few months of treatment, I felt empowered, alive, and ready to take on new challenges.

And right in the middle of my feeling better about life, there came this nagging sensation that something was not right. The sessions between Dr. Smith and I began to shift. Maybe it was a change in his fatherly tone. Perhaps it was the direction of his eyes in our sessions or the way he sat in his chair with his legs spread wide. One morning, while mulling over my uneasiness, I grabbed my Bible and watched it freefall on the story of King David coveting his servant's wife, Bathsheba. The king seduced Bathsheba and slept with her. He then sent her husband to the frontline to fight. The man died in battle, and the king moved in on Bathsheba.

After my quiet time, I went to Tyrone and showed him the story. I also told him—in supposed confidentiality—that I felt that Cirrus, many times, was crossing boundary lines with me, that he was even willing to destroy my marriage to get what he wanted. Tyrone carelessly said, "If Dr. Smith is really trying to seduce you, God will deal with him."

That day I walked out of my sister's home empty. I went to Tyrone because I saw him as a righteous man of God. I believed that he, as an associate minister, would intervene. Perhaps he could talk to Cirrus, set him straight, and I could continue my healing process. But Tyrone was also a disciple of Cirrus and as unionized as the next member, closing his eyes to the evil and supporting Dr. Smith in all things. After my talk with Tyrone, I spent less time in therapy and more time out in nature. Dr. Smith took me fishing all the time. I wanted his help, yet I knew what was going to happen. I wanted to run from him, but I was drawn to him.

It was when I was fishing with Dr. Smith that I saw his real intentions.

Dr. Smith had a bass boat. He would drop his boat in the water, start the engine, and guide us across the lake. From five in the morning until late at night, we fished and talked and fished some more. On the water was when Dr. Smith was no longer a pastor or counselor. He insisted that I relax and call him Cirrus. Cirrus knew everything—and I mean everything—about fishing. As I watched him catch fish after fish, he explained the system.

"Mrs. Wolfe, he said while baiting his hook, if you want to catch a fish, you have to understand what they want. Once you are inside their mind, and you know their desires, you can catch 'em all day long. But to do that, you gotta know who they are and where they come from."

Cirrus always educated me about the fish we were after.

One day he hooked one and pulled it in the boat. As he extracted the hook, he held the fish in front of me. "Ms. Wolfe, this is a largemouth. It's a sun fish, not a true bass. Its life begins in cool water. They keep their nest close to the shore. This particular fish will take any bait you throw out there."

When we first started fishing, Cirrus half-heatedly tried to talk to me about my problems. He promised that our time on the water would be similar to our therapy sessions. If not just like the sessions, they would at least be therapeutic. Cirrus connected our fishing with the Bible, church, and daily problems; but as we got more familiar, his pastoral demeanor waned, and he became another person.

He started drinking Jack Daniels; lightly at first, just a few sips here and there. Hiding the bottle from me as he poured drinks, he slipped it into cokes and chewed peppermints to mask the scent. Sometimes, he got so drunk his face looked swollen, resembling an oversized pickle. That day, he drove his bass boat so fast it looked like Pharaoh sending chariots of fire after Moses on the floor of the Red Sea.

Another day, in a drunken stupor, he fished hard until he got a bite. The fish trapped himself and fought back by yanking the line and trying to escape. As he reeled it in, Cirrus laughed. The fish had glowing, red eyes. "Mrs. Wolfe," Cirrus said as he held the fish up, "This is a smallmouth. It will take any bait you throw at it. Look how hard it fought for its life. That little bugger fought hard for his life. He just didn't know he was on the end of Dr. Cirrus Smith's line. The damn thing was so desperate to eat, it even went after artificial lures." He smiled jubilantly and slid the fish into the live well.

I was just a sport to Cirrus; and nothing more.

"It's all about the presentation," Cirrus would boast, "you have to know your fish, study it." I learned, very early on while fishing with him, the importance of presentation, the actual baiting of the hook and making the death row meal so appetizing, the poor fish could not resist the temptation to take the bait. There are many fish in Oklahoma. To name a few of Cirrus favorites, there are stripers, channels, blue catfish, flathead, walleyes, and black and white crappie. Each species comes with its own desired bait. For instance, because crappie are known to get excited over live minnows, a good, well-educated fisherman would never fish for crappie with chicken liver or corn kernels.

When I was a child, I thought all one had to do was put a worm on the end of a hook. I was wrong. Fish *can* be caught by chance, but a real angler knows that most fish have to be manipulated to strike the bait. Cirrus was a genius in the art of manipulation. The first few times I fished with him, I caught nothing while he reeled in the catches of the day. After about four trips on his boat, he finally laid out his gaming techniques:

#1) Presentation was paramount. While baiting your hook, make it look so good to the fish, that when he sees it, *he will by- pass safe food and feed ferociously on that which is not.* Once he takes the bait, reel in slowly and tighten the line to secure the hook. *The second you know the hook is in the fish's mouth, yank back with steady force and reel him in.*

#2) Cirrus's second rule in catching was true technique: know thy fish! How you secure the hook in a crappies mouth would be different than how you'd hook a catfish. While the catfish has strong jaws, the crappie is known as the *paper mouth*. You have to be delicate when setting the hook with crappie or you'll lose the fish altogether.

After many lessons with Cirrus, I became a skilled fisherman.

One day on the water, Cirrus said, "After reading your journal, I know what I'm going to call you! I'm going to call you My Little Rabbit!" I wanted to know why such a nickname. He said, "Oh, now, that wouldn't be fair if I told you, would it? But I will challenge you to figure it out. The clues are in John 5:1-8. But I have to warn you…if you ever figure this out, you will probably despise me for the rest of my life!" His words should have alarmed me, but when you are as far in as I was, your eyes are covered and your ears are shut.

What could make me hate my teacher? I didn't understand.

Death of a Parasite

Eddie and I were talking about trying to salvage the relationship. Things were not quite dead, but they were close. I did not want to go through another divorce. I hoped we could fix it. Eddie was an irresponsible individual. He had been unfaithful in the past. He was a parasite and had wounded me badly. However, there was something pushing me. It wasn't so much that I couldn't live without him; I just wanted to be accepted.

I wanted Rosa and her cronies to accept me as a valid Christian; I loved God as much as they claimed to. Trying to retrieve my relationship with Eddie would make them invite me to their gatherings; it would make them stop talking behind my back. *If I could fix it*, I thought, *I would be right in the eyes of the church*. The insidious gossip of the church was funneled back to me through my sisters friend, Shelly. She would give me the 4-1-1, always emphasizing that the most scathing remarks were made by Rosa. Shelly was struggling with bipolar disorder, sometimes *in the circle* and sometimes out. When she was out, she ran to my gallery to report all the horrible things my sister and others had said. After speaking with Shelly, I began to see a new side to Rosa.

My heart burned when I learned that Rosa gossiped a lot and was self-righteous. I wanted her to stop disparaging my character. Instead of addressing the issue with Rosa, I tried to fix my marriage. I thought if I salvaged my relationship, Rosa would quiet down, Pastor Smith would move on, and everyone *except me* would live happily ever after. I was dead wrong on all counts.

Eddie lived in a tiny apartment in the heart of town. Brian wanted to see him and find out why he missed such an important event as his scholarship ceremony the previous night. After convincing me to take him, we got in the car and headed unannounced over to Eddie's place. After parking we walked up and found that, just like the shop and our perpetually unlocked home in Atlanta, the front door was ajar. *Wow*, I thought, *same old Eddie*. Brian pushed the door open with his finger, and I walked in. There was rustling in the living room.

We found Eddie and his coworker Anita, naked on the couch, having sex. I lost control. The room spun as I ran toward him, sobbing and hoping the nightmare would go away. Anita jumped up and raced to his bathroom. I ran to the kitchen, looking for anything that would inflict pain. The room smelled awful.

Brian, in an attempt to stop me, pulled at my clothes, begging, "Please, Mom, lets go."

I kept screaming, "Why? How could you do this to our family?" Eddie stood there, looking empty-headed.

Brian, amidst my crying, continued to scream, "Mom, don't touch anything. It's filthy....don't touch anything. Please, let's go."

I refused and ran, beating on Eddie's bathroom door where Anita had barricaded herself. I lamented, "Why, Anita! Why? What did I ever do to you?"

She replied behind the locked door, "You've never done anything to me. You've always been nice to me. I'm so sorry, Wanda...please forgive me. I'm so sorry!" Brian left in a panic.

I sank into the floor as Eddie stood nude in the middle of the living room, apologizing and scratching his head in disappointment. I struggled to get up. The moment I gained my balance and lunged toward him, a large set of hands grabbed me from behind. It was Dr. Smith. Brian had gone to a neighbor's house and called him. Dr. Smith lifted me up and slung me over his shoulder, carrying me out the front door. I couldn't get the scene out of my head; it played and replayed over and over again, threatening to overtake me like quick sand swallows up the weak. The more I thought about it, the deeper and lower I sank into its suffocating hold.

Dr. Smith shoved me into his pickup truck and drove me back to the church office. He shut the door, threw me a white baptismal towel, and with zero ounces of compassion, said, "Wipe your face. You look a complete mess. Eddie has made his choice. Get over it. You've got a wedding cake to make. If I were you, I'd get going quickly." I buried my face into the towel and, hoping to find safety in the darkness it provided, I cried my life away.

The next day, I prepared and delivered a flawless wedding cake with tears in my eyes.

*   *   *   *

Early Sunday morning, everyone was talking. The night before, I'd cried on Rosa's shoulder, and before morning, the whole congregation knew all the sordid, humiliating details. People I didn't even know were calling, giving their condolences.

When time came to get dressed for Sunday service, I didn't want to go. I didn't want to face those judgmental eyes and sharp tongues. However, Tyrone called and insisted that I would find my healing at church—and only at church. After pondering the thought, I decided to go. After all, God could fix anything. I didn't have the energy to wait on the boys, so I went alone.

I shoved more hurt and disappointment into my closet, wearing all black to mourn the death of a longtime dead situation. As I walked down the aisle of church, whispers flared underneath church fans and heads turned. I sat on the second row to the far right-hand side, alone. No one came to sit beside me. No one offered comfort, not even my sister Rosa. I was a glutton for punishment. Instead of finding the proper place to worship, as any sane person would do, I came back to Unionized Baptist Church every Sunday and drowned myself in the vicious whispers. Like a penitent sinner, I felt the gossip was all my fault.

By Monday morning, I was unable to stand. The thought of facing the day was too much to bear. I called the church for prayer. Dr. Smith's secretary, Jeanette Saul, rudely informed me that Dr. Smith was out. "Probably fishing, because Monday is his off day," she said, trying to hurry her good-bye.

Before she hung the phone up, I cried out in distress, "I realize Dr. Smith is out, but I need someone to pray for me."

She sat quietly as I waited for her to volunteer. She did not, so, all choked-up, I begged for mercy. "Jeanette, will you pray for me?"

Without emotion, she said, "Oh, o—kay," then prayed to somebody—I don't think it was God—"Father God, I come to you right now on behalf of Wanda. Forgive her, Lord. Help her to understand your will, Lord. I don't know exactly what she did to bring this situation on herself, but, Lord, right now I want to ask forgiveness on her behalf. Lord, show her the error of her ways. You know all the things she did to bring her to this point.

Lord, forgive her." At that point, *I* went into my secret closet and closed the door. I don't remember saying good-bye. Jeanette always prided herself in being nasty and rude. She considered it her duty to God to tell it like it was. She knew how bad she hurt me. I have no doubt that she relished the pain inflicted by her tone and words.

I came to understand Jeanette's behavior and the vicious whispers of the church. They all had secrets, and focusing on my issues diverted attention from their own. All of the preachers training under Cirrus desired to pastor their own church. They tried to protect their reputations and keep bad things off their resumes. And it wasn't just the pastors-in-training; even Rosa, the paragon of virtue, struggled to hide the birth of Tyrone's illegitimate child. The whole church, including Cirrus, looked like Pharisees and Sadducees to me. They focused more on teaching the Word of God and less on living it.

The day Brian graduated from high school was the day my divorce from Eddie was finalized, proving to be bittersweet. With a dead marriage, my sister blacklisting me, and nowhere to turn, I kept going to Cirrus for counseling. In my most vulnerable state, it was open season for rabbits.

One of my clients informed me that right next door to my business was a newly remodeled condominium. After a brief conversation with the owner, I moved. The new home was beautiful; all white, cozy, and clean. The distance from Cirrus's home did not decrease his visits; it simply emboldened his pursuit.

Cirrus had always flirted with me, as he flirted with so many other women. But while I was unpacking, and my children were gone, Cirrus came over to have a serious conversation. Grabbing my arms securely, he told me about his feelings, challenging me to love him, because he had never known love. He told me that he had never loved anyone like he loved me; that he wanted to keep me safe, to possess me, that he would never allow any more harm to come to me. He was skillful in baiting the hook for fragmented souls to bite. Without questioning anything around me, as I had done so many times in the past, I did exactly what the man told me to do, no questions asked. And there, in my new house, we had sex. I had become everything that I did not want to be. The vicious whispers at church were a self-fulfilling prophecy. I just shut down and let Cirrus have me. Not only had I slept with a married man, I'd slept with a preacher.

My God, what had I become?
Who was the man that took me?

The more Cirrus pulled me in, the more I saw of his corrupt life. Cirrus was a disaster of a man, and I really wanted no part of him, yet I felt no way out.

This relationship devastated my soul. In the midst of all the filth that Cirrus brought into my life, community leaders honored him as Dr. Cirrus Smith THDD. MIN. He boasted successfully completing not one but two doctorates. Dr. Smith, as his public knew him, was a man of God, and he knew the Word better than any other individual in the entire state of Oklahoma. To his congregation, Cirrus was the light, the power, the glory, forever and ever.

And while he was the light, my life descended into blackness. I grabbed my problems—the brokenness and pain—and quietly entered the darkest corners of my secret closet. What had I done to myself? Why could I not break away from these debilitating relationships with men? All the while, Cirrus laughingly called me his little rabbit and reminded me to read John 5:1-8.

I lost myself in darkness. It was worse, much worse, than all the things that came before, combined. I cried myself to sleep. I spent entire weeks alone. My self-image dissolved into an acrid pool of hateful nicknames: whore, slut, sinner, terrible person. There is no way to convey to you how my self-hate transcended words into a realm of raw emotions. When Unionized Baptist church disparaged my name, I agreed with all the nasty words that spewed from their mouths. All the while, my sons watched as their pastor—their counselor in Christ—came in the middle of the night to have sex with their mother. My children never forgot those days. Cirrus showed them what a so-called *real man* should look like. And that hurt worse than death.

Cirrus was correct when he said there were certain things that did not sit well with me. Each time sexual activity occurred, I spaced out. I was not the type of woman who would become involved with a married man; or so I thought. He used his influence and knowledge of my personal life to enter into a *No Entry* zone in my home. My sons and I succumbed to his presence. He crossed boundary lines with very important information about me, and to make matters worse, he played with my mind by challenging me to figure the puzzle out. Not only that, but Cirrus taunted Sean, my youngest child, threatening him with failure for his life. Standing over Sean, Cirrus would tell him that he had nothing but disaster to look forward to in life. In the same breath, he spoke of a great future with Ivy League schools awaiting his and Michelle's children. As time passed, he became more forceful, physically pushing Sean into walls and doors, yet he was the only male role model that existed in Sean's life.

One day while traveling to Tulsa, I expressed my desire to remove myself from the relationship. I told Cirrus I wanted him to have nothing to do with my sons. He abruptly pulled his truck over to the side of the road, put his hands around my neck, and shouted, "Brian, Jason, and Sean belong to me! If you ever mess with the scenario that I have put together, I will kill you!" Frightened from this exchange, I begged him to take me home. He obliged. When one has a history of abuse, many times that person is more familiar with violent exchanges than not. For me, violence, sometimes physical and other times, verbal, was all I knew.

I was the queen of secrets. No one could keep their mouth shut better than me. My loyalty was always to the perpetrator rather than myself. Cirrus, as my counselor, knew who I was, because he studied and observed how I responded in my relationship with Eddie and in conflict with my sister Rosa. In each situation, Cirrus watched me remain quietly devoted and loyal to my abuser. Conquering me was not a hard thing to do. In this case, remaining silent took almost an entire decade of my life away from me. I now know a better way and believe, deep down in my soul, that I have a responsibility to other broken women to share the things I learned while living through my Babylon experience and finding my way out.

Because my consistent desire to break free always set off a *violent* Cirrus, there was no civility in our arguments; they always got out of control, ending in physical abuse. Any inkling of my wanting to be free prompted a violent response from him. Knowing that I survived that incredible darkness may give some tormented soul the gumption *to get up and go*!

I quickly forgot about the beauty of my newly remodeled condo and moved deeper into the darkness. Every breath I took, every word I spoke, reflected the shadows around me. I mastered Wanda's Cake Gallery by day and served Cirrus by night. Each day he came, stayed a while, and went home. Each day I cried for the sinful state I was in.

Every Sunday, Cirrus got up in the pulpit and preached sermons people actually believed. Outside of the pulpit, it was hard to believe he was a preacher. There were times when he portrayed the hopeless and unloved. This supposed helplessness prompted sympathy within me. As jacked up as I was, there was a part of me that desired to save him from himself. The day he said to me, "I can't live without you," was the day I stopped thinking about my own well-being. One day he posed the question to me, "Do you believe that Solomon was an afterthought of God?" His convenient theory was that Solomon was born through Bathsheba and David, and that God must have known beforehand that David would put Uriah, Bathsheba's husband, on the frontline to be murdered, then have sex with Bathsheba, lose their first child, then later give birth to Solomon, the *Wisest man of all men*! Cirrus cunningly attempted to make logic of the darkness, and it soon became clear that I was but a pawn in his and Michelle's dysfunctional marriage.

One day Michelle asked to chat with me after Sunday service. She told me she was happy Cirrus was not disturbing her living arrangements; that she did not have to be bothered with him, and this suited her just fine, "But I need you and Cirrus to be discreet. That, my dear, is my only concern," she said, "because I'm the *queen*. I have *always been the queen* and will *forever be* the queen." She questioned me, "Do you think you are the first one that has walked this road with Cirrus and me? Cirrus and I are best friends. He leads stupid women on to believe they matter. He tells me how stupid and vulnerable you all are and how you want my crown. There have been so many before you. I wouldn't get my hopes up too high if I were you. My household is very secure—just don't bring about a scandal." And she leaned back in her chair and laughed. Owning the air around her, Michelle leaned in, pointed her index finger into the table and said, "You can have him! He's all yours, But the queen's chair and crown belongs to *me*." The queen had spoken. Embarrassed, I told Cirrus about Michelle's comments. He laughed it off, making light of a dark situation. I just wanted it all to end.

The following Sunday, the king replied from the pulpit. Cirrus preached a sermon on Queen Vashti being deposed from her throne, for being disobedient to the king, and on Esther, the King's mistress, becoming the queen instead. Cirrus looked back and forth between Michelle and me as he spoke. We sat on opposite sides of the church, so he slowly rotated from one to the other. The heads of the congregation did the same. Heads bobbed back and forth, resembling a crowd at a tennis match. Pastor Smith told a captivated congregation that this sermon, which he claimed came directly from the Holy Ghost, was the first of a three-part series.

Cirrus didn't seem to value the words of God, nor did he respect his position as pastor. He used the pulpit to preach sermons suited toward his personal agenda. This time the congregation, to their credit, approached Cirrus and told him his three-part series was inappropriate and distasteful. The next week, he changed his message and went back to thundering away against sin.

Moving Deeper into Babylon

I spent a major amount of my time trying to make everything okay in Cirrus's life. Besides his son and daughter, he painted a picture of a gloomy, empty house. When he came to our home, it was always with Jack Daniels and Coke. He sat for hours, trying to drink away the outside world. It was his hidden life. I did not want to see how ugly the situation really was. I saw what I wanted to see, convincing myself that he was a fragile bird with a broken wing. I had no desire to see Cirrus for who he really was; instead, I saw him for who I wanted him to be. The truth was that as many times as he called me smart, he also called me stupid and dumb. Second-guessing my abilities as a mother and businesswoman, he frequently compared my organizational skills to that of Michelle's. I placed all negative comments in the back of the closet and pretended the world to be whole. Living in complete fear and dread of the possibilities, I didn't want to see or pay attention to what was really going on.

One day, Jason was at the mall, and a woman from church walked up to him and said, "Your mama is a ho!" Shattered, Jason did not respond to her comment. Instead, he came back home and cried about how devastated he was to hear that about me. It is dangerous to close your eyes to the truth around you. When we walk with blinders on, not only do we fail to see the person we are dealing with, but we also fail to see ourselves. Cunning and calculated people, if given the opportunity, will prey on our inability to see. I allowed Cirrus to use the garbage, locked away in my secret closet, to feed the demons in his.

The Creator has a way of interjecting people into our lives to help us to understand who we really are. He keeps bringing us back to the same scenario with different people until we get it right. I did not know how sick I was. Cirrus, on the other hand, fully understood that he could get away with the abuse as long as he heroically came back to save me. I lived in self-denial about the closet I allowed him to place me in. The longer I stayed there, the more fearful I became about coming out into the light. After a while, his dark closet, instead of my own, became the reality of my being. It was not a good situation. It did not matter how many candy-coated letters he wrote to me; it was, and is, what married men do. And I, in turn, did exactly what wounded, broken women do; I made up excuses of why I could not leave him.

When Cirrus came to my house, I never knew what I was going to get—the mean and abusive Cirrus or the depraved preacher from the pulpit. I had not yet learned that, whatever baggage he came with, was his and not mine. Lifting his heavy load, I saw him as being all I had. And he understood that, manipulating the utter of that one issue until it was completely empty and void of milk. Looking back on this awful situation, I know now that it was impossible for me to gain control of the contents of my own baggage, consumed with other people's issues. I found myself trying to save Cirrus. Sacrificing my reputation and integrity was one of the most painful things I've ever done as a woman, but I found it incredibly hard to think independently of the sewage hidden in his dark closet.

Overcome by darkness and lost deep in the bowel of Babylon, the seventeen miles of double walls around the city, built by Nebuchadnezzar, walled me in. Looking through the peephole of Cirrus's closet, I saw no light in sight. Babylon lay along the

Euphrates River and, like the Jewish people, I was deep in exile with no one except me and the Creator to deal with the true issues. As the Jewish people did, I worshipped God in this dark, lonely, and dry place. And while I could not see, at that time, any true value in falling on my knees, I worshipped him anyway. I had no idea that through this emptying out, I was growing stronger and more independent of Cirrus's belief system every day. Yet I understood, without apprehension, that I was as deep into Babylon as one could get. Cirrus's mind became more reprobate as he embraced a world of debauchery. I perceived no exit out of the darkness that possessed my soul. The average woman, I believe, does not realize the power of the word *no*; that it's okay and perfectly fine to say no if a situation does not feel right. Each time we, as women, say yes, it is a sacrifice. We may not see or understand that we've sacrificed ourselves, but the word *yes* always means a giving of ourselves. We must be clear and ask ourselves, "Who is this individual that we feel drawn to make this sacrifice for?" The only one who deserves sacrifice without question is the Creator. He is the only one who should have unlimited access to our heart and soul. Everyone else needs to be carded. Over time, I have learned to use the 5-W challenge: Who are you? Why are you? Where are you? When were you? Where were you?

While my method seems a little invasive, I have found that it works for me. We must be willing to ask questions until clarity proves itself. This day and age presents a host of deceptions, therefore, we, as women, must be willing to take off our rose-colored glasses and pay attention to the details. It may seem like the small things don't matter, but many times, it is the little stuff that gives us a glimpse into the future. We must find the motivation to think past our lonely hearts, fragility, pains, and prior brokenness to exercise our right to say, "No! No, I'm not going there! No, I don't feel led to do so! No, I think not! Yes, I think I'll move on!"

The Escape Artist

In May 2000, Jason graduated high school and enlisted in the army. Unlike when Brian left for University of Arkansas; Jason's leaving caused me to shed rivers of tears; I was grief-stricken. During his last year of school, we became so close. I'm not sure why we waited so long, but it seemed irrelevant at the time, for all I could think about was him leaving me in a town where the black folk loathed the very ground I walked on. When he hugged me good-bye, I wanted to scream, "Don't leave me, please!" Instead, I held him close, affirming his choice to serve our country. Jason never knew that my heart was broken.

He and Brian saw Cirrus as their spiritual father and witnessed only the beginning stages of boundary lines being crossed. I'm sure they were confused, but they revered and respected him even more than they did me. After all, he fixed their mother's problems, rescued her from a terrible marriage, and understood the Bible better than anyone they'd ever known. Every time I tried to break away from Cirrus, the violent acts perpetrated against me were seen by them as my fault. Looking back, I can see that they were searching for their father as well. The stuff in my closet was running out and spewing over into my son's lives. Embracing the empty space around me, Sean and I were left to deal with Cirrus and each other.

Writing about Sean is extremely painful and difficult for me, because he saw so much, much more than a child should see. Cirrus despised Sean (maybe because he knew that Sean did not feel the same as Brian and Jason). Each time Cirrus came to our house, he searched for ways to demean and tear away at Sean's self-esteem. There was never one good word uttered from Cirrus's mouth. Speaking of his children, Cirrus would say, "My son had a straight A report card. How many Fs did you bring home today, Sean?"

Cirrus's mode of operation was the stripping away of Sean's confidence as a young African American male. Repeatedly put down and told by Cirrus that he should not get his hopes up too high about the future, Sean bought much of what he said. How could he not? After these daily ego beat downs, Sean would watch as Cirrus retired to his mother's bedroom. Each Sunday, he was subjected to Cirrus's messages from the pulpit.

Sean hated Cirrus and knew that he not a rescuer, a brilliant preacher, or a positive role model. To him, Cirrus was a hypocrite, an enslaver, a snake-oil sales clerk, and a crooked philanderer. The things my son saw caused him so much pain and agony that he escaped into another world through drugs and stealing from my cash register. If I had not been a business owner, Sean would have gone to jail. I was so thankful to God that I was the only one from whom he stole.

Every child deserves a safe environment to grow up in. Because of the sickness inside of me, I failed to provide that for Sean. He saw his pastor come and go as he pleased. He dealt with other children whispering about the affair his mother was having with Dr. Smith. From the age of twelve to eighteen, Sean watched the most indecent exposures in his own home. The things he saw and heard would cause him to wander angrily and aimlessly through life for another seven years before moving in a positive direction. He was mad at the entire world and had not one clue why. It would take years for Sean to come to terms with the physical and emotional violence perpetrated against him.

Rosa and Tyrone eventually moved away to the suburbs of Tulsa escaping the *embarrassment* of my life. Before leaving, she said in the choir stand to the other members as I was leading a song, "Some people ought to learn how to walk their talk." I was numb as the rest of the choir sat humiliated *for me!* Even though Rosa and I rarely spoke and she wanted her children to have nothing to do with me, I went back to my condo and cried uncontrollably when told of their move. I was devastated and blamed myself for their decision to leave.

I cringed at the thought of Cirrus coming to my house after dark. Each time he left in the middle of the night, I jumped in the shower, scrubbed my skin, and attempted to wash the night's filth away. He and Michelle were going on with life as usual. As Michelle had said, I was not the first and probably would not be the last. I resented them. Heck, I resented me.

Each year, Cirrus planned a church marriage retreat for his church members. Each year, he lied to me and said he either went for show or didn't go at all. His sister always told how Cirrus and Michelle had bonded and recommitted their love for each other on each retreat. If it wasn't the retreat, it was vacations. He was with his wife but would call, pretending to be somewhere else.

Attempting to cover himself, Cirrus doubled over, buying Michelle and me the same gifts. Once, I went to a church function, and Michelle and I were wearing the same dress with slightly different prints. Cirrus had purchased them while he was on vacation in Mazatlan, Mexico. When I confronted him about it, he said he had to purchase her one, just in case she examined the credit card statement.

He used *my* company checks to put food in the house or gas in *my* car. I paid for everything on the fishing trips we took. Cirrus, for years and years, used *my* money to buy me things. Though it was my money, the sickest part of all was that I was grateful. All along, he continued to taunt me with his puzzle. He told me daily that he knew what was wrong with me, but he could not tell me as it would crush his little rabbit's heart.

One day, Cirrus decided he no longer wanted to be my counselor. He suggested that I go see a friend of his. "Dr. Simms is more than capable of helping you." Amidst my zealous protest, he informed me that my appointment had already been made for Monday. He then said to be careful about how much information

I shared with my new counselor, as it would jeopardize his name and image.

The moment I sat down in Dr. Simms's office, he informed me that Dr. Smith had already briefed him on my condition, giving him the pieces to the puzzle needed to aid in my healing. After I answered a few general questions, Dr. Simms took a huge, red marker and wrote something on an oversized sheet of paper. As if it were an afterthought, he tore the page away from its hinges and lifted it up for me to see, requesting that I read the words he had written aloud. My jaws dropped as I struggled to get the words out of my mouth. Before I knew they were coming, tears rushed pass my eyelids, blinding me as I attempted to roll off my tongue what I saw into the atmosphere. I whispered it at first, shuddering as I spoke. Dr. Simms stopped me and said, "I'm sorry. Can you read it a little louder?" I didn't want to; I wanted to die right there in his office. As if trapped in time, he repeated, "Can you read the words a little louder?" Sinking low in my chair, I pushed pass the tears and read the words: "I have never belonged!"

I said it once, then again, then one more time. The truth of those four words knocked me down out my seat. In that little statement, I saw Daddy's distaste for me, I saw Sam slam against my head, I saw my baby drowning in the commode, I felt all the fierce whispers and a lifetime of insecurities spill out of me, and on, and on, and on.... Scenes from my life flashed between the spaces of each word as I collapsed on the floor into a ball of hopeless grief and tears. Dr. Simms had to lift me up out of the floor and place me back in the chair. After allowing me to gather my composure, he said he wanted to see me the following Monday.

I went back to Cirrus and told him what happened. He forbade me ever to go back.

I never saw Dr. Simms again.

I Have Never Belonged

Little rabbits may be timid creatures, but they know how to do one thing. With their wide back feet, long ears for balance, and powerful legs, rabbits are born to run. Worse than all the others, Cirrus knew why I ran, why I failed, and why I let it happen over and over again.

He could sense the session with Dr. Simms affected me, so he stepped up his game of lies and deception. He began making promises to leave Michelle. *Where did that come from?* I thought. I never wanted him to leave Michelle; we were all clear on that. I had only requested that we be platonic friends, but Cirrus was not having that. I became his silent but bitter partner.

One morning, while on my way to Tulsa to buy supplies for the gallery, my truck spun out of control. Driving seventy-five miles an hour, I tried to come to a complete stop by slamming on my brakes. Instead of bringing the vehicle to a halt, the driveshaft snapped in two, causing the truck to violently shift in the opposite direction. It then jumped the median and went airborne, ramping off an incline and launching into oncoming traffic. The truck then became a death chamber; the only way it could stop would be to collide with some great structure like another vehicle, pavement, or embankment. Once it hit the pavement, its impact caused the truck to roll over. There was sheer pandemonium in the cab as I cried, screamed, and prayed for a swift death. There was no way to make it out of this one alive. Each time the truck rolled, I screamed, "Oh God, receive me. Forgive me of my sins!" By the time it finished rolling, it had flipped over three times and left me hanging upside down, suspended in my seatbelt.

Paramedics came and could not believe what they found. All the windows were broken, half the cab was crushed, yet there were only a few scratches on my hands and feet. The police officers attending the scene of the accident said that if there had been a front seat passenger, his head would have been decapitated. As they yanked me out of the mangled vehicle, one paramedic said, "I have no idea how one could survive this accident as you did. Angels must have been present."

Impacted greatly by the accident, a week later, I wrote Cirrus a letter, telling him that the relationship was over. I was leaving Oklahoma to go to Tennessee. There were many similar letters throughout our relationship, but the accident changed my timidity to courage. Cirrus, of course, flipped out. He rushed over to my house and attacked me. He shoved me down. Each time I attempted to rise, he stood over me, pushing me down. I kept rising and fighting to stand. With each attempt, his fury grew. A deep anger boiled inside me. I decided I was going to rise up or die right there on my kitchen floor. Cirrus swung at me, choked me, and pushed my face into the floor. I rose, at last, and broke for the door!

I ran out of my condominium, into the streets, but Cirrus was bigger, faster, and stronger. He caught me a block away and tackled me onto the pavement, laying his heavy body on mine as I wailed for help. In an effort to silence my crying, he grabbed my hair and slammed my head against the concrete street. The fight in me left, as the world washed languorously by my eyes.

Cirrus was drunk and out of control. Once he understood what he did, he sobered up quick. He looked me over. All threats transformed into panicked breaths. Cirrus gained control of himself. He cried out remorsefully for his actions, "Oh my God! Oh, Father in heaven, I didn't mean to hurt you! I'm so sorry, Wanda!" he said. "Please forgive me! You are the one somebody who cares about me!" He picked me up off the street and took me to Jane Phillip's hospital; the same hospital I went to a week before.

He dropped me off at emergency and parked on the far side of the lot. When the triage nurse questioned me, I told her that I was working late and slipped. "There was a puddle," I said meekly, "I fell into a table and hit my head."

"I see," she said, "did you fall four or five times?"

The question went unanswered.

After four hours in the hospital, I walked across the parking lot where Cirrus sat in his truck, watching me walk unsteadily through the darkness. His coming to the front door of the hospital was too risky for his pristine reputation. "I'm so sorry, Wanda," he said as he placed his hand on my knee and drove me home.

A few weeks later, I packed up my house, closed the shop and moved to Tennessee.

The distance between Oklahoma and Tennessee was nothing but a new big outdoor adventure to Cirrus. He interjected himself into my life in Tennessee. Once a month, he pushed his whale of a butt into his truck and made the long drive down, sipping on Jack Daniels the entire way. Everyone in Tennessee knew I was sleeping with a married man, because Cirrus made it a point to tell them. Far away from his ministry, his worry of destroying *his* reputation no longer concerned him. He was far enough away to finally manage his two-faced life.

As time passed, his trips grew more frequent, and his drinking got worse. Sometimes, he would call before he showed up. Most times, he didn't. But always by the time he arrived, Cirrus was roaring drunk. There were fights and more fights. He would hit me, apologize, then have his way. "Oh my little rabbit," he would say, "running won't solve your problems."

With every visit, Cirrus became more agitated and irrational. One trip, he downed a fifth of Jack Daniels during the seven-hour journey. By the time he made it to my house, he pulled right up over the curb into my front yard. He had not even realized that there was a police car behind him. Without looking back, he stumbled out of his truck and urinated right in front of the cops on my front lawn. I saw it all from my living room window.

I was so embarrassed for him. He was totally out of control. The city police questioned him and threatened to take him to jail, but I came to the door and told him I was James Super Wolfe's sister, and that I had been waiting on Dr. Smith to arrive. That one statement about my brother, who was a city councilman, saved Cirrus from arrest. After the cops left, Cirrus was irate that I chose to use Buddy's name. Even though I saved him from embarrassment, he acted as if I humiliated him.

Not long after this incident, Cirrus arranged a trip to Russellville, Arkansas, to fish at Lake Dardanelle. This trip would ultimately change the very ground I walked on. The first day, we fished. The next day he invited me to go for a drive. Without the boat, he drove his truck to the edge of the lake and parked. His demeanor was different from any other time in the years I'd known him. With a quiver in his lips, he nervously said that he, as a counselor and pastor, had been so unfair to me. Over the years, I'd heard him say this very statement many times. Each time I asked him why, he said the answer would cause us to lose our friendship. This time was different. Cirrus reminded me that I had to remain calm through this process, that he was coming to me as my counselor only, and that he fully understood that what he was about to tell me would most likely destroy our relationship. This thing that he had to tell me was about my *core fiber*, he said. It was about your being a rabbit.

Many times in my life I've listened to the words of associates and acquaintances and knew in my heart that their words were pure rhetoric, but the words Cirrus spoke on this day burned like hot coal or molten lava from a blazing fire within my heart, spirit, and soul. Not like anything I'd heard in my life. The words he spoke ripped the foundation from under my feet. It was too painful for me to sit; much too painful for me to stand. The words he spoke caused me to reflect over my life: shattered pieces of glass, fragmented, broken, dismantled, running, stopping, sick, depressed, running some more, dissatisfaction, disdain, and dead, fallen, stupor, forty-one years. It was as if someone had come and flipped the light switch on in a dark room, and I could finally see, but what I saw was so ugly, I wanted him to shut it off quickly... too much for me to digest...but at least the light had been turned on. There's something about the truth—you know it when you see and hear it, for it pierces the thickest darkness and tumbles the mightiest of walls; the secret was finally revealed to me, and it astonished me that the words were not long and drawn out. Cirrus had held onto these seven words for five years to keep me in his dark closet. He sat calmly, looking directly at the water and away from me, and said, "No one is coming to save you!"

That was it... seven words that caused me to scream as if someone was choking the life out of me; seven words that caused me to hyperventilate. "God, I can't breathe!" I sat crying. "Oh God, Oh God, please take me back to the hotel... Please God help me. Please take me back!"

Cirrus took me back to the hotel. As if I were a fugitive on the run, I ducked in through the side door, found my way to the room, slid the card in the key slot, went into the bathroom, turned the water to the shower on, pulled my clothes off, got in, and started to scrub my skin, until I sunk down into the floor of the shower, limp; no words, no need to talk. Forty-one years had been enough.

I remembered back when Dr. Simms wrote the words: I have never belonged. It fit together. It all made sense; the running from place-to-place. I sat in the shower until the water ran cold, then crawled out as if I were a helpless child. I put my clothes on and walked into the room where I found Cirrus, sitting on the couch with a Jack Daniels in his hand.

He said, "You know it's too late for you to try to change now? You do realize that, don't you?"

I stood silent.

He went on to say, "These are core issues. You are searching for the father you never had. You go from one relationship to another, and when you discover the person can't save you, you run like a rabbit. I tried to give you the clues when I told you to read the fifth chapter of John. You're looking for someone to save you, to pick up your mat for you. Well your mat belongs to you, Wanda. Oh and by the way, I am not charging you for this information. Any other counselor would charge you a fee," he said with a smirk on his face. "You're a classic in the study of Messiah syndrome. I know you don't like living in Tennessee, so what I will do is help you get back to Oklahoma. This will be the last time I help you move. If you ever want to leave again, you're on your own!"

With his Jack Daniels in his hand, he said, "You've actually lived longer *with* the disorder than not. Chances are…you will be this way when you die." I stood in the hotel, amazed at the callousness of this individual. I had a sudden impulse to take one of the hotel lamps and slam it across his drunken face. He had exposed me to the filthy underworld of preachers. This position that Dr. Smith held within the church had been set in place biblically to help mend the hearts of broken individuals like myself. He, like many preachers, misused his power to feed his own demons. Dr. Smith was the only person I allowed into my secret closet. He had gone in and done a chainsaw massacre of every life-altering event that had ever happened to me.

I stood there, listening to his drunken words until they eventually trailed off into nothing, not because he stopped talking, but because my mind shut down to his words of discouragement and opened up to the reality of words like *messiah trap. What did that look like?* Without ever reading a book on this condition, I imagined a woman caged, imprisoned, in bondage, with shackles on her feet and locked inside Dr. Cirrus Smith's dark and hidden closet. For one brief second, I believed him. I would never find my way out. I was doomed. I had walked with this condition for forty-one years, all my life. That would be over half my life if I were blessed to live another forty more years. *Why should I try? What is the need?* I thought to myself. Of all things that had occurred in my life, this one revelation was the most earth shattering for me. It was the *eye of the storm*, the vortex of a category five tornado.

For a brief moment, I wanted to lie down and let the storm take me out. For one brief moment I wanted to shut up, stop, and exit this world. But it was just one brief moment, and then the intuition to survive, as it had always done, kicked in. I smiled at Cirrus and, on that day, at that moment, I willed myself to survive; and addressed him as *Dr. Smith*. I don't even think he noticed it, but from that point on, the name Cirrus would never be used again.

Dr. Smith, as he had promised, helped us move back to Oklahoma. I determined that I didn't want to live in his city, so we moved to Tulsa. He graciously found a tiny crime- and roach-infested apartment with the closet doors hanging off the hinges for us to live in. When I protested, he promptly told me to shut up and be thankful that he made the choice to help me. He became angry when I selectively chose what would come off the moving vans and what would go in storage. I moved only the necessities into the apartment: one couch, a TV, two beds, and a few dishes. The rest went in storage. He became irate when he found no artwork hanging on the walls; I wrote scriptures on large blank sheets and hung them instead. "This is our artwork!" "For my thoughts are not your thoughts neither are your ways my ways declares the Lord. As the heavens are higher than the earth, so are my ways higher than your ways and my thoughts than your thoughts." And then I placed under that a reading from Isaiah 59:1, which read, "Surely the arm of the Lord is not too short to save, nor His ear too dull to hear."

The hanging of scriptures in my new apartment infuriated Dr. Smith. Each time he came to visit, he looked at the different scriptures on the wall and balked like a spoiled child. As I searched diligently to find my healing, Dr. Smith sought to undermine each scripture on my wall, from a theological approach.

"Ms. Wolfe, Make sure that when you put these scriptures up, you know why the writer felt like he did. Are you sure you understand the context and conditions surrounding these passages? The Israelites were in the temple and…. What's wrong with you?"

More scriptures went up. I was troubled about the crime patterns of the neighborhood, so I searched and found protection in Psalm 91:5-12. I posted it right inside the entry to my apartment. When Dr. Smith saw this, he said, "You probably don't want to take these scriptures too literally. These were written for the Jewish people in those days. Don't make too much of it."

One day, I opened my Bible and ran across the most beautiful psalm. It reflected where I was, having no one to turn to as a friend. The reading was the most powerful prose I ever read. It sent shock waves through me, calming all fears. It read:

> I will lift up my eyes to the hills. Where does my help come from? My help comes from the Lord, the maker of Heaven and Earth. He will not let my foot slip- He who watches over me, will not slumber; Indeed He who watches over Israel will neither slumber nor sleep. The Lord watches over me. The Lord is my shade at my right hand; The sun will not harm me by day nor the moon by night. The Lord will keep me from all harm- He will watch over my life. The Lord will watch over my coming and going both now and forever more.

The simple beauty of such prose covered me like a fresh blanket. I wrapped myself inside the warmth of the phrases and let it sooth my troubles.

I must have looked like I was out to lunch to Dr. Smith by posting these large signs throughout this tiny apartment. I'm sure he felt I was one step from flying right over the Coo Coo's nest, yet I was far from having a breakdown. I was beginning to see Dr.

Smith for who he really was: my enemy. Come hell or high water, I was determined that I was not going to live the latter part of my life in the dark. Recovery and survival became my number one priority.

I searched the Sunday paper and found a job as a pastry chef at the Philbrook Museum. The first day on the job, I set to improve the place, by reinvigorating their desert menu. Working alone, I found ways of providing my new employer with some of the finest and most delicious pastries without breaking their bank. I went back to basics and created old-fashioned desserts with a flare of elegance. A client from Bartlesville was having lunch at the museum. She ordered dessert and, after tasting, swore she knew the pastry chef. She told the waiter it had to be a *Wanda* cake.

That chance encounter led to my meeting with a banker in Bartlesville who wanted to help me go back into business. Even though my credit was not the best, Cecil Epperly, the president of Arvest Bank, took a chance on me. He was a delightful person and admonished me to work hard, make beautiful cakes, and pay the loan back. That customer who saw, tasted, and recognized the desserts at the museum was Susie Hautman, Kathy Epperly's best friend. She had gone back to Bartlesville to share her experience at the Philbrook.

With the loan from Arvest, I set out to start a business again. First, I needed a place. I found a 1,400 square foot space in a small shopping center. Brian, who had come home from college to work with me to open the cake shop, protested the excess space. I didn't mind the extra room. The place just felt right. Knowing it was going to be a success, we signed the lease and went to work on renovating the space. We worked from early in the morning until late at night, cutting corners by ordering our own tile and laying the floors ourselves.

In September 2002, we reopened Wanda's Cake Gallery. Though amazed at the grace extended to us, still, our shop was balanced on the abyss of success or disaster. Neither Brian nor I lived extravagantly, yet there was never enough money to make ends meet. Nearly every penny went toward survival. We both hated that! We prepared desserts for the wealthiest of the wealthy but struggled to pay our own home light bill. It was exhausting and taxing on the mind. Yet, caught up in the day-to-day structure of Wanda's Cake Gallery, business was all I knew.

And with Dr. Smith living on the brink of severe insecurity, he started to come to Tulsa almost every day to make sure he wasn't completely losing ground. I sought to find normalcy amidst a maelstrom. However, life isn't like the movies, where change comes instantly. In the real world, failures and success happen by a matter of degrees.

Guilty by Reason of Insanity

My favorite Author, Dr.Iyanla Vanzant, penned a wonderful book about her meantime experience. "What do we do while we are waiting?" she asked. I found myself asking similar questions: What do you do in the meantime when this offender, pastor, and counselor has used you as his whore for five years, then opens up a can of worms in your life, and they are crawling out of control? There seemed to be worms everywhere. What do you do when the biggest, fattest, and slimiest night crawler of them all is still setting up camp in your living room and has the audacity to complain if anyone even inquires about sitting in *his* Lazy Boy chair?

I became obsessed with healing. Many nights I scoured libraries, searching for books to help me deal with my core. When I could not find the subject anywhere, I looked back and examined my past.

For forty-two years, I traveled the same road, running from place-to-place, from man-to-man, always looking for others to save me. This winding, crooked road came to a dead end and dumped me off in Dr. Cirrus Smith's dark, perverted closet. For over five years, he hid me away deep in his secret dungeon.

To all who viewed from afar, I looked like a whore, a wayward woman who interjected herself into his marriage. The truth was the complete opposite of public perception, but who cared at this point; I sure didn't. *No one was coming to save me.* The only way out of this trap was to save myself.

After much searching, I stumbled upon two priceless pearls. The first one was T.D. Jakes's *Woman, Thou Art Loosed.* The second was Dr. Vanzant's *Interiors: A Black Woman's Healing Within.* I delved into these books and embraced the possibilities. For the first time in my life, I began to believe that I was going to be okay.

Although not a lot in the beginning, I embraced myself. I took baby steps, moving the journey of my healing along. When you have hated yourself all your life, it takes time and systematic effort in learning to love and accept the beauty that resides already inside of you. We, as women, tend to buy other people's analysis of who we are. Family members like Rosa had used the word *shiftless* on many occasions, in regards to my character. In the back of my mind, even though I was a respected and well-known businesswoman, I secretively saw myself as ugly, insignificant, and as they said, *shiftless.* I wore a constant mask for the outside world. My clients would make remarks about my beautiful smile and graceful demeanor, having no idea of the tumultuous battle and war of words inside my mind. For forty-one years, I bought other people's rhetoric, taking possession of their analysis of me as if they were my own. In truth, another person's value of our character has absolutely nothing to do with us; that is, unless we take ownership of their analogy of us. I had to learn to treat the words of other people like a piece of catfish, eating the good meat and throwing the harmful indigestible bones in the garbage can.

During this very important time of healing, I allowed my sister Rosa to kick, cry, and connive her way back into my life. Even though I hated how she ostracized me, I willed myself to forgive her, giving her another chance. One day, while visiting her, I saw on a shelf, a book titled *The Messiah Trap.* I immediately pulled it down and noticed that the honorable Dr. Cirrus Smith had donated it, along with most of the other books. He had stamped his name on the cover pages, *Property of Rev. Cirrus and Michelle Smith*. Amazed and shaken, I pulled the book off the shelf and approached Rosa. With a straight-flush poker face, I calmly asked to borrow this book. Rosa exchanged a stare with her husband that spoke volumes, but agreed to lend it to me. I went home and plowed through the entire book that night. The more I read, the more I saw myself. Each word moved me further along on my journey of healing. In the meantime, I worked hard to keep my company afloat.

I moved from the awful apartment to a moderately nice home where I proudly pulled everything out of storage and replaced the scriptures with my beautiful art. Underneath... no beauty in the world could cover over the continual burning sensation to heal the woman within. The search through my problems garnered my son's attention. Many times, Brian said, "Don't make too big of a deal out of Dr. Smith and this thing called *Messiah Trap*." I protested, because this was a big deal; it was Mount Everest.

I had run all my life searching for my father, releasing control to my offenders. Each one felt entitled to a free reign over my life, taking no responsibility for their own behavior. In each relationship, when I had had enough, I ran. These escape routes caused pain, insecurities, and many other problems for my three sons and me. Because of my running, Brian, Jason, and Sean never knew what it felt like to be settled in a community where they felt like they belonged. Living with *Messiah Syndrome* affected their schooling, home life, and friendships. It would be years before they realized the impact of these perpetrated offenses against their lives.

My own sons listened while the Simpletons dehumanized my character, leaving an indelible impression that continues to this day to concern me. Rosa and Tyrone told my boys that I was an unfit mother, a bad person and an emotional wreck. My sons believed the words they heard and felt these emotional molesters had my best interest at heart. Elevating Dr. Smith and Rosa's family to be ones of reverence and purity, they were torn in their perception of me, even casting a few stones of their own. I was not angry, because like me in the beginning of my journey, they all comfortably wore blinders, seeing what they wanted to see. In this case, it was easier for them to blame me and me alone. Years would pass before Brian confessed that his Auntie Rosa and Uncle Tyrone began poisoning their minds against me right after the move from Atlanta to Oklahoma. My sons believed at one point, they, by listening to the Simpletons, were disconnecting themselves from my bad decisions. They didn't know that they were being injured, not just by me, but by the Simpleton's lies as well. I was obligated to pen these pages for them and millions of other misguided broken-winged birds. The truth had to be told.

An avalanche of questions filled my mind. *How would Rosa and Tyrone feel if I chose to chip away at their children's self-esteem by filling their heads with garbage about their parents?* The possibility of doing so was not a part of my character or nature. *How could my own sister treat me like this? Why would she try to turn my family, even my neighbors against me? Why was she so hateful toward me? What did she want from me?* In the middle of seething about Rosa's behavior, I sat down and prayed for her. I asked God to help me understand her and bring us together. I wanted to forgive her, and I wanted her to forgive me.

Maya Angelo once wrote, "Once you show me who you are, I believe you!" One wants to believe that no matter what…family will be there for you. God built us that way! Even though Rosa had shown me her true character on many occasions, I still wanted to make her out to be something other than what she was. I thought about our relationship. I remembered Rosa angering clients while she worked the front counter at my cake gallery. One day a client asked to speak specifically with me, and Rosa screamed out "Wanda, Wanda, Wanda, it's always Wanda. It's always about

Wanda. I'm so sick of hearing that name." That day I started to believe there was a hint of envy in her heart for me.

Rosa went to college, received a Bachelor of Science degree in Computer Engineering. Upon completing her education, she went to work as a programmer for Phillips 66 and married her high school sweetheart, Tyrone Simpleton. After working six years with Phillips, she became pregnant with her first child and determined that she wanted to become a full-time mother. This decision was a noble one, but clearly, I could see that she wrestled with her choice by her indecisive words and actions, becoming more and more critical of my success through Wanda's Cake Gallery.

Even though the storehouse in her life was overflowing, Rosa could not see it. Because education and self-sufficiency was a huge deal in our family, she was constantly concerned about how the rest of the Wolfe's saw her. Because I understood her discomfort of fully embracing her unpopular decision to be a full-time mom, I built her up, encouraging her to be the best mother she could be. It was a good decision, from my perspective. The net result was three beautiful children: Meggie, Nicolette, and Tyrone Jr. She and Tyrone, Sr. were active in the church, and Rosa became a professional hockey mom.

I once read that the eyes are the windows to the soul.

As the years passed, the light in Rosa's eyes went totally out. She remained beautiful, but I could see that she was worn out, tired, and growing old. She did lots of whispering about other people's shortcomings. Because Tyrone was one of Dr. Smith's disciples, he was involved in the ministry of counseling. Everything he heard from the brokenhearted, he ran back, relaying confidentials to Rosa. The outcome was never a good word. There was lots of finger pointing and critical remarks about other hurting people. Over the years, Rosa became the judge and jury of everyone else's problems and circumstances.

If confronted, Rosa always shut the door in your face. Asking forgiveness was not a word that you would ever hear from her or Tyrone. Someone once said, "Be ye healed or bleed all over everybody!" Well, Tyrone and Rosa had become self-righteous church folk, bleeding all over everyone. On the surface, they were all smiles, but trouble was beginning to show even through their children's actions. They did not know it, but they were leaving blood trails behind them.

One day, I took their eleven-year-old daughter, Nicolette, to dinner. Out of nowhere, she started to question me about why I had a problem with Dr. Smith. Caught off guard, I wrestled to retrieve an answer from my discombobulated brain. Too late… Nicolette quickly responded, "Auntie Wanda, I know what your problem is, but you may as well get over it, because Dr. Smith is the man!"

Tyrone and Rosa had not spared their children's ears when discussing adult issues.

My parents had all kinds of issues when I was a child, but I never once heard them discuss grown up business in front of us. They respectfully told us to leave the room, and we promptly did so. I sat at the dinner table in utter disbelief as this miniature Simpleton grilled me about matters much too complicated for her underdeveloped brain.

I was shattered to hear this child question me as if she were a grown woman. I got up from the table and told her that I was taking her home. Leaving a part of my heart at the table, I silently resolved, *Never again. There are those who are for you and those who are against you. Blessed is the woman who knows who's who in the scheme of things*! It had taken many painful years to acknowledge that these people, though related by blood, were not for me. Clearly, they were against me. This was a painful reality. Nothing could make it okay.

The next day, Brian and I shuffled through a box of photos. Hundreds of pictures cluttered my dining room table, as I emptied every box, attempting to jar my memory to aid me in healing. There were a few pictures of my children when they were small, a few of other family members, but the crux of the mountain was made up of Rosa, Tyrone, Meggie, Nicolette, and Tyrone Jr. I could not believe that I had taken that many photos of their family and so few of my own. Right or wrong, Rosa had been my heart's desire, and her children were even more than that to me.

When Rosa was a little girl, I watched out for her. I did not want her to feel the pain I'd felt growing up. I felt more than the simple need to protect her as my sister. Somewhere in the back of my own shattered mind, in my own sickness, I had wanted to be her *Messiah* and save her.

In second grade, when Daryl Anthony asked the teacher if he could move to the next row, because I smelled like pee, I never forgot that and vowed to protect Rosa from such shame. Unsure of how to properly care for ourselves, we went to bed in our clothes, peed on ourselves in our sleep, got up, roasted like rotisserie chickens in front of the potbelly wood stove, and off we went to school. It was a horrible life for a kid with a name like Wolfe.

Once when Rosa was a little girl, the neighborhood rug rats, Dee and Peel, made a sandwich out of her in the kiddie pool in our front yard. I happened to catch a glimpse through the window of our house. Peel, the younger boy, was on the bottom while Dee lay on top. I ran out and forcefully pulled the older boy off her. Rosa stumbled out of the pool and ran inside as I chased the boys away, threatening to kill them.

I went into the house and found her in a closet. She was ashamed. I pulled her out and sat with her and talked with her about boys, about her body, and what a decent young lady would and should not do. That day, I told her how beautiful she was and how I expected great things from her; that I could see her being so successful in life. I explained to her what the boys' intentions were; that the end results could have been devastating. I committed myself to helping her grow and blossom into a virtuous young lady. I taught her all the things that a girl should know about her body: personal hygiene, the birds and the bees, choices, good and bad. I wanted her to succeed in life.

By the time Rosa left home for college I was married and living in Michigan with Ray. She, on the other hand was madly in love with Tyrone, whom Mama loathed but, out of regard for Rosa, tolerated. Mama's constant complaint to me was that Tyrone, who was only eighteen years old, offered her no respect as a fifty-four-year-old mother of nine children. After Rosa graduated from college, she moved to Oklahoma, married, and financially supported Tyrone as he struggled to attain his Electrical Engineering Degree.

Tyrone was the first and only son in his family to attain a college degree, and he was seen as *the one that made it out.* When Rosa was at holiday gatherings with his family, Tyrone's mother, out of envy, would belittle my mother and her children's accomplishments, putting Rosa down especially. She experienced that same envy during holidays that Rosa unconscientiously exemplified toward me. It was exacerbating to watch my sister and her husband fall into the same old churchy rut as so many other preachers. They, without assessment, lived duplicitous lives like their mentor, Dr. Smith. They maintained two separate standards of living and operating; one, the good ol' religious way, and the other, do what you want to do, and say what you want to say. However two-faced, they were the only relatives I had, and family meant the absolute world to me.

After their children were born, Rosa and Tyrone used them as a rod of correction to keep me in line. When things were going their way, they allowed me to interact with their children, if not they would shut off all contact. Nothing I did was good enough for the Simpletons. I literally gave them the rugs from under my feet to manipulate them into loving and accepting me. Anything they asked for, they got. During this season of my life, I didn't know why I gave them everything they asked for, I simply knew I felt compelled to do so. Tyrone noticed this trait and told me, "I can ask you for anything... and I am quite sure that you will give it to me... if I said that I wanted all the paintings off your wall you would jump to please me." He then added, "When I get finished using you, I'm going to throw you away like an old dish towel!" He laughed. I had not found his statement funny.

The Simpletons built their world around their children, the Smiths and the world of ministry. Rosa and Tyrone praised Meggie, Nicolette, and Tyrone Jr.'s achievements and talked of my children as if they were outlaws. Their love, grace, and mercy extended no further than their own front door. I regretted the move from Atlanta to Oklahoma. All my life I had believed that my sister was the one person outside of my mother who loved me unconditionally. She, within a span of just a few months, shattered that belief. Her love was not only conditional, but her heart was riddled with envy and deception.

By the time I made it to Oklahoma, I had very few clothes. Most of my clothing hung neatly in Rosa's closet, so I asked to borrow a few dresses that I purchased for her the year before. She had a better idea. Since she was no longer pregnant, she took all of her old hand-me-down maternity dresses, twice removed from her previously pregnant friends, put them in an old, black garbage bag, and brought them to my house for me to wear. I smiled and said thank you, but inside I was angry and disappointed. Granted, if you're in need, you should be grateful for whatever you receive, but I had made a silent rule for myself to never give a person something that I didn't want. I never wore the maternity dresses because... well... because I was not pregnant, nor was there a chance that I would be in the future. I took the bag and set it outside for the next day garbage pickup.

A couple of weeks later, Rosa confronted me about not wearing the clothes. I tried my best to let her down easy, but she insisted that I return them back to her. There I was, caught in the middle of a nothing situation and trying to make up a lie to smooth things over, when I really should have told her, "I threw the damn dresses away. I'm not pregnant!" I did not have the guts to tell her what I really thought. In retrospect, if I had known what I know now, I would not have fought so hard to have a relationship with them. I was so desperate for love and family that the many webs woven of lies and deceptions didn't matter to me.

One day, I went to their home and, upon entering, found that every picture of me had been removed from their walls. I hugged everyone, then turned around and got back in my car. I drove down the street, parked, sat, and cried until it seemed I had no more tears left. The Simpletons had shown me numerous times that they wanted nothing to do with me. I moved from Atlanta to Oklahoma; they moved to Tulsa. Hurt and inconsolable, I moved to Tennessee, then back to Oklahoma, making Tulsa my new home. Even though I knew they had no desire to connect with me, I secretively hoped that some day we would sit at the table as a family together. We would *learn* to love each other. I allowed the Simpletons to come in and out of my life, back and forth, during my first few years in Tulsa. There were days where Rosa loved me, but the moment she heard my beloved clients speak with respectful adoration of me, she would burn with anger, shutting the door for months on me.

During one of our *in times*, Rosa and Tyrone invited me to go to their church. It was a very small church with not many members, but I enjoyed myself. Rosa introduced me to their new pastor and his wife. They both seemed genuine. Pastor Jones had a warm smile, and Clemmie, his wife was very engaging. Rosa informed them that I owned Wanda's Cake Gallery. Clemmie told me they were familiar with our cakes and our reputation. We became instant friends.

Rosa and Tyrone then took me to the finance office where Tyrone worked. Sitting at a table near the entrance to the office, was an older man who was later introduced to me as Clay Braxton, the only trustee of New Road Fellowship and Pastor Jones's best friend. Clay, Pastor, and Mrs. Jones, along with two other members, were the founders of this newly planted church. Clay seemed a little odd but nice enough. We chatted about unimportant things. After a while, I realized that Rosa and Tyrone were pushing me to talk to him. Their reasoning was that we both were broken individuals who needed love.

When Bill Cosby came to Tulsa, and Tyrone allegedly asked Clay to purchase me a ticket, Clay said, "No woman is worth a fifty-dollar ticket!" When I got whiff of his comment, I, in turn, made a point by giving Tyrone $100.00 to purchase tickets for Clay and me. I asked Tyrone to deliver the ticket with a message that read: "Friendship is worth far more!" Pastor Jones and Clemmie accompanied us to see the show, opening the door for a new friendship.

Clemmie and I grew fond of each other quickly. Each time I visited their church, Pastor Jones acknowledged my presence by talking of his wife's newfound friendship and suggesting to the congregation that they get to know me a little better as an entrepreneur. After three visits to their church, Rosa pulled me aside and expressed her anger, "Tyrone and I have been coming to this church. Pastor Jones has never called our name like that. We are tithers—we have done so much for this place. And you come here for a couple of Sundays, and he can't shut up about it! I'm sick and tired of this!" It was a new church, but the same old Rosa. To keep the boat from rocking, I promptly wrote the pastor and his wife a letter, asking them to never call my name again during church service. I explained to them how important my sister was to me and that I didn't ever want her to feel slighted or uncomfortable. They didn't understand, but agreed with hesitation, to never welcome me by name again. Meanwhile, Clay and I were getting to know each other better by spending our free time hanging with the Joneses after Sunday service.

Clay was a math teacher for a community college and lived miles away from Tulsa. He traveled almost sixty miles to attend church. In the few years the church existed, Clay never missed a single service. Each Sunday, after church, he would stay behind, balance the church books, and then head over to the Jones's house for dinner. One Sunday, Clay missed service, and Pastor Jones called me and asked me to check on him. Apparently, Clay was not answering his phone, and the people at church were worried.

After doing a small amount of probing, I found out that Clay's mother was ill. He was going to drive to Minnesota to visit her in the hospital. However, the scenario did not add up, because his school informed me that he was expected in class to teach by the evening. I told Pastor Jones that I would drive out to Clays to check on him to alleviate their fears. Moreover, while I wanted to check on him for the Jones's, a small part of me wanted to get to know him. He was attractive, educated, had a job, a car, and a good faith in God. Those are rare traits in men these days.

Pastor Jones gave me directions to Clay's house, and I took a trip to the tiny Oklahoma town where he lived. There was no one home, so I pulled my car in the driveway and waited for him to return. As I sat alone in the darkness, I shook with fear. The *black of the night* and I had never been friends. The thought of being alone in the unprotected night brought back a painful memory of my past.

One night, after performing at a football game as a flag majorette, I waited near the high school gymnasium for Daddy to come and pick me up to take me home. As time passed, the crowd of other children began to thin out. Eventually, there was not a female in sight. Slightly apprehensive, I made my way into the gym. The moment I stepped inside, a group of boys approached me. At first they were laughing and saying I had no need to be scared. Then someone pulled at my coat, and the next thing I knew, I was on the gymnasium floor, and the boys, at least eight males, were all over me. I cried, kicked, and screamed for them to let me go, but someone said, "Ya'll ready to pull this train?" Their tug at my clothing became even more ravenous as the testosterone built in their bodies. Then all of a sudden, someone of value and worth shouted out, "Man, ya'll get up off her! Let her go!" He physically started to pull the boys off of me one-by-one. The young man's name was Samuel Ealy, a star athlete for our school. After the boys disappeared into the night, Samuel asked me why I was in the gym in the first place. I told him I was waiting on my father, but he never came. He carefully put me in his car and drove me safely home. From that point on, *darkness* and me lived on opposite sides of the street.

I often think about what would have happened to me had Samuel Ealy not intervened that night. The mere fact that I was *almost* raped is sometimes too much for my brain to carry; one can only wonder what would have been the condition of my soul had those boys been victorious in their conquest. Today, Samuel Ealy is a minister, and the idea that he is, challenges me to think that there are *some* good ones out there. I sat in Clay's driveway, scoping out my surroundings and hoping he would return soon.

On the side of Clay's small house, only a few feet away, was an old Indian cemetery. As darkness continued to fill the space and shadows of tombstones stretched across the landscape like fingers of the dead, crawling out of the ground, I began to have second thoughts. I looked at the clock on my dash. If Clay did not come by 10:00, I would leave.

At 9:45 p.m., a car pulled directly behind me. Clay, perhaps concerned about my presence, left his lights on as he paced toward my vehicle. A strong voice snapped me back to reality, "What are you doing here?"

I responded "I'm checking on you. Pastor and Mrs. Jones were worried about you. I was worried also. Are you okay? Is everything all right?"

He shot back coldly, "Everything is fine."

I said, "Well, I've driven all the way down here; I'm starving... Can we go grab a bite to eat?"

He slightly smiled and nodded his head in agreement.

Never have I said this to anyone, but I was so relieved that Clay said yes. We sat there at the diner, and I was so happy to sit with an unmarried man. I was ecstatic about not hiding. When ordering my coffee, I ordered it *not* in secret. When I went through the buffet line, I felt so good that the person critiquing the food was a single man. It did not matter how his breath smelled, nor did it matter that he was wearing a sports jacket with a pair of polyester jogging pants. I did not care; nothing mattered outside of *Clay was not a married man.* I eagerly paid for his dinner.

Every decision to come would be based solely on my *closet* experience with Dr. Smith. Clay had been by himself for over fourteen years, and I was pleased to hear of his abstinence from affairs and sexual activity. The very thought of dealing with the possibility of contracting AIDS stopped me right dead in my tracks when I entertained leaving Dr. Smith's closet. So when Clay put his arms around me to say good night, I felt secure. I drove away, seeing a way out of the darkness.

A couple of days later, Clay called and asked me out to dinner. I put my phone on silent, and he and I went to Atlantic Sea Grill, a moderately expensive restaurant in Tulsa. That night, before we could really get off to a decent start, Clay held my hands and told me how rough and awful they looked. They look like a man's hands, he told me. I looked at the calloused roughness of my hands and thought back on my life. The picking cotton, the army, the endless decades of grueling labor etched into my palms, gave him a glimpse into my past. His words cut to the core.

Clay told me he could tell that I had worked hard all my life. I was hurt as I sat there, listening to him tear me down. As much as I did not like what Clay said, I knew there was nothing he could say that would drive me away. Anything was better than being locked in a dark closet. If I had wanted to be cruel, there were plenty of things I could have said to him, but I chose to be polite. Once again, I paid for the meal, and Clay and I left the restaurant.

After eagerly saying good night, I took my phone off silent and immediately, it started to ring off the hook.

Dr. Smith had called nearly a dozen times while I was on my date. He had felt that something was not right, "He couldn't put his finger on it," he said, but he had a gut feeling that some cataclysmic thing was about to happen. I was silent as he rambled on into the dead of night.

The following day, Dr. Smith came in with a fifth of Jack Daniels and a fist to fight. He didn't know why, but he said he felt like he wanted to draw blood, and before the night was over, he was sure to show me who was in control. He staggered into my home, pre-empting war. Time had shown me that he was as erratic as the next neurotic person. Struggling to maintain control of his little rabbit caged and locked away in his dark closet, the night fast-forwarded as Dr. Smith walked around, looking intently to see if anything was out of place. Instead of going to the bathroom, where one would go to urinate, he opened up the backdoor to my house, whipped out his business, and peed right there on my concrete patio, marking his territory like a pit bull terrier.

I don't know where the gumption came from, but I raced to the backdoor and informed Dr. Smith that this lewd act was unacceptable behavior. He drunkenly stared me down and staggered back in the house. He was angry, but I was tired and fed up with the darkness and everything around me—especially this big, black, oversized blubber of a whale.

I walked back into my den and sat as he stood over me. Reaching down, he grabbed my braided hair and tightened his grip by twisting it snuggly between his fingers and pulling as hard as he could. "Did you know that you are stupid, worthless, shiftless, and ignorant? I'll bet you didn't even know that, did you? I have wondered for days why I would deal with someone as shiftless as you. Michelle has even asked me. I know you didn't think I was going to leave Michelle for someone as shiftless as you, did you?"

I did not say a word.

He continued, "I would never leave Michelle for someone as pathetic as you!"

My desire to fight back was gone, dead... probably resting in the Indian cemetery besides Clay's house. I sat, shivering and crying, until he finished with his drunken rage and left. Once he walked out the door, I got up off the couch, walked into my bedroom, lay across the bed, and cried myself to sleep.

Blood On the Side of the Bed

His apology came—though it took longer than usual—a few days later. Cirrus arranged a fishing trip to Paris, Texas, for the two of us. The ride to Paris was quiet. Not a lot needed to be said. I was ready to fish. I had actually grown fond of fishing and looked forward to my time on the water.

We arrived at a dilapidated motel. He went in the office, checked us in, and I reluctantly went inside the small room (As I revisit these events, I now realize Dr. Smith understood that the conditions of this room would disturb me). Not much bigger than two average bathrooms put together, the room was thick with a repugnant odor. The bed was full-sized, but the room was so small I had to inch around the mattress. There was blood all over the side of the bed. Frightened out of my wits, I thought, My God, was the blood from the killing of a deer or a person? It was insane for me to go from one far-fetched scenario to another. I showed Cirrus, and after looking at the blood for a half-second, he said, "Get over it, Wanda, it's not that big of a deal. It's just blood, for God sake!"

I took the cover I brought from home, wrapped myself inside, and lay on top of the comforter, not allowing myself to come in contact with the bed. Dr. Smith eventually fell asleep with his Jack Daniels in his hand. I got up and lifted his glass, carefully, out of his hand. He looked awful: spit rested in the corner of his mouth as he drooled from too much alcohol. In the dimness of the room, I looked again at the blood on the side of the bed. I found myself wondering why. *Why had Dr. Smith chosen me?* The things he did as my counselor and Pastor baffle me to this day. I've yet to understand the cold ground underneath his heart and mind, but that night I decided that this twisted immoral relationship would come to an end. I made this decision, looking at the blood on the side of the bed. Just like that, I determined that I would no longer allow my counselor to use me for his sick, demented fantasies. No longer would I subject myself to his abuse. I didn't know how, but this pile of lard had to go!

We woke early in the morning. We were out on the lake before sunrise. Cirrus, the master angler, didn't get a single bite all day. I left Paris, Texas, with the thought of never fishing with Dr. Smith again. He was so drunk he didn't even know.

Upon returning to Tulsa, Clay had a small bouquet of flowers delivered to me. I was so grateful. He called later and set up a third date.

One of my problems had always been that no man had to work to get me. I was never a promiscuous woman, but I always settled for the first man that showed an interest in me. I knew no better. The *savior complex* came up repeatedly. Some man; somewhere was going to come and save me. That thought today seems unreal, but while I was living it, every detail of my life connected with *Someone... Please come and save me!*

One night, Clay came to my house and said, "We are both older, you like me, and I like you. We can either have a long and drawn out courtship or we can go ahead and do what we know is inevitable." Clay, the math teacher and historian, had broken down our lives into a simple equation. He made the argument that a long and drawn out courtship would be unnecessary and costly. Why waste money on dating, when we can save all that cash and buy our dream home? I pushed aside his ugly remarks about my worn out hands, his remarks about not believing in a higher power; I pushed aside many other little things that spelled trouble, went against my gut feeling, and said, "Yes." Saying yes to Clay was a *no* to Dr. Smith's dark closet!

How to Kill a Vampire

Saying yes meant one thing in particular for me. Yes, was the blessed word that I used to drive through the vampire's heart that fed off of me in the middle of the night for seven years of my life. Saying yes would ultimately destroy the cannibalistic behavior of this bloodletting monster. Killing a vampire is not an easy thing, but it can be accomplished in several ways.

One way is to touch led items to the gravestone of the walking corpse. My problem with this method was that Dr. Smith had not yet taken possession of his own grave, nor did he do much standing. This creature of the night was usually in a drunken stupor slouched in my Lazy Boy chair with a Jack Daniels in his hand. The second option in ridding myself of this ghastly night stalker would be to behead the beast and hammer a wooden stake through his dark and corroded heart. I saw jailtime in using this method.

The third, and final, method that was considered a surefire way of ridding oneself of such evil that walked and fed by night was to expose the hideous creature to light. This is the method I chose to use.

In Asian culture, they believe that a Vampire can be lured and trapped by sprinkling Red peas, rice, roses, and garlic while the body lay in its grave. I knew that these healthy items would not work for this type of Dracula. This was a great big fat vampire, who, during the day hours, slurped down Burger King, McDonalds, and other greasy foods. He would *never* go for red peas, rice, and roses. No this bloodsucker would have to be lured in with fatty foods and Jack Daniels.

The first few nights were quiet as I waited for him to come. He did not. He chose to go back to Paris, Texas, with one of his fellow lackeys. He called and bragged about the four-star hotel they chose, miles away from their fishing site. I in turn, told him that when he returned, a stake (Did I misspell that), a nice juicy steak would be waiting on him with Jack Daniels. They would be sitting right next to his Lazy Boy chair. I hung up the phone, eagerly awaiting his arrival.

A week passed with no word from Dracula. I fell asleep, not even thinking about my blessed sword that I would use to pierce him with, should he come. At about two o'clock one morning, I woke up and saw the huge beast standing over me. For one quick moment, I shook with fear. He stood over me, telling me he didn't want to talk, that I was not to say one word, just turn over. I took the blessed sword (the word of God that I had hidden) and told him sleepily that my body was the temple of The Living God and would never be used again for bloodletting. I told this blood sucker to lay the key to my house on the dresser and never return. He screamed back as Brian slept in the next room, "You better be sure about this!"

My reply was, "You have no idea how sure I am. You were my counselor, and you took advantage of me to feed your demons! You destroyed parts of my children's and my life that we can never get back! And all the while, you looked like the victim. You're no real minister. You are a parasitic monster! Get out, right now." He left, and just like that, the bloodletting was over! For one moment, I exhaled and fell asleep. My Babylon experience was over.

Many times, I blamed myself just as Rosa, Tyrone, and the rest of his congregation would have wanted me to do, but the truth is that Dr. Smith had a responsibility as a pastor and professional counselor to create a safe environment for healing. He did not do that. Instead, he took very personal and sensitive information about my past hurts, pains, and disappointments and used them to create a duplicitous lifestyle for himself. With manipulative wording and seductive phrases, he instead created an environment that appeared safe, one filled with illusive mirages. With my eyes closed from suffering with the *Messiah trap* all those years, he was able to manipulate me by acting as my Savior in all areas of my life. The price, emotionally and physically, was great. I doubted ever trusting another preacher's words from the pulpit.

After I was able to break free from this awful bondage, I wrote Rosa and Tyrone a letter, telling them of the painful abuse that I experienced. I explained to them how Dr. Smith used information from my past to lock me in his own personal closet and keep me as his whore. I shared with them all that I could stomach about these very painful seven years of my life. They, in turn, appeared compassionate toward me. Rosa in particular said, "How could he do this to my sister, when he knew how much she had already gone through?" She then hugged me, commended me for my strength, and resolve to tell Dr. Smith I was no longer asleep; my eyes were finally open.

Tyrone, a preacher and counselor, himself, offered to help. Rosa and I sat in his office together as I told him the story.

During counseling with my sister and her husband, I felt maybe, just possibly, everything was going to be all right. What we were discussing was so sensitive and confidential. It had taken so much out of me to open up this volatile closet. Nevertheless, in my heart I felt that they were family and were ultimately on my side. Rosa even affirmed this notion by saying that, because this abuse was perpetrated against her sister, she could never associate closely with Dr. Smith. She even went on to say that they, meaning the Simpletons and the Smiths, had not seen each other in years.

I was encouraged by that. I needed my family in my healing process. I knew from things that Dr. Smith had said about his family that they knew how to love and support each other. His family adored and supported him, even when they knew he was wrong. My family on the other hand—I'm not sure what I expected from them. Maybe I expected truth, honesty, authenticity, empathy, and even maybe a little sympathy. I wanted them to rally around me and celebrate my healing, in progress. After all, it was not Dr. Smith who opened up his volatile closet, exposing it to light; it was I who told him, "No more!" I cried on their shoulders, believing them when they said to me, "We understand. We are troubled and angry that this awful act has been perpetrated against you. We will always be there for you."

Even though the darkness that enveloped me in Dr. Smith's closet was over, still the desire for someone to save me overwhelmed me. I had no idea what was in store for me with Clay. In fact, at that point, I did not care. Nothing could be worse than being hidden in a closet and coming alive at night while other normal people slept. Nothing could be worse than that graveyard experience. Not even marrying a man who lived in the midst of a historic Indian cemetery *and this* he coveted as his own.

Clay

On December 26, Clay and I were married. During the ceremony, Rosa and Tyrone rudely interjected themselves into places they did not belong. They switched the music I selected. The decorations were not to their liking, so they switched them too. They'd never had a wedding. By the time my ceremony was over, I had felt as if I had attended their wedding, not my own. Had it not been for my ploy to change the unity music at the end of the ceremony, everything would have gone their way. They both looked on in disappointment when C.C. Winans's *I Surrender All* rang through the church sanctuary. The liberties that I allowed people to take at that time were incredible. I had not felt like fighting battles with anyone, especially Rosa. She reminded me of a category five twister, completely out of control.

Even though I had asked her to be my matron of honor and included her entire tribe in the event, it simply was not enough. After the wedding, she and Tyrone—as usual—walked away and did not speak to me for at least six months.

Right before the wedding, Rosa and Tyrone talked me into telling Clay about the events that that occurred with Dr. Smith. I was reluctant to tell him. All the hurtful things in the past were not old enough for me to sort through. I was not ready to tell him. But, Tyrone counseled me and held up the no-secrets flag. They pushed every day to get me to come clean.

Month's into the marriage, Clay revealed that my secret had not been a secret at all. Five years prior, Rosa had talked about her sister Wanda being a whore and sleeping with her ex-pastor. Clay, before we were married, allowed me to sit, cry, and lean on him while I struggled through the process of opening up, even though

Rosa and Tyrone had already discussed their perspective on the matter with him years before.

It was the secret that everyone already knew, that began to tear apart my new marriage. I was beginning to feel duped and sometimes afraid. There were moments when I would catch Clay looking at me as if he wanted to kill me. Over night, he began to act strange, very strange. Sometimes, I would wake up and find Clay standing over me. Occasionally, I received a glance that was full of hateful emotions. The marriage had gotten off to an awful start. Every chance they got, the Simpletons threw their spoon into the pot to stir up trouble.

Clay and I placed his house on the market and set out to find a new home. About the same time we found a home, his house that I feared would never sell, because of the graveyard, sold. It was divine intervention, and I was excited, where Clay on the other hand, fell into a stupor of violent depression. I had not understood what was happening. It was almost as if he was another person. It would be months before I found out that he suffered from bipolar disorder, also known as manic-depression. This illness ran in his family.

Upon the sale of his home in the country, I volunteered to go and help him pack up the house to move into our new home. The moment I touched his belongings, he became irrational. "Don't touch anything in my house! I will do all this by myself." I watched in misery while he slowly packed with anger. I asked if I could assist him in lifting any of the boxes. I assured him that I would be very careful. He angrily said, "No! Don't touch it."

He had four vehicles dating back to possibly the 1930s, sitting in the front yard. There were at least ten bicycles carefully stored in the attic. Clay even had boxes of clothing, dating back to when he was two years, hundreds of old model cars (which I thought were wonderful), albums, tapes, Jet magazines dating back to the first publication, and receipts of every bill that he paid since he was eighteen. Clay threw nothing away, and the more packing he did, the angrier he became.

I got up, walked out on his back porch, and looked at all of the headstones in the Indian cemetery. Before I could process my thoughts, a huge red wasp slammed into my arm. I screamed and ran back in the house, in tears. Out of breath and transported back into my childhood, I cried like a baby while Clay assured me in laughter, "That aint nothing but a nasty old wasp." I nursed my wound alone. Many times as a child, I experienced the awful pain of bee and wasp stings. It is interesting how one event or happening can force you out of the reality that you presently live in, dump you off on a dirt road, leave you there for a few minutes, and then bring you back to your present, and at the same time, show you that your present is not so different from your past. I cried even harder. But more importantly, I cried alone.

Clay was 100 percent absorbed in his own world. He was unwilling to share his universe with anyone outside of his daughter, her three children, his ex-wife, her two daughters, and a step-grandson. There was absolutely no room for anyone else. I was alone in my new marriage.

Not long after Clay and I were married, my gynecologist determined I needed a hysterectomy to detach my rectum from my uterus. The two were glued together. The sick fantasies that I fulfilled for Dr. Smith damaged my body so badly that I needed surgery. My doctor said he had never seen anything like it in all of his years of practicing medicine. The surgery involved a five-week painful physical recovery, but nothing compared to the psychological wounds left by my pastor.

Before surgery, I asked Clay to keep an eye on the business. I put him on as a signer to make sure that the accounting side of our company ran while Brian accommodated our clients. I was off work for three weeks. It was supposed to be five, but I sensed things were falling apart. My keen intuition was on track. While trying to nurse myself back to health, Clay drained the business account, paying only his personal credit card bills, leaving no money in the account for business matters. I was livid to say the least. When confronted, he had no answers why he would operate in such a careless and callous manner.

I may have stated before in my writings that I believe firmly that the truth shall set one free, but for almost one week, I pulled away from my memoirs, because I had no idea how to connect the dots of this relationship. So many things just did not make sense. My hairdresser once said, "Insanity is impossible to figure out, but should you figure it out, consider yourself insane." After giving this statement much thought, I decided to provide you with a brief clinical description of bipolar disorder. While I am in no position to elaborate on why and how this disorder occurs, I am in a position to express what I experienced, living with a person with this very grave illness.

The bi-polar person goes two distinct places. Each situation is an extreme journey either to a mountaintop or valley experience. During Clay's hypomania phase of bipolar, he was very hyperactive, even though he slept very little. He had grandiose beliefs about this ability to drive anyone who stepped on his toes insane, as well. He believed that he was the smartest man on the earth, and everyone around him was trying to play catch-up with him. During these episodes, he was unable to concentrate on any one subject for a long period. He was highly irritable, picked fights, lashed out at me when I was unwilling to agree with his plans or if I critiqued his behavior. Clay, during this phase, did things that were reckless without thinking of the consequences *like draining the business account* or carelessly maxing out his credit cards and placing us in debt for over $70,000.

From the opposite spectrum, if he went into the valley, it was virtually impossible to pull him out. His energy was very low, and he suffered from extreme fatigue. He lost interest in everything regarding life. He was easily agitated and, many times, lost his grasp on reality. But my biggest concern during these valley experiences was that he loathed me and even himself. He would become very angry with me when I would say, "I simply can't go there with you."

There were things about Clay that seriously disturbed me. His mental illness reminded me of who I almost was and what I could have become…had I stayed in Detroit. Attempting to help him deal with his illness, I opened up to him about my painful past. In doing so, I placed myself in an extremely vulnerable position. When Clay had episodes of unrealistic grandeur, beliefs about his ability to control my mind, he would scream out, "Before this is over with, I am going to drive you looney!

It became Clay's goal in life to drive me off the edge. "Wanda," he would say in his Oklahoma country accent, "You say you been lookin' for your father; Well, you've finally found him." On one occasion, he ran out into our cul-de-sac in only his underwear, screaming like a mad man. "Awwwhhhhhh! Awwwwwwwh!" He screamed as he ran in circles in the streetlights. Clay, bearded and wearing spectacles, danced through our front yard as my neighbors looked out their windows in the middle of the night. The truth is I became fearful of losing my life. For all his crazy—and Clay was a lunatic—it took his ridiculous behavior to show me that he was no savior. No man was. I had to save myself.

Many times, I awakened and found Clay sitting straight up in bed and staring into space. There were also times that he woke up, screaming in complete terror of what he saw in his dreams. He was a man on the edge. When Clay calmly told me how easy it would be for him to poison me, because I allowed him to administer my medicines as I lay exhausted from my day's work, even I started to backtrack by pulling some of the power out of his hands. "I could just put anything in there, Wanda. You take whatever I git ya. You'll just go right on ta sleep, never wake up. People would come by the house to check on you, and I would tell them that you just died in ya sleep," he reminded me.

"Thanks, Clay, but no thanks. I can get my own medication from here on out," I said. These shifts in his personality were not just mood swings as the Simpletons had put it. If ignited, Clay would explode. I was sure of that. I became as quiet as a mouse in my beautiful, spacious house. The moment we left the privacy of our house, I pretended, making up excuses for his obtrusive behavior. He was rude beyond the bounds of normal society, threatening people and handing out insults.

One night I fell asleep while Clay lay with his back turned toward me. I dreamed there was blood all over my feet and legs while I was lying helplessly in bed. I woke up in a panic. The light in our bedroom was off, and Clay sat, staring into the void of the dark. I turned on my lamp to make sure I was okay. He continued to stare blankly into space.

In church and even on his job, Clay was functional and able to carry on with his responsibilities. At home, after the rest of the world was on the other side of the door, he carefully wrapped himself in a tattered blanket and curled up in a fetal position on the couch in our den. His condition worsened as time passed. He looked at his unnecessary credit card spending and said to me, "I don't know what I was thinking when I spent all that money. I don't know where all that money went." He then consumed himself with trying to find a way out of debt. I, on the other hand, was not willing, be it right or wrong, to go into those dark places with Clay, for fear of being trapped myself.

During this time, the Simpletons were *in* rather than *out*. I cried on Rosa's shoulder as she cried to every ear she could reach, using the excuse, "Every little prayer helps." She and Tyrone lived in contentment when there was chaos in my life. As long as they could be the saviors, they were completely at peace with me. Moreover, I privately resolved that as long as there was no physical violence, I would continue to try to make the marriage work. It would not be long before his illness took him down the street of *No Return*.

One night, I woke up to Clay holding a knife to my throat. I lay still as he played with a white-handled pocketknife. The day before, he threatened me with his fraternity pledge paddle, saying, "I would like to take this big ol' piece of wood and crack your skull in half. That sure would be easy for me to do!" I was petrified with fear but couldn't give him the edge of knowing, so I silently prayed and told him in a firm voice to remove the knife from my throat. "Ah, you ain't no fun! I was jus playin' witcha while you were sleepin'," he laughed and said. After Clay removed the knife from my throat, I called his only friend.

Pastor Jones headed over to our house at three o'clock in the morning, sat with Clay, and told him that his behavior was unacceptable. In the midst of his own agitation, Clay laughed and said, "Oh this ol' knife wouldn't cut through butter. She's making a big deal out of nothing." His friend assured him that it was a big deal. When Pastor Jones left, Clay laughed and asked, "Are you scared?" Silently, I walked away from him, grabbed a blanket from the closet, went to the den, sat in the recliner, covered myself, and sat, wide awake, for the remainder of the night.

Clay had crossed the line. A big line; a line so clear and bold that even I, a person who allowed people to walk on me my whole life, could not accept his transgressions. I sat, thinking about my life and just a few of the events that had happened on my journey. I never saw myself as a person who struggled with boundary lines, but in the pitch-black darkness shone a blinding light that pierced the dusk that over shadowed the dawn of day. I had the epiphany of all epiphanies. It was the size of a thirty-five pound blue catfish. I briefly remembered a statement Dr. Smith made on one of our fishing trips. He said, "The system will take what you give it!" I turned the light on, grabbed my journal, and read a passage from one of my entries that blew my mind.

In my household, my children give little or no respect at all to my personal belongings. They don't respect my truck when using it. They eat foods that I've designated as my own. They simply have no respect. They are all males, and I am a woman. They constantly let me know that what I think and feel does not matter not to them.

I turned the light back off. All my life, I had seen myself as the victim. *Poor little ol' me.* While living the life of an innocent child, one is able to see that a child needs protection from the elements. If that child is not protected, as I was not, we can safely say that this minor is a victim of his or her own circumstances. *But at what point should that person begin to take responsibility for his or her own life?* I questioned myself in the dark. I had opened myself, my life, my home, my heart, and my soul up to the system I placed myself in, searching for my father. I had not drawn any boundary lines for anyone. People came, took, and abused me, because I allowed them to do so. There was a welcome mat at my front door for abusers that read, "Come right on in—doesn't matter who you are or what your agenda is. Have me; have what you want and take what you need. Walk on top of me; leave me listless and nonresponsive. I am the victim. That is what you do to and with victims."

For the first time in my life, I took a good look at myself in the dark, and I realized I had no idea who I was. I knew how to play the role of businesswoman, but in my personal life, I was a stranger to myself. *How can one build healthy relationships when you don't even know who you are or what healthy looks like?* I thought if I gave away all I owned, people would love the unlovable. The universe is such that it takes you around in circles over and over again until you get it right. I had not set healthy boundaries for the people I met. In fact, I had no sense of what a healthy boundary line looked like. Without defined boundary lines, I exposed myself to people who were unsafe for me to be around. I openly exposed myself to abuse, and then beat myself up, complaining about the unbelievable circumstance I had come through as the victorious victim.

I found myself sitting in the dark, thinking of how I'd always felt responsible for others, how I, with low self-esteem, feared being abandoned. Nonetheless, I had a high tolerance for someone else's inappropriate behavior. I found it difficult to be real or authentic. Charles Whitfield in his book *Boundaries and Relationships* calls these *core* issues. I had victimized myself. By hiding all the hurts in my secret closet and not dealing with them, I placed myself on life's not-so-merry-go-round. I regarded other people's feelings and situations as more important than my own. I put all my energy into the other persons' needs and neglected my own as I mindlessly trekked throughout life. While this epiphany did not excuse the bad behavior of the people mentioned in my memoirs, it allowed me to focus inward for the first time in my life on true healing.

The following day, Clay got up and quietly went to work as usual. I prolonged my stay at home by jumping into the spa tub and allowing it to invigorate my body. Afterward, I put my makeup on and went to work refreshed. Even though the night's events had been horrific, I had been blessed with a huge revelation, and it had little to do with Clay. I was energetic about the possibilities for the day.

Teri, Clay's stepdaughter, at the last minute, called the shop, requesting a five-tiered cake on Saturday, for her cousin, an ex-pro football player. Brian and I obliged. This party would bring in almost three thousand dollars. Wanda's Cake Gallery was struggling and needed such an injection. Before we could finish closing the deal, Teri called Clay and told him the cost of the cake. Her mouth couldn't hold water. The moment I opened the door to the house, his comments poured out like slippery oil.

Clay was deep in debt and wanted the money to pay his credit card bills. I told him it was out of the question because this business deal was like any other. I had to account for every penny I spent and earned. When I explained this to him, he launched into a tirade. "That money is as much mine as it is yours! You my wife, aint ya?

At two o'clock on Saturday morning, Brian and I went in to the gallery and worked hard to bring the party together. By the afternoon, we both were extremely tired. I went home and found Clay lying with his tattered blanket wrapped around him. *The blanket is out. This can't be good,* I thought.

I asked him if he would drive us to his hometown to deliver the cake. Clay abruptly said, "No." Instead of accepting his answer, I told him I was too exhausted to drive and that I was not sure if we could safely make the sixty-mile trip. He then said, "Good. I don't care if you die on the highway."

I said to him, "That's fine. I got to go before I'm late." I headed back to the Gallery. Brian and I loaded up the truck and headed toward the countryside. Once we were on the freeway, a driver ahead of us, carrying a mattress and box spring on the back of his truck, switched into our lane. He was moving so fast that the box spring went flying off, forcing vehicles to swerve in every direction to save their lives. The box spring was coming directly at my truck in full force. At the last minute, not knowing what the outcome would be, I quickly steered over into the grass. Somehow (I'm really not sure how), I missed the box spring and skillfully drove back up on the highway. Miraculously, even though it was a rough ride, every décor and detail on our Mad Hatter cake was still intact. Brian, with his eyes shut tight, held onto it as if he were protecting a baby. We had started out exhausted, but this near crash left us wide-awake and alert to the world.

Once we arrived at the party site, we took the cake out of the van and began to work our magic. Brian stacked the five tiers and worked with icing to complete the detailing. While he and I hurried along to finish our set-up, I noticed a woman standing to the side. Intuition told me that she was Clay's ex-wife. On first glance, I thought that it would be better not to speak, but there was a nudging inside me to say hello and introduce myself. Clay said she was the vilest awful person in the world, but that she was also the only woman he had ever loved.

I walked over and introduced myself. Without thinking, we both extended our arms and embraced each other. She told me that she had heard so many good things about me from her children. I lied to her and said, "Same here in regards to you. Clay speaks so highly of you." It had been just the opposite. Every time Vanessa's name came up in our house, Clay roasted her as if she was the prize turkey for Thanksgiving dinner. He called her a lazy, philandering witch. In fact, he said if we, by chance, encountered her, to look the other way. "Do not talk to her," he warned. Clay made it sound like she was a monster. My husband's characterization of Vanessa proved to be as off-balanced as his bipolar reality.

When Brian finished his work, he came over, and Vanessa grabbed his hand, telling him how pleased she was to meet him. After a pleasant fifteen-minute conversation, we said good-bye. When we were getting in the truck, she told him to take care of me. On our way back to Tulsa, Brian and I discussed how soft-spoken she was. Vanessa appeared nothing like Clay portrayed her. Their divorce happened twenty years ago. She re-married and moved on. To Brian and me, she seemed genuine in her demeanor.

The moment we hit the door to my house, we found Clay pacing the floor, back and forth. History had already taught me, *Don't even ask*, so I tried to avoid Clay, hoping the storms of his emotions would die out in the silence. Brian went into the den and, exhausted from the day's events, fell asleep in the Lazy Boy chair.

"You met my wife?" Clay shouted a few feet behind me.

I did not respond. I assumed that he was mistaken, so I let the slip of his tongue go. He closed in on me and pushed me into the kitchen. "You met my wife?" he screamed at the top of his lungs. "You met my wife?"

Brian woke up out of his sleep and said. "No Clay, we met your ex-wife. My mother is your wife."

Clay exploded. "You are nothing but a whore! You're a whore! You slept with your pastor! You let him use you as his whore. You are the scum of this earth, the absolute scum of this earth! You are a good for nothing, lying whore!"

I silently picked up the phone and dialed Rosa and Tyrone's number. After they answered, I laid the phone down so they could hear all the horrible insults. Clay rambled about the three thousand dollars we made off the party. He then worked himself into a thick lather of hatred, grabbing me and pushing me against the wall. "You met my wife?"

In the midst of his ramblings, I mentioned that we almost wrecked the vehicle. I reminded him that I invited him to help us transport the cake, and if he had contributed the smallest amount of effort, I would have paid him an income.

"I wish you would have wrecked," Clay said, "I wish you had died on the highway—you and your lazy son. Look at him, sitting in that chair. He's not a man. He's a boy. If he was a man, he would not let me talk to you the way I just did.

Brian looked over at Clay. He looked at me. Then, he stood, shook his head, and left. *Why did he leave me?* I thought. There was no one to protect me. *Why did he leave me?* I didn't understand. My tears gave Clay more fuel. Pushing my shoulder and nudging just a little bit closer to insanity, he screamed, "You met my wife? You are a whore! Whore! Whore! Whore!"

"Clay," I said, "please stop! I can't do this! Please leave me alone!"

He screamed back, "Leave you alone? Leave you alone? Well, I can't do that! You think I jus' found out you were a whore? Nope, I knew it when I married you! I said to myself, 'Well now, Clay, you know she's a whore, but go on and marry her anyway." So that's what I did. I married a whore! If I hadn't married you, you would be alone, cause no one wants to be with a whore!"

After about forty-five long minutes, there came a knock on the door. Even through Tyrone and Rosa lived only five minutes away, they listened for almost an hour before coming to help me. *Better than not at all,* I thought. I raced to let them in. It was Tyrone and his friend, Corey. They came inside and tried to calm Clay down. The presence of the two men did not temper his anger. His threats got louder, his pushes turned to shoves. All the while, Tyrone was telling him to calm down. "Why were these two good, Christian men allowing Clay to continue to physically push me up against walls?"

"I've had enough, Clay. I can't do this anymore! It's over," I lamented! "It's over!" My words set off a ticking time bomb.

Clay began slamming against my head with an opened hand. The strangest thing—something I will forget—is that with each open-handed slap, Clay yelled, "Bam," never like the bubbled dialogue of a comic book superhero. "Baam!" Clay slapped at my face. "Baam!" In the midst of my tears, my jaws dropped. He was so far disconnected from reality that he added sound effects to his physical abuse. I was thankful the palm of his hand was open when he hit me. *Why was no one coming to stop him?*

I yelled out, "You can't let him hit me! Please, Tyrone, don't let him hit me!" As if awakened from a deep trance, Tyrone tranquilly asked, "Clay, why would you do that? Why did you hit her?"

Tyrone's calm voice, juxtaposed to all of the screaming and threats, seemed out of place. His cool irritated even Clay, because the moment it registered in his head that the villainous Tyrone Simpleton from *Planet Hypocrite* was there to save the day, Clay pulled his rusty pocketknife out and said, "I have always wanted to cut you, Tyrone! I have never liked you. I always think when you are in the pulpit, preaching those sermons, you're such a phony. You aint no real preacher!"

In a not-so-calming voice, Tyrone shouted, "Okay, that's it Clay! I've had enough! Get some clothes, Wanda, you're coming to our house."

While Clay switched his knife back and forth at Tyrone, pouring on the insults, I grabbed my purse in tears. As I drove away from the house, I felt a wash of emotions from being physically and emotionally drained.

The moment I arrived at the Simpletons, Rosa invited me to rest in their bed while she wiped my tears away. I had felt oddly uncomfortable as she tried to comfort me by stroking my forehead and face. For by the time I reached their house, their children knew all the details of my dreadful night. I was sure the church members knew as well.

The next day, I went to church and sang on the praise and worship team as usual. After service, instead of going back to the Simpleton's, I chose to go back to my house. I wasn't going back to the marriage, but I wasn't going to be afraid either. So I went home.

I walked in, and Clay was up under his blanket. He was in a depressive state and didn't say a thing.

A little later in the evening, Brain came to my front door. He stood at the door, apologizing for leaving the previous night, but he said he felt like his leaving would possibly diffuse the situation. I disagreed with him but silently accepted his excuse. My sons, like the rest of my loved ones, turned their heads and backs on me.

While Brian was at the door, Clay came out of his stupor and pushed me out of the way, saying, "Brian, don't you know it ain't proper to come to a man's house without saying hello?" Brian quickly turned around and headed for his truck. As Clay ran antagonistically behind him, Brian opened the door to his truck and quickly jumped inside. He started his motor as Clay was shouting obscenities at him. As insane as this sounds, Clay then jumped on to the back of Brian's Honda CRV, latching himself on and daring him to drive. "Come on and drive, Brian," he shouted! "You wanna kill a sixty-something-year-old man?"

I watched from the doorway on pins and needles as Brian shifted gears, putting his truck in reverse, then forward, then reverse until he was able to throw Clay off into the street. I didn't know whether Brian was going to run over him or what. This time

I wanted him to diffuse the situation, by leaving. He revved up his motor as if he was about to commit the unthinkable, but after sitting for a moment, he drove away. I was so thankful no harm was done to Clay's body.

Clay got up and ran frantically in the house, threatening to press charges against Brian. I didn't say a word. I went into the den and picked up my dogs, holding them close as I sat in the Lazy Boy. Out of nowhere, Clay came in the den with a kitchen knife, pulled Poncho, the male dog, from my arms, and put the knife to his throat. I got up and fell to my knees and, securing Blue, my other dog, pleaded with him, "Please, Clay, don't hurt my dog! Please let him go!" Clay talked to Poncho as if he was human, saying, "This is your last day on this earth. I am going to slash your throat." I cried buckets of tears as I called the Simpletons. "Oh, my God! He's going to kill Poncho. He has a kitchen knife! Please help me, Rosa!" I slammed the phone down. Clay opened the backdoor and hurled Poncho to the ground, then snatched Blue from my arms and threw her violently to the ground also.

I told them, as calmly as I could, "I don't know what the problem is, but I will tell you this, I went through abuse when I was younger. I will not die in an abusive relationship. If Clay is ever violent to my dogs or me, I will do my very best to protect myself. I will not subject myself to violence anymore! I will not tolerate any form of abuse!" This was my first clear-cut boundary statement. that I had ever made! What was to happen next was unthinkable.

The uncomfortable feeling I had when Rosa touched me became clear in the next few moments. I always felt that my sister thought I was beneath her, but I never knew her opinion could stretch into the depths of hell...

Tyrone came over to me. In a sanctimonious pose, as if he was drawing power from heaven, Tyrone placed his hand firmly on my forehead. The tips of his finger gripped my skull as he began to shout. "In the name of Jesus, I call this demon out of Wanda.

Stunned, I said, "What are you talking about? Tyrone, let me go! What are you talking about?"

Tyrone screamed, "I don't want to talk to you. I want to speak to Wanda."

His hands shook as he screamed while pressing down harder on my head. I felt my brain rattle as he pressed in more for a firmer grip and shouted to the heavens, "In the name of Jesus, the Savior, the Lord of all, I want to talk to Wanda! Demon, you have no place here in this house, in this body! Come out! Be gone!" I was dumbfounded, suspended in disbelief!

I slapped at his grip. I said, "Get your hands off of me!"

He became louder saying, "No, I demand that this demon flee. I want to talk to Wanda!" His grip became stronger. I looked to Rosa and burst into tears. Watching Tyrone try to draw the demon from me was something that even crazy Clay could not even fathom. Clay stared at him in utter amazement.

I finally snapped.

Get your hands off of me! Now, Tyrone! Get your hands off me!" Tyrone released his grip. I cried out, "You are as insane as Clay! This man hit me several times last night, and tonight he had a kitchen knife on Blue and Poncho's throats, and you are calling out demons from *my* spirit! It's perfectly fine for him to hit me, to pull knives, Tyrone? Because I have said no to this violent behavior, there is a demon inside of me? This is crazy! I said it before, and I am going to say it again so that everyone understands: I will not tolerate violence in my life! Call that demonic if you want, but nobody is going to hit me again!"

The room stood silent as we all looked at each other. There was nothing left to say, so after a few terse minutes of silence, Tyrone and Rosa left. The moment they walked out the door, Clay fell over into the floor laughing hysterically. "Now that was funny," he said. "You get up every morning to do your so-called *quiet time* while I lay in bed. When Tyrone put his hand on your head, I thought I'd crack up or die trying. I said to myself, he just don't know; the demon is over here, sitting on the couch inside of me."

"Oh boy," Clay laughed. "Those Simpletons are something else."

Clay laughed so hard he couldn't contain himself.

Without a word, I picked up my dogs, my purse, my keys, and drove to the Broken Arrow police department. On the way there, I thought about the events of the night...

Rosa had recently taken a call center job from home for Christian mega ministries. The Simpletons connected their home computer and phone to Mega church orders all over the United States. It was the perfect job for her. Faith and healing ministries like TV Evangelists Benny Hinn, World Changers, PTL, and Dan and Paula Crouch had orders pouring into Rosa's home. While she sat on her couch, watching soap operas, lost souls would call the Simpleton's house, begging her for prayer and ordering the latest item from their favorite television evangelist. Rosa saw Benny Hinn perform miracles, and she desperately wanted Tyrone to have the same gift. A few days before the so-called demonic exorcism, Rosa told me she had been praying for Tyrone to possess the power to heal and cast out demons. As I drove, I thought, *Who better to start on than me?*

There is something sinister about covering up violence. We, as women, think that if we sweep the events under a rug, they will go away. Nevertheless, when it's all said and done, after the dust settles, we, in an effort to hide it away, have played as much of a role in keeping the violence alive as the perpetrator. When I was a child, I prided the fact that my parents never argued. Looking back, however, I see that their lack of confrontation was not a good thing. It is important to learn to disagree and, more importantly, disagree healthily. Daddy and Mama never modeled what healthy boundary lines looked like; it was just the way it was in our household. No one was allowed to show his or her true emotions. Everyone in our family was expected to act and emote the same. Claiming uniqueness would have been considered rebellious and made for a bad seed. I knew very early on in my life that I was different, *but unable to show my feelings*, my point of difference quickly turned into low self-esteem, guilt, and shame. When people abused me, I thought I deserved it. Nonetheless, when Clay hit me, I knew that his actions were not only wrong; they were illegal. I was tired of putting up with and covering over abuse.

The moment I filed the police report of the incident, the officers connected me to a domestic abuse counselor. A silver-haired white woman with wise eyes and a kind voice assessed my situation. I was beginning to see that, in order to recover from the years of abuse, I had to be real with myself. I could not blame anyone else for the absence of boundary lines. I had to claim responsibility and take charge of my life and my own recovery. No one else was responsible for me. In Charles Whitfield's *Boundaries and Relationships* he wrote that one had to "let go" of prior rigid or unhealthy walls to facilitate true recovery. I told the counselor that, as a Christian, I didn't want to leave my husband, for I would be a failure in the eyes of the Lord. She placed her hand on top of mine and said, "Sweetheart, Don't worry! The Creator will be in the midst of your recovery. You allowing a man to slam up against your body is not a part of His plan for your life. It is impossible to serve or keep your mind on God, if you are constantly afraid of where the next abusive blow is coming from!" She reassured me that protecting *myself* was the right thing to do. I needed to hear that, because I felt like I was all alone.

Undaunted, the counselor explained the danger of violence perpetrated against animals. Authorities have found that the killing of a pet is the precursor to many violent acts such as murder perpetrated against human beings. It was important to be brave and have courage in filing a restraining order to protect myself. This wise woman said, "Challenge yourself to do more than exist....live!"

The next day I went through the court system and took measures to protect my life. My home was a toxic environment. I sought not to take control of the environment, but to gain control of my life. I could not live with the abuse any longer. When Clay came home, I informed him that I had filed a restraining order against him. He looked up from his chair and calmly said, "Oh well, I guess you tied my hands. There's nothing I can do now." He packed his clothes and told me he would be back later for the bulk of his things with a moving truck and left.

The next time I saw Clay was in court. His beard was so thick, I hardly recognized him. I sat right behind him and didn't even know he was making an appearance. Three times before, I had shown up in court, and each time the Judge said he had not been properly served. On this particular morning I almost missed the proceeding, and even though I made it there on time, I sat, thinking about the waste of expensive gas and time that I put in only for the system to say they were unable to locate him. The judge, as with times before, called his name. This time Clay answered by standing up. He looked like an African American version of Ted Kaczynski, the *Unabomber*. My heart trembled as the judge asked if he felt the request for a protective order was needed. Clay answered, "Yes, absolutely." The courts granted the Order of Protection for three years. Somehow, the light of truth shines through even the darkest of days, because Rosa and Tyrone refused to come and testify to what they saw and heard. I was concerned about having a witness to help validate the event. Looking back, I had not needed them after all. My marriage to Clay was over and once again, I was alone.

Digging up Old, Dead Bones

During the winter of 2007, the state of Oklahoma was hit with a tremendously harsh ice storm. Even the strongest and oldest of trees bowed down to Mother Nature's grip and blast of wintery blues. In my home, she brought along with her *death*. The lights went out all over Tulsa and its surrounding cities, and a cold, emotional chill enveloped my spirit as I watched the unthinkable happen. Blue, my female miniature pinscher got out of the yard and killed two of the neighbor's rabbits. The neighbors came over upset and demanded that Blue be put to sleep. To keep the peace, I allowed the city of Broken Arrow to put her down. A few days later, I came home from work and found Poncho, her male companion, strangled with an unraveled cord from his own blanket. I was shattered and inconsolable.

Almost every tree in my backyard had succumbed to the ice storm. There were limbs everywhere. Earlier in the fall, I had planted a weeping willow tree. It was tiny and frail, yet it remained intact. Not one limb was lost. Its fragile arms had submissively bent, bowed, and hung just the way nature intended. When the storm was over, I walked out, cried, praised God for my lights, and buried Poncho under the willow tree.

I mourned Blue and Poncho's deaths for months. I had not understood why they had to be taken away from me. As crazy it seems, I had felt they were all I had. Brian decided, because of my grief, to leave his Weimaraner, Gerald Ford, with me. Ford quickly attached to me and his new lifestyle. There was plenty of room to run and play. I reciprocated by falling deeply in love with him. One day while delivering a wedding cake, Brian and I saw the most beautiful chocolate miniature pinscher. We questioned its owner, and she promised to find out if her little guy, Malcolm, had a brother. Within days, Ford and I welcomed Sydney Malachi into our home. He was so handsome with light hazel eyes.

Of all creatures great and small, the dog is my favorite of God's creations. Upon first impression, the dog is just a typical beast of burden. Live with one or two or even three, and your mind will change. They are the most beautiful of all things in this world to me. I watched as Malachi and Ford shared their world together; working closely to guard me. Somewhere in my past, I was told that Weimaraners and miniature pinchers would never get along.

Their breeds and personalities were so vastly different. I respectfully received the information but chose not to accept it as gospel. A dog, regardless of its breed, I believe, takes on the personality of its master. I find it hard to imagine anyone connecting with me the way my dogs do.

One evening Ford and Malachi came in with an acrid odor on them. After giving them a bath, they immediately wanted to get back outside. After letting them out again, they came back in with the same foul smell. I went out and found that the dogs had discovered Poncho's grave and pulled his bones to the surface. It was very disturbing to me. I redug his grave deeper and cried as I reburied him, placing heavy stones over his gravesite. I was upset, but I understood that Ford and Malachi were doing what dogs do. I found no excuse for the Simpletons when they chose to do the same thing.

For three long weeks I had cried and lived in utter turmoil, because Rosa and Tyrone determined they were going to bring Dr. Cirrus Smith in to do their installation as the new pastor and wife of New Road. Pastor Jones had finally given up and placed the church in their hands. I got the news through the grapevine. A friend happened to mention during a phone conversation that Dr. Smith was totally shutting down Unionized Baptist on October 12, to go and conduct installation service for Tyrone and Rosa. I immediately asked to be released from the phone conversation and raced back to the shower to wash the filth away once again as tears mixed with water soaked my face. My hands and arms hung as limp as the fragile willow tree during the ice storm. I slid down in the shower floor and allowed the water to run fully over me from head-to-toe. *Baptize me, Jesus. Wash this filth away once and for all.* No matter how hard I scrubbed, I still felt dirty. Just a few months before in May, Tyrone, and Rosa wrote a letter, saying they would never do anything to intentionally cause me any pain.

The letter, I felt, was as good as it gets when dealing with the Simpletons. Tyrone never took responsibility for wrongdoing. He simply stated that he was sorry if his and Rosa's choices offended me. I was not stupid. I understood everything he was saying, but I forgave them anyway. A few months after the writing that letter, while I was working, Rosa brought me Judas bread and meat for lunch and made a big deal out of my health. She said, "Wanda, you work too hard. You've got to take better care of yourself. You've got to take a break and eat sometimes! Take some time for yourself and get away from this place. You need a break!"

After Rosa walked out of the shop, I took one bite out of the sandwich and looked at Brian as I chewed away, satisfying the hunger in my stomach. Brian shook his head and said, "Okay, what is she up to? Auntie Rosa is weird. Something cataclysmic is in the pot and ready to stew!" We both felt uncomfortable, because random acts of kindness were not a part of Rosa's personality. I began to feel like Jesus must have felt right before the big betrayal by Judas.

A couple of more days passed, and Rosa came back to the Gallery, announcing that she and Tyrone were taking Pastor and Mrs. Jones's positions in New Road. I congratulated her on their accomplishment. Clay had remained Pastor Jones's best friend, but when we divorced, he left the church altogether, leaving Pastor Jones alone with the Simpletons. The Simpletons had done a private smear campaign, telling people that pastor Jones was worn out and erratic in his behavior. Rosa told Brian and me that she felt so sorry for how bad his leadership had turned out to be. To validate Tyrone and her position even more, Rosa talked about things finally changing under Tyrone's competent leadership.

I felt horrible for Pastor and Mrs. Jones. He and his wife were good people. I had come to love them. Almost every Sunday, Clay and I ate dinner with them. Each gathering became a political debate. Pastor Jones was Republican, and I was middle of the road. We argued with fervor, converting our political positions. At the end of the evening, we would all hug and kiss good-bye until next Sunday.

When Clay and I divorced, he divorced the church as well, leaving all office matters in Tyrone's hands. Pastor Jones burned out quickly. Clay always said, "I'm only ay New Road to protect my friend, watch over the money matters, and keep those Simpletons in check. You see, if I wasn't here, Pastor Jones wouldn't have a chance. The Simpletons would seize all aspects of this church." Repeatedly, he reminded me of this.

Over a year had passed since our divorce, and Rosa was announcing this great blessing that had been *miraculously* bestowed upon her and Tyrone. I hugged her and congratulated her again. A couple days later, another piece of Judas bread and meat with mayonnaise arrived, and Brian and I agreed, death of something was eminent. We didn't know what it was, but we knew one thing: whatever it was, it was connected with me.

Their choice to bring Dr. Smith to do their installation was a painful ordeal for me; more painful than all other times of betrayal by them. I closed my eyes shut, for when I opened them the tears blinded me. I had not wanted to see. To see it for what it was, meant that I would no longer be able to pretend that I mattered to my sister and her family. The thought of belonging had kept me coming back for punishment. To see would mean I had a clear understanding of what was and what was not. It would mean that the skewer in the middle of my eyes would have to be removed. To see would mean no more defective lens. It would mean accepting the Simpletons for who they really were and not who I wanted them to be. The scales from my eyes were being painfully removed, and again I was faced with another truth. Sometimes, before things get better; they get worse, while truth is having her say.

I got up, ran from room-to-room, then falling to my knees, drug myself across the floor in tears, begging God to remove the pain that was being inflicted by these *good Christian folk*. There was complete silence, for truth comes in its own time. Even if you feel you can't handle it, it reveals secrets by removing the dark veil of deception. Truth uncovers *Who's Who* and what role they came to play. But there is none so blind as she who refuses to see.

Dr. Smith and my sister were close. The truth was the Simpletons purchased and drove his old truck. Rosa lied when she said she hated the fact that it was in their driveway. They removed all the pictures of me, because they didn't want to see my face. Hanging instead were pictures of Dr. Smith and his family. They did not regard the situation with Dr. Smith as abuse of power. To them, it was an affair, no more than that.

I had not wanted to see, but through the night, my anger grew. I opened my eyes and saw the situation for what it was. The next morning I called Tyrone. Before I could speak, he hung up the phone. I then dialed Rosa's number and as soon as she heard my voice, she slammed the phone down also. I looked at the figurine that Rosa had purchased for me when I had my hysterectomy. It was of a woman, who had a cheetah with her. She was beautiful, but her gown was seductively falling off of her. Months ago, I had taken a marker and written on this statue, "Krazy Kinfolk. This is who I am not! She does not know me."

I became angrier. I got in my car and raced over to their house.

I came to a halting stop in the driveway. I marched up to their door and knocked repeatedly. Even through Rosa's van was home, and I could clearly see movement upstairs, she refused to answer the door. When I think back, she probably made the right decision. I was beyond angry. *I was livid!* I got back into my car and noticed a sharpie marker on the seat. I looked at the marker, and then at their driveway.

Following Tyrone's pseudo-exorcism, I felt this time, God had chosen me. He had marched down from heaven and miraculously placed the magic marker on my seat. I grabbed the pen and held it in my hand, like King Arthur held the sword after pulling it from the stone. I felt its power coursing through my veins.

I got back out of the car with the marker in my hand and got on my knees in their driveway. I uncapped the marker and touched the stone. The felt tip of the marker appeared to chisel right into the concrete. I carefully scrawled out the words "Hypocrites and liars…no more!"

Wanda

On October 12, 2008, Dr. Smith came and gave an awesome sermon on forgiveness. I'd heard through the grapevine that my sister, Sophie Mae, and her daughter, Courtney, had come all the way from Texas to attend the celebration. They described this event as an event of a lifetime. I was told that Dr. Smith had said that regardless of what you've done or where you've been, God forgives you. My sister, Sophie Mae, had described his sermon as totally moving. She spoke of how she lovingly hugged Dr. Smith, praising him for his awesome words. Afterwards they shared a close, intimate time together.

All day long during the festivities, I was writing and fully understood that if I didn't tell the story, the truth would die with me. It was even possible for me to take their lies to *my* grave. My freedom was in my story. Liberty would come in the truth. Until I wrote on their driveway, I had not realized just how angry I really was. My relationship with Rosa had been based upon the perfect lie. Because I was so hungry to be loved and because I wanted to believe in her so badly, I bought her story. But the truth is: you know when someone is not dealing with you earnestly. Wherever and whenever we spent time together, I felt very uncomfortable, like I was walking and talking with the enemy. I would talk to God about my feelings, and each time, He would tell me to set a guard over my mouth, to keep my personals to myself when dealing with them.

On the day of Dr. Smith's installation sermon, I had written until I had writer's cramp and hunger pains. I decided go grab a burger, no need to groom myself. I remembered thinking, *God, I look like my mother in one of her not so finest hours. Worse than when her wig was on backward!* No worries…I rushed to the car anyway, raced to Burger King, grabbed my dinner, and headed back home. As I pulled up toward my cul-de-sac, there sat Rosa's silver van. With dread, I pulled up into my driveway and sat in the dark, hoping the people inside would pull away and find someone else to terrorize. They did not.

I saw the shadow of a person at my window, motioning me to roll the window down. It was a friend of the Simpletons. I reluctantly pressed the button to release my window. I politely asked, "How can I help you?"

The person standing in the dark said, "Oh, I just wanted to give you a hug."

I returned, "I don't need a hug." I said, "You all have a nice night."

She backed away, then turned and raced back to the van. Rosa, who was ducking under the seat, rose up like a demon from hell as they got in, closed the door, and drove away. I sat there thinking to myself, *Thank God I've started the memoirs. I'm hungry as heck.* I went inside and peacefully ate my meal and continued to write.

Later that night, a family member called and asked if I was okay. Word had gotten back that I was shattered and on the verge of suicide. God once again reminded me, "Tell the truth, or they will tell lies." This time there was not one tear in my eyes. Truth was looming within my penned words. Freedom and liberty was finally at hand.

I had no idea how many Mary Magdalenes existed or what their stories were, but I knew on the inside of my lonely heart that my purpose would be in finding out. I knew that the world was riddled with lonely, broken hearts. There were so many; they were countless. I knew God had called me to reach out to those who had found themselves in Babylon. Getting in was easy; finding my way out took a miracle. It was Babylon for God's sake. Yes, the Simpletons dug up dead bones. No, they were not supportive of me. No, blood was not (In this case and in many cases), thicker than water, but truth always prevails!

I remember reading a passage in the Bible where Paul charged Timothy to remain faithful to the Word of God and to always remember the things that he had seen and been taught. He said that evil people and impostors would flourish. They will go on deceiving others, and they, themselves, will be deceived. Paul reminded Timothy that all scripture is inspired by God and is useful to teach us what is true and to make us realize what is wrong in our lives. When truth raises her graceful head, you can rest assured that once she has had her say, if you are bold and wise enough to hear and accept her words for what they are, your life will forever be changed.

One day I walked inside my house and decided to do a makeover to represent my newfound commitment of taking care of myself. I wanted and needed my home to represent safety, peace, and tranquility. The majority of my life, I neglected my true self. I nurtured everyone around me while I neglected self-care. My boundary lines had been almost nonexistent, and I had allowed other people's toxic waste to come in and pollute my life. I neglected everything that pertained to a healthy me.

This, in no way, excuses the actions of the people mentioned in my writings. They did what they did, but their shortcomings, debauchery, and hypocrisy have nothing at all to do with my healing within. If I took any one my offender's closets and tried to separate their messes, the result would yield the same type stew that had cooked, boiled, and burned in me for over forty-seven years.

One has to come to a point where they declare, "That's mine," or with courage, declare, "That does not belong to me." As I looked at the house that was to be made into my home, I got excited about reaching deep inside for the answers. Most of the time, the complex answers to one's brokenness resides inside of that person. To go outside of oneself and the Creator to connect the dots is a grave mistake. The true answer is to take responsibility for the fuel that makes your engine *go*.

Whether it be an abuser, enabler, over-achiever, martyr, perfectionist, or in my case, victim, the answer resided inside rather than out. My first step was to create a sanctuary. I remembered going into Clay's home in the country. I'd noticed that the walls were pristine white, but the carpet was atrocious with stains from God knows what. While living in our new house, he had attempted to do the same thing. The floor would be where I would start.

Because most of the violence perpetrated against me happened in the bedroom, I decided that I would begin the makeover there. I got down on my knees in the corner of the room and lifted up the edge of the carpet. I thought to myself, *Have I lost my mind? This will be a gigantic project.* Something *inside* said, "Keep going! When it's done, you will be renewed and blessed." I kept moving. After a huge amount of hard work, the carpet and foam was removed, exposing the concrete underneath. Sometimes it takes removing things, and many times layers of things, to get to what is really underneath. I sat amidst the dust that had been created from the pulling and tugging at the carpet.

On the surface, the carpet appeared clean. In fact, I had, many times, cleaned it myself, but upon removing it, stains that I had no idea existed, remained hidden underneath. Dust was everywhere!

With an extremely bad back, I tugged and pulled with all my might to get the carpet to the garage for disposal. I walked back into the bedroom and decided at that moment that I wanted to acid wash and stain my floors. There was paint around the very edges of the room that the original house contractor had dropped. They felt no need to clean it up, because the end result would be that the imperfections would be covered up with carpet. No one would notice, because it would be hidden underneath. This paint would have to be removed with paint thinner. Visionaries are able to see beyond the distance, depths, or height presented to them. On this day, for the first time, I saw myself as a visionary. I understood that my life had not and would not fit neatly in a little, square box.

The well-known scholar, Socrates said, "An unexamined life is not worth living." At the beginning of this project, I did not understand that the uncovering of these marred and imperfect concrete floors would lead me to uncovering my authentic self. It was too big to tackle the entire project in one or two sittings, and so I thought, *How do you eat an elephant?* The answer is one bite at a time.

There was so much crud hidden underneath the carpet. When I initially looked at the work at hand, I became frightened that my own handiwork would look worse than the imperfections covered up by the original contractors. I had no idea what steps to take next, so I went to Home Depot, purchased a book on staining concrete floors, and before long, I was deep in the midst of my DIY project.

From acid washing to degreasing and flooding my floors with water, I became immersed in the art that was soon to play out from my heart through my hands to my floors. Instead of using a paint roller, I took weeks off work and used a two-inch paintbrush to detail my floor with precise lines. My house was turning into my sanctuary.

During the staining process, I realized something I had not known about my core. I am an artist. It had taken all these years to come to understand this God-given gift about myself. My artwork on the floors in my home illuminated my soul and changed my life.

I mothered and nurtured three young men into adulthood, affirming each one according to their special individual needs. I knew more about my sons than I knew about myself. Somehow as a parent, I was so consumed with making sure their lives turned out right that I neglected my own. I was much more familiar with the tapestry of their core than my own. But here on my floor, the light switch was once again turned on for me to get a clear view of myself. I liked what I saw. I admitted to myself that seeing the world through an artist's eyes was a bit different from how the rest of the world sees it.

This project, without proper directions from the *How to Stain a Concrete Floor* guidebook, my floors have looked much like the misguided life I'd lived. Unfortunately, by the time we engage in self-help books, it is after the damage has been done. They are more or less self-recovery books. We find ourselves trying to pick up the fragmented pieces of ourselves for damage control.

When I decided to stain my concrete floors, I had no idea that there was a cleaning process that went beyond sweeping and mopping. After clearing every heavy piece of furniture out of the room, the floors not only had to be swept thoroughly of debris and degreased with the proper solution, but then the dreaded process of acid washing had to be done to open the pores to receive the stain solution. I felt sorry for the concrete, but each step was critical to bringing out its true beauty. Once the acid etching was completed and the floor was properly dried, the concrete was finally ready to receive the artwork that I so eagerly wanted to release from captivity. The end result was sheer eclectic beauty with tones of earthy browns and sunset gold. I found myself even experimenting and changing the tints of the stains by mixing colors to achieve the look I desired. Then there was one final step that needed to be done to *protect* the beauty of my floors; a sealant had to be applied. The look was breathtaking; moreover, I found myself in my floors.

Through the process, I found my right to grieve my losses, abuses, and traumatic experiences of my past. I found my right to release the individuals who had chosen not to be supportive of me by invalidating the experiences of my youth. I found my right to protect my own well-being by not allowing others to control or manipulate me. I found my right to love myself and not feel guilty about my accomplishments. I have the right to not carry the weight of other people's dysfunctional behavior—my right to be happy, sad, angry, frustrated, whatever the emotion— is my God-given right. I have the right to reject any and every negative message, belief system, or attitude that is meant to tear me down. I have the right to say no. I realized while immersed in my artwork that I also have the right to close the door permanently on those hell-bent on hurting and manipulating me. I have the right to terminate those relationships by preempting the use of *The Gift of Good-bye.*

Enough cannot be said about the vulnerability of a person who has been abused. I have found that I have to constantly be on guard and in touch with my authentic self to avoid falling back into old habits and negative conflict—the type of conflict that leads me down only dead end roads. I have to remind myself that I have not yet arrived. Each day of my life, I conscientiously work on being my best self. Because so many years have passed and have been riddled with pain, each moment at hand is so precious to me. I can't change my painful past, but the emotional fact-finding and my commitment to myself to figure it out has brought freedom—freedom of my mind, body, and spirit. Yet I am not so rigid that I leave no room for falling, knowing that falling does not mean failure. I'd like to think of each fall as a fall forward.

A Series of Misfortunate Events

After the death of my marriage to Clay, some of the most complex business years I can remember occurred. It was a time of contemplation, second-guessing, and great struggles. Fleas, flies, ticks, mites, and other hideous bloodsuckers in human form came out of the woodworks. From a ban of Scalawags, who did everything in their power to take over Wanda's Cake Gallery to wayward employees and ghetto hood rats, who stole my company blind while I scrambled to figure it all out. These people saw empty, vulnerable spaces and jumped in to see how much they could plunder while I grappled to save my business. All the while, I continued to smile when my clients walked through the doors. During this season, Brian married the girl of his dreams and decided he needed new business partners. We were both burned out from our demanding company. I had not had a vacation in ages, so with fifty approaching, I welcomed the change. With a few minor stipulations, I decided to let Brian have a hand at working alone. Brian, on the other hand, had become so burned out on working with family, he almost *gave* our company away. Struggling with a little *Messiah complex* himself, when Todd and Kris Ann Hamilton told him they could save the business and make him wealthy quick, he jumped inside their boat, headfirst. They promised him a better life and more efficient way of doing things.

Instead of doing two weddings a Saturday, Kris Ann scheduled six and seven with a three-man crew. She scheduled so many weddings, they asked me to come back and do paid consultation. This so-called consultation assignment soon turned into an overseer position, the person who kept the slaves in line. Wanda's Cake Gallery was becoming a *Famous Amos* production line with complaints coming in daily and people wanting to know *Where is Wanda?* If pressed hard, Kris Ann would reluctantly tell the client that I was in the back and had no authority to come and speak with them. While we slaved in the kitchen, the Hamiltons, complete with Grandma, grandpa, little Susie, and Sarah sat in the office, counting thousands of dollars from our hard labor. By the time the Hamiltons finished with Brian, he didn't even have the authority to sign a company check. Still, Brian was two days away from signing the contract, when my attorney asked to review the terms of the agreement. With much coaxing, we were finally able to get the Hamiltons to open the contract up to us. We were appalled by what we read. They handed us a three hundred-page binder, filled with small print. If Brian were to sign the agreement, the Hamiltons would own all tangible, intangible, and intellectual properties of Wanda's Cake Gallery. (They would own even Brian's thoughts!) The only thing left out were stipulations of whips, shackles, and provisions of slave quarters. The Hamiltons were so gung-ho on gaining control of our business that they moved in before gaining proper legal control. They sent a red flag up by continually squabbling with Brian over meeting my minor stipulations. I refused to sign the document Brian needed to go forward with the Hamiltons, and he was advised to disband the idea of a new partnership. When I found out they removed Brian's name from the business account, I ripped their credit card terminal from the wall and changed the locks on the door.

The Hamiltons demanded that I put things back intact, or if I didn't, I would never be able to do viable business in Oklahoma again. Either I handed them my business on a silver platter, or they would ruin me. In essence, *crack the whip and get back to work, or else!* To make sure I understood their threat was bona fide, they secretly trademarked every name associated with Wanda's Cake Gallery. Forced to change my company's name, I was devastated by this final revelation: *Brian decided he was leaving Wanda's Cake Gallery.* Without any warning, he and his wife felt that his life should take a different direction. This small decision was life-altering for me. Brian and I had pulled together through thick and thin for many years, and all I could think about was *What about the parties we already booked, the cakes he booked that only he could perform? What about the clients who expected his hands to specifically work on their cake?* I was good at what I was good at, but he had specific things he promised certain clients, yet the moment the Hamiltons left, he was gone too. Nevertheless, I tried to make due. The stress level in my life accelerated and did not stop growing until it matured into a monster. I tried to think fast—quick enough where the outside world would not know that I was wounded. There was no time to sulk or pout; I had to come up with something, so I decided to move the shop into the heart of Midtown, hoping that my client base would help to see me through the storm approaching. With no bank account, I worked hard to keep it concealed that I was uncovered and vulnerable, but even in the wild jungle, wounded animals are sniffed out and devoured. I pressed on anyway and moved in an attempt to save face. There I was in Midtown Tulsa with no money and alone. When I talked with Brian and his wife about fulfilling the obligations that were already on the books, it felt as if I was intruding. I was in trouble. I opened the new Wanda's Cakes and Epicurean anyway and tried to make it work, but disaster loomed in every breath I took.

To further complicate matters, our great country was brave and bold enough to elect an African American man to be commander-in-chief. My customer base, made up mostly by white Republicans, went berserk! The day after President Obama was elected, clients with extensive orders, called into the shop, declaring mysterious illnesses and misfortunate events to keep from picking up their already prepared desserts. Many of my clients were angry, afraid, and wanted to know, "How could something like this happen?" *A black man in the White House?* People called the cake shop, cancelling their orders, and many who did not cancel, came in and inspected their cake for a fraction of a flaw, as if they were new recruits of CIA. Some clients came in, declaring the world was about to end, because, "Obama is the Antichrist," they said! While I have always made it a rule to keep discussions of politics and religion out of the shop, I kindly assured them, "No, President Obama is just a man, no different from President Bush or Clinton!"

One night I woke up and found my bed soaked with urine. Attempting to get up, I struggled to make my way to the bathtub to clean myself up. My legs were weak, trembling and failing to support my body. With my heart racing and beating erratically, I, with great effort, pushed myself to get in the water, but once I was done, I could not pull myself out. Holding onto the side of the tub, I crawled out and forced myself to stand. One of my greatest fears was about to play itself out. Something was wrong. All my life as a businesswoman, I wondered what would I do if I became ill. *How would I provide for myself? How would I make good on the promises I made to my customers?*

Months passed as mysterious symptoms began to take over. From severe anxiety, irritability, and diarrhea, to a rapid and irregular heartbeat, I had no strength to even lift a mixing bowl. Sweat poured from my face as if someone dashed a bucket of hot water on me. My neck was so enlarged that it felt like something was lodged in my throat, causing me to gag when I swallowed. My eye bulged as weight dropped from my body.

On one of my morning walks, I attempted to stretch and fell forward. My friend Jane held onto me as I struggled to keep from falling. Disturbed by my condition, she suggested the possibility of Parkinson's disease. The mere likelihood of those words caused me to drown in my own tears. Jane hugged me, reassuring me that everything was going to be fine, but as time passed, the symptom got worse. With no health coverage and *no Brian,* the weakness and tremor in my legs and hands forced me to entertain the unthinkable. Sinking deep in quicksand and depression, during my busiest season, I made the tearful, unimaginable decision to close my beloved business.

People, after hearing that I was ill, were astonished and dumbfounded at my decision to cease doing business. Many clients understood and empathetically told me to take care of myself, but many called and cursed me out. Some even used the dreaded *N word* over the phone! After fourteen years of impeccable business reputation in the state of Oklahoma, a few disgruntled people used the *power of internet* to diminish my good standing in the community. I shuddered in anguish over the untruthful things I read. Still the decision to close the shop to take care of my physical and emotional self fell deep within the heart of my writings. When the rubber met the road, what would I do? I chose to take care of me!

When the Church Fails Us

At each crisis in my life, I deemed the magnitude of a storm greater than the last, but that's just our nature as human beings. Each time

I, with the help of God, miraculously overcame each event. I have always been victorious and triumphant for angels have constantly surrounded me. Even I was amazed that I'd mattered so very much to God. I often think that had I not become disciplined in starting my mornings off with the Creator at an early age, I most likely would have missed out and thus not been the benefactor of these angels of mercy.

My moments alone in silence with God enabled me to survive and overcome. Great beginnings allow for triumphant and sweet endings. Case and point: this book has had many beginnings, many of them good enough, but they were angry pages, filled with unforgiveness. I first attempted to write about the unfairness and injustices that had occurred in my life. I especially wanted to pen my anger and frustration toward Rosa, Tyrone, and Dr. Smith. One day in my quiet time, truth lifted her head and challenged me to look at my past experiences from a very different angle. She pointed out the difficult circumstances that I had come through over these forty-eight years. They hardly represented who I was. They are not the sum total of me. These experiences, however harsh, helped to define my place and purpose in life. Each circumstance, however challenging, were simply chapters in my life. Amidst all of the harsh realities were also unbelievable successes. These penned words evolved and became a story of self-evaluation, determination, and affirmation of my love for the Creator, because of who he has been in my life. He has always guarded, hidden and kept my life with amazing care.

Many times during the writing of these memories, I grew weary and angry at the self-righteousness and hypocrisy that exists in the church today. In my case, there was a systematic dismantling of my children's lives and my own. I'd found, through discussions with other women, that this type of abuse was common in the church. I was amazed at the response of so many women. "Been there, done that." It happens in the church all the time. The bondage, the abuse—mentally and physically—occurs from the pulpit more often than one would think. We find ourselves as lost souls, searching desperately for something to believe in. Once we believe we've found the sanctuary of believers that we feel we connect with most, we begin putting our faith in man's hands rather than God's, by placing ministers, in particular, on pedestals and making small demigods out of regular, rag-tag souls, certainly no better than our own.

Not all men who are in the pulpit are saved, nor should we as intellectuals, be so stupid and void to think that they all have faith. Yet we find ourselves looking up to them and expecting them to lead us to God. We challenge the preacher rather than ourselves to get us to our mountain top experience. We believe everything they say from the pulpit, because we are either too busy or too lazy to go and investigate the Word of God through our own Bible study, our own quiet time, and personal experience with the Creator. Spending time alone with God promotes that intimacy that is needed for us to become whole. It is that very same intimacy that I searched so diligently for through man, only to be, time and time again, disappointed.

Meditation alone with Him makes us steady on our feet, not being so quick to fall for the empty words of mere mortal man. When the church fails us, it becomes our responsibility and our responsibility alone to take ourselves—our mind, body, and spirit—back. I have found in my own personal life that one of the greatest forms of empowerment is the gift of service. Through humble, sincere service, my ego and the thermostat of my heart is quickly checked at the entranceway. Helping others forces me to take my eyes off of me and the circumstances around me while I pour myself back into those in much greater need than myself.

Dr. Laura Bilbruck, a very close friend of mine, during a conversation about personal intimacy and worship, invited me to spend a Sunday at Light of the World Ministries. She warned me that nothing about their church was conventional. Her husband Greg, served as pastor of the church. Their meeting place, she informed me, was at the VFW. I asked about the time of service, and she answered, "Oh between eleven and eleven thirty." At my church, First Baptist, the deacons and trustees would have definitely called a special board meeting for such an answer. Even I, because of my years of traditional thinking and conditioning, felt uncomfortable with her answer. Nevertheless, I decided to keep my word by visiting her church.

Upon arriving at VFW, I, in disbelief, found homeless people crowded at the entranceway—poverty stricken mothers along with their hungry children, people who were clearly in dire straits—gathered to experience praise and worship, a sermon, and a warm meal. Many of them, I was told, waited specifically for Sunday to arrive, knowing that for certain, they would get food to eat.

This awakening hit me like a ton of bricks. I had chosen a church probably the same way most of us do. It was important to me to connect with people who looked like me, had a similar forecast as mine for the future, with a similar desire to lock away and forget the past and near homelessness in my own life. More money had been invested in church edifices and seat cushions than the lives of battered and broken women. As a matter of fact, our own secrets of abuse, battering, and lies were neatly hidden under our beautiful Ralph Lauren dresses. Anguish had been weaved into our hair and pinned up securely with the most magnificent adornments. We wore our history well; no one knew, and no one was about to tell.

Every once in a while one needs a cold dose of a reality. There are lots of hurting people in this world—people who don't even have a bed to sleep in, some who sleep in boxes under bridges. Truth had again lifted her head and said, "With all of the things that have happened in your life, Wanda, you could have very well been one of these people." Sobering... totally sobering! Rosa, Tyrone, and Dr. Smith, at that moment, seemed insignificant. I had wanted to know, "How could I help?" I'd later found myself making dessert, singing praise and worship with the homeless and helping to serve dinner after the sermon was over.

Skimming the Scum

Cooking for me is relational and almost equivalent to a love affair. When I am cooking, I am in my own world. It is what I do. It is a great part of who I am. Soups, in particular, are one of my favorite things to prepare from scratch. They warm my guests on the inside and prepare them for the height of the evening, which always ends with the grand finale: dessert. There is something very sensual about the preparation of soup, which starts with the making of the stock.

Every good chef will tell you that the key and foundation to a good soup lies in the quality of the stock. The two keys to success in making a high quality stock rest in the art of simmering and the continuous skimming of the scum as it rises to the top. Home cooks will tell you that you'll need to start with the finest of ingredients to create a fine stock, but a commercial cook or chef will tell you otherwise. Stock is made from things that one would probably throw away like the scraps and peels from vegetables, or bones from fish, chicken, or of even the carcass of beef. The rule of thumb in the preparation of food is to make use of all you have, throwing away as little as possible. Sounds like life, doesn't it?

A good stock begins with placing the meat, vegetables, and seasoning in a large pot of cold water. Dropping the meat in hot, boiling water would result in loss of flavor and disturb the clarifying process that naturally occurs during simmering by boiling the impurities into the surrounding liquid. The less you disturb your stock, the more beautiful and clearer the end product will be. As your stock comes to a simmer, you will notice fat and blood protein slowly rising and accumulating on top. This is what is known in the food world as *scum*.

With a long-handled ladle, disturbing your stock as little as possible, one must begin skimming away the scum. This murk and slime is deceptive, because it looks as if it is taking over the pot and the liquid underneath. Do not become alarmed at the ugliness that is rising to the top, continue to ladle and skim away! There is beauty hidden underneath the murkiness. This long simmering process must be completed. There are no cutting corners. A good stock could simmer for up to four hours. It is important for you to carefully baby your ingredients and liquid by continuing to skim the impurities away as your stock simmers. While this process may get a little tedious and even messy, skimming is a necessary step in the making of a clear stock. If the impurities are allowed to boil back into its surrounding liquid, the result will be a thick, cloudy stock with a muddy, greasy flavor affecting the outcome of your finished product and inevitably affecting the flavor of your soup. After the flavor has been extracted from the bones through the simmering process, the last step is to strain your stock through a cheesecloth, catching the bones and other crud left behind. After you strain your liquid, set it aside and cool. You are now ready to make your soup du jour.

I spent my entire life allowing the scum of this earth to infiltrate my existence. I was too afraid to let them go. It wasn't until my life was totally compromised that I took a long look at myself and realized these negative influences were no good for me. In order to save the recipe of myself, I had to let certain people go! This was not an easy thing to do. In fact it was one of the hardest things I've ever done. In my case, it took years, a whole lot of effort and secret prayer. And by the mighty hand of God, he set me free. I found that one must be prepared to lose in order to gain; for when I lost my life, that was when I found it.

We as women must be willing to let it go. Negative people and the minus effect that accompanies them; are of absolutely no value in our lives. Their sole purpose is to drain and subtract all of our virtuous energy to fill the empty void in their own life. Skim it and flush it down the drain. Immersing our precious God-given energy in someone else's filth causes our lives to resemble cloudy stock, keeping us from truly seeing ourselves and dealing with our own issues. It inevitably zaps our strength. When that, that is positive finally comes... we are all played out with no energy to entertain. Like me, take the time to get selfish about yourself. I realize that is a bold statement, but a little bit of selfishness is necessary to clean up your act. If you have no love for yourself, trust me, no one else will find the beauty inside of you.

Each time we give of ourselves, we lose not only portions of our virtuous energy, but we lose valuable time. Our time becomes wasted, and we can't get it back. I lost two decades to bad relationships. The lost years are gone forever. Don't allow this to happen to you. Take your future, time, and energy back! It does not rightfully belong to anyone but you.

Take your body back. We must never forget that each time we lie down with the enemy, with the minus effect, virtue goes out of us. I don't care what lie has been told to get you in this place of subtraction, get up and get out. This place can *only* be a place of loss and losing. Gird up, put your clothes on, and say no to this supposedly easy way out. Lose it, grieve it, and let it go. Even if it feels like you are going to come out with the short end of the stick and lose your mind in the process, still lose it. That unrighteous minus effect would want you to believe that it can't be done, because you're not smart enough, not educated enough, and so on. Well guess what? You made it this far. And if truth be told, there is a great, big world with awesome experiences awaiting you. And if you become willing to subtract that which is already a negative in your life, the creator will honor your effort by adding to your life good, wholesome things and bring you to a positive and spacious place.

Some losses, however painful, are necessary in order for us to focus, grow, and spread our wings to fly. If we hold onto that which is negative and that which serves no good purpose, many times it places us in a position where we are in *mark time*. *Mark time* means that we are moving our feet to the beat of walking, but we are marching in one place, going nowhere. This energy takes us hostage and holds us back from being our best self. Negative people bringing their own baggage filled with negative energy, weighs more than our own baggage. We increase our load by inadvertently picking up their issues and lugging them along and cross mingling them with our stuff and oh, what a sincere mess!

Usually the baggage we choose to pick up is of people who would dare not even attempt to touch, let alone assume the weight and responsibility of our issues. When I understood that my sister, Rosa, Tyrone, and Dr. Smith had used the cross as a tool and method of control, abuse, and hypocrisy; it was up to me to skim the scum, serve cut-off notices, and change the locks on my doors. While I don't advocate writing on anyone's driveway as I did, do yourself well and find an hour and place of release. For as I fell on my knees in anguish and despair in their driveway and started to write the word *hypocrite* I felt a cathartic release from being the subject of abuse that spanned for well over two decades. Do not write it on a driveway, but write it somewhere to release the pain.

Forgive Them...
They Know Not What They Do

While the skimming of scum is of the utmost importance, I can't say enough about the gift of forgiveness. Forgiveness is a choice between freedom and bondage. There was absolutely no way to move forward in my healing until I at least entertained the possibility of releasing these people from the debt of betrayal and ultimately forgiving myself for the part I played.

When digging deep into the possibility of forgiveness of the Simpletons, I struggled in a dark place. Of all things, the tampering with my sons' minds and my relationship with them was the hardest to conceive. Every day, before the liberation of forgiveness, I lived with the pain of knowing in my heart that I had given my complete all in parenting, yet for a long time, my relationship with my sons did not mirror that reality. Instead, my children saw me through the Simpletons' eyes. With all this said, forgiveness was still necessary for me to move forward.

One day, my son, Jason, said, "Mom, forgiveness is not for the Simpletons, it is for you. It is for your health and vitality." Jason was so incredibly right! I had to will myself into a place of light or perish emotionally in the dark. I will not tell you that it has been easy, but I will tell you that I made a conscientious choice to release these trespassers from their debts. Since I let go, I can celebrate my relationship with my sons, their wives, my grandchildren, new friends, and new family. Jason was right; forgiveness was for me!

Clearly, I had a choice between healing or bleeding all over everyone I met. I chose to heal, move on, and celebrate the wonderful triumphs I'd achieved in my life. After the scum was skimmed away, I was able to clearly see the beauty and gift of friendship around me. I realized that I had wonderful friends who knew the authentic *me*. These friends were multi-racial, multi-cultural, and diverse...

I've chosen to celebrate the goodness of life. I've chosen to celebrate my evolution and the strength, knowledge and wisdom I've acquired during the process of evolving. I've chosen to celebrate and dance like crazy like no one is watching. When I think about the miles I've traveled, the bridges I've crossed, the cities and states I lived in, the people I touched, the people who touched me, I get excited. I choose to celebrate my new ability to take life not-so-seriously, allowing room for mistakes and some room for overtakes, intakes, and a garbage bag fill up every now and then for seasonal outtakes. And even though tying the garbage bag tight does not guarantee that some stray alley cat will not come and try to tear the bag apart before the garbage truck comes to take it to the landfill, I celebrate my awareness that I will not always get it right. I am human. I celebrate knowing that I am not perfect and neither are those who I chose to break bread with.

I celebrate the wind blowing and the rain dancing on my windowpane, the autumn leaves emptying themselves onto the ground, the return of winter's cold, and the rising and setting of the sun. I celebrate the art inside of me, the transference of that art to a cake, and my beautiful floors. It had taken almost all of my life to embrace the goodness of living and the good that resided *on* the inside of me. Knowing that I am now awake *during* the process of living ignites a fire within me to keep on living and tell the story!

As I look back on some of the circumstances surrounding my life, I am amazed at the strength and bold flavor that developed in me while I was simmering in all my abuser's pots. In many of my darkest hours, I was forced to call strength forth and, in my amazement, I found it in the oddest places and at some of the oddest times. I had run so much in my life that I had not known what true womanhood looked like…

Occasionally Stocks
Come out Cloudy…

To clarify a troubled stock, one must drop about a cup of egg white inside the simmering mixture, allowing the particles and impurities to attach themselves to the protein. And voila—just like that the stock is saved.

Not everything in life ends up perfect, but there are always solutions. However complex and impossible a problem looks, there is always an alternative answer. There were times when I simmered, then reached a boiling point, and many times went back and forth, allowing toxic relationships to permeate my soul, but I never gave up. As long as I am breathing, I'll continue to skim off the negative that weighs me down, keeping me from being my best self. Like cloudy consommé, with life, sometimes we have to throw in a cup each of self-confidence, commitment to endure, and assurance; to clean and clear up the cloudy aspects of our lives. We must know, without even a shadow of a doubt, that we will come through the process, whole, fresh, and new, loving ourselves even more for our boldness, strength, and resilience to weather all storms however devastating they may appear.

Cooling Down

I had come into true womanhood in my late forties. It only came after years of living and examining my life: the hills, valleys, and mountaintop experiences. With all of the scraps I had been given, I had found a way to save the recipe of me. I had many times reached boiling points where it seemed that the temperature was simply too hot to survive, let alone, turn out to be a productive member of society. But I think it was Eleanor Roosevelt who said, "You never know how strong a woman is until you drop her in hot water." She was right.

When you control a person's mind, you control his or her destiny. Dr. Smith controlled me, knowing from a clinical standpoint 'cause and effect'. The secrets that I kept for ten years shy of half-of-a-century caused me to walk, and many times, run in a hypnotic state. I built dark closets and crawl spaces to guard the misguided choices I'd made in my life. It was not until I made a conscientious choice to open the doors to these private places, exposing them to light and air, that I began to heal and find the missing ingredients. One day I thought to myself, *If I'm artistic enough to do a topsy turvy cake where it looks as if it's falling in all directions, certainly I am able to do the same for myself. I can do me!*

Through an analytical approach, I found that I am a true survivor with an incredible zest for living. I am no longer walking in the dark, and I now know my worth. My worth is far above rubies. I am a virtuous woman. I am a Queen. I once saw a newspaper article about Oprah and her spiritual life. The article showed a picture of her looking up toward heaven with her eyes closed and her hands clasped together. It asked the question, "Is she divine or not?" Certain people had tried to figure her out. They had placed more emphasis on Oprah's spiritual life than they had on their own. The same had been done to Iyanla Vanzant and even Jane Fonda. Strong women have always been put under the microscope. The world had unfortunately tried to gauge the temperature of these and many other strong, intellectual women's hearts. They had determined that, because we did not fit into their square box, we were unfit to see and experience God. No one knows the context of a person's heart, except God.

Healing can only take place when you stop eating from other people's plates and borrowing their eyesight to view the world around you. Pastor Anthony Scott once said, "We, as humans, should see our problems as a gift and opportunity to look in the face of God. We mortals, tend to have a narrow view through a wide window, but seeing our problems through the eyes of God changes how we see the entire universe, for God gives us a wide view through a narrow window." In this analysis, I found that learning to eat what was on my plate was plenty for me. I have been blessed with angels, guarding my every step. However tempestuous the journey, I am still here and have yet more traveling to do, with more lives to impact. Yes, life has been good to me.

My Oak Tree

Outside my window, I noticed my oak tree. Its leaves were turning brown. Winter was coming, the leaves were dying, but the tree itself was so firmly rooted in the ground that it still stood tall. Old bark was wearing away, exposing new skin as if its interpretation of this yearly process was metamorphosis *rather than death*. The new skin exposed seemed to say, "I welcome the coldness of the winter months. These leaves will die and fall to the ground. My branches will sleep. They will rest during the winter. For I am so deeply rooted, I am not concerned of these cold months to come. For when spring arrives, my girth and limbs will grow even wider, longer, and stronger, and new leaves will appear. This is God's way of pruning me, for He made me capable of growing so big, man could not. Each year I grow bigger and stronger. Remember how tiny I was when you first saw me. I looked so fragile. When the wind blew and the rains came, I'll bet you thought I'd snap right in two. Look at me. I am still here. When my leaves begin to turn brown, I don't shake, draw back, or tremble. I calmly stand still and allow my metamorphosis to take place. I allow nature to run its course. Each year, from spring to summer and fall to winter, you watch me turn from green to beautiful vibrant yellows and oranges, then brown to gray. When the gray comes, it appears that there is no life left in me. But I am so deeply rooted in Mother Earth that even though it appears that I am dead—I am not. I am only asleep. When spring arrives, and the rain comes with sunshine, *as it always does*, little green buds will burst out my once-dried branches. God's eyes are watching over me during my change. If I, the tree, know this and speak this loud and clear every changing season, why do you shake, shiver, and draw back with the changing of your season? Learn to stand still and watch God in his continuing re-creation of you. I'm just a tree—I am only a tree. Then, finally my good friend and watcher of me, whatever things are true, noble, just, pure, lovely, and of good rapport—if there is any virtue and anything praiseworthy—meditate on these things while you stand still. Do these things while you are going through your winter season, and the God of peace will be with you."

Dedicated to the memory of my Mother:
Malinda Smith-Wolfe
February 12, 1930-December 31, 1995